Robert Song is Tutor in Ethics at St John's College, Durham

D0146174

OXFORD STUDIES IN THEOLOGICAL ETHICS

General Editor
Oliver O'Donovan

OXFORD STUDIES IN THEOLOGICAL ETHICS

The series presents discussions on topics of general concern to Christian Ethics, as it is currently taught in universities and colleges, at the level demanded by a serious student. The volumes will not be specialized monographs nor general introductions or surveys. They aim to make a contribution worthy of notice in its own right but also focused in such a way as to provide a suitable starting-point for orientation.

The titles include studies in important contributors to the Christian tradition of moral thought; explorations of current moral and social questions; and discussions of central concepts in Christian moral and political thought. Authors treat their topics in a way that will show the relevance of the Christian tradition, but with openness to neighbouring traditions of thought which have entered into dialogue with it.

Christianity and Liberal Society

ROBERT SONG

CLARENDON PRESS · OXFORD
1997

Oxford University Press, Great Clarendon Street, Oxford OX2 6DP
Oxford New York
Athens Auckland Bangkok Bogota Bombay
Buenos Aires Calcutta Cape Town Dar es Salaam
Delhi Florence Hong Kong Istanbul Karachi
Kuala Lumpur Madras Madrid Melbourne
Mexico City Nairobi Paris Singapore
Taipei Tokyo Toronto Warsaw
and associated companies in
Berlin Ibadan

Oxford is a trade mark of Oxford University Press

Published in the United States
by Oxford University Press Inc., New York

© Robert Song 1997

All rights reserved. No part of this publication may be reproduced,
stored in a retrieval system, or transmitted, in any form or by any means,
without the prior permission in writing of Oxford University Press.
Within the UK, exceptions are allowed in respect of any fair dealing for the
purpose of research or private study, or criticism or review, as permitted
under the Copyright, Designs and Patents Act, 1988, or in the case of
reprographic reproduction in accordance with the terms of the licences
issued by the Copyright Licensing Agency. Enquiries concerning
reproduction outside these terms and in other countries should be
sent to the Rights Department, Oxford University Press,
at the address above

British Library Cataloging in Publication Data
Data available

Library of Congress Cataloging in Publication Data
Christianity and liberal society / Robert Song.
(Oxford studies in theological ethics)
Includes bibliographical references and index.
1. Christianity and politics. 2. Liberalism I. Title.
II. Series.
BR115.P7S6324   1997   230'.046—dc21   97-7805
ISBN 0-19-815933-1
1 3 5 7 9 10 8 6 4 2

Typeset by Joshua Associates Ltd., Oxford
Printed in Great Britain on acid-free paper by
Bookcraft (Bath) Ltd., Midsomer Norton

JESUIT - KRAUSS - McCORMICK - LIBRARY
1100 EAST 55th STREET
CHICAGO, ILLINOIS 60615

BR
115
.P7
S6324
1997

For my parents

ACKNOWLEDGEMENTS

I should like to thank the following, who kindly read and commented on early drafts of one or more chapters: Nigel Biggar, Duncan Forrester, the late Peter Hebblethwaite, Tariq Modood, Alan Ryan, Nicholas Townsend. This book is a revised version of a doctoral dissertation submitted to the University of Oxford, and I am grateful to my examiners, Rowan Williams and John Finnis, for their suggestions, and to St John's College, Durham, whose grant of a term's study leave enabled me to complete the revisions. My greatest debts are to Oliver O'Donovan, who supervised the thesis, Philip Wheatley, and particularly Margaret Masson; in different ways their friendship, wisdom, and generosity over many years have been of inestimable worth.

R.J.S.

CONTENTS

ABBREVIATIONS

BT   Reinhold Niebuhr, *Beyond Tragedy: Essays on the Christian Interpretation of History* (London: Nisbet, 1938)

CLCD Reinhold Niebuhr, *The Children of Light and the Children of Darkness: A Vindication of Democracy and a Critique of its Traditional Defenders* (1944; repr. London: Nisbet, 1945)

DST   Reinhold Niebuhr, *Discerning the Signs of the Times: Sermons for To-day and To-morrow* (London: SCM Press, 1946)

ESJ   George Grant, *English-Speaking Justice* (Sackville, New Brunswick: Mount Allison University Press, 1974; 2nd edn. Notre Dame, Ind.: University of Notre Dame Press, 1985)

FH   Reinhold Niebuhr, *Faith and History: A Comparison of Christian and Modern Views of History* (New York: Scribner's, 1949)

FMW Jacques Maritain, *Freedom in the Modern World*, trans. Richard O'Sullivan (London: Sheed and Ward, 1935)

ICE   Reinhold Niebuhr, *An Interpretation of Christian Ethics* (1935; repr. London: SCM Press, 1936)

IH   Jacques Maritain, *True Humanism* (1936), trans. M. R. Adamson (London: Geoffrey Bles, 1938)

LN   George Grant, *Lament for a Nation: The Defeat of Canadian Nationalism* (Toronto: McClelland and Stewart, 1965; 2nd edn. 1970)

MMIS Reinhold Niebuhr, *Moral Man and Immoral Society* (New York: Scribner's, 1932)

MNHC Reinhold Niebuhr, *Man's Nature and His Communities* (London: Geoffrey Bles, 1963)

MP   Ronald Dworkin, *A Matter of Principle* (Cambridge, Mass.: Harvard University Press, 1985)

MS   Jacques Maritain, *Man and the State* (Chicago: University of Chicago Press, 1951)

NDM i, ii Reinhold Niebuhr, *The Nature and Destiny of Man*, i: *Human Nature* (London: Nisbet, 1941); ii: *Human Destiny* (London: Nisbet, 1943)

NLNR John Finnis, *Natural Law and Natural Rights* (Oxford: Clarendon Press, 1980)

PCG   Jacques Maritain, *The Person and the Common Good* (1947), trans. John J. Fitzgerald (London: Geoffrey Bles, 1948)

PH   Jacques Maritain, *On the Philosophy of History* (1957), ed.
        Joseph W. Evans (London: Geoffrey Bles, 1959)
PL   John Rawls, *Political Liberalism* (New York: Columbia Uni-
        versity Press, 1993)
RMNL   Jacques Maritain, *The Rights of Man and Natural Law* (1942),
        trans. Doris C. Anson (London: Geoffrey Bles, 1944)
RMO   Oliver O'Donovan, *Resurrection and Moral Order: An Outline
        for Evangelical Ethics* (Leicester: Inter-Varsity Press, 1986)
ST   Thomas Aquinas, *Summa Theologiae.* T. Gilby and T. C.
        O'Brien (eds.), *Summa Theologiae* (60 vols., London: Eyre &
        Spottiswoode, 1964–73)
T&J   George Grant, *Technology and Justice* (Toronto: House of
        Anansi Press, 1986)
TE   George Grant, *Technology and Empire: Perspectives on North
        America* (Toronto: Anansi Press, 1969)
TH   George Grant, *Time as History* (Toronto: Canadian Broad-
        casting Corporation, 1969)
TJ   John Rawls, *A Theory of Justice* (Oxford: Oxford University
        Press, 1972)
TRS   Ronald Dworkin, *Taking Rights Seriously* (London: Duck-
        worth, ²1978)

I

Introduction

Ever since Karl Barth's inversion of nineteenth-century cultural Protestantism in the early decades of this century, the predominant attitude of Christian theology towards its surrounding culture has been one of critical distance rather than uncritical legitimation. Barth showed how Protestant theology had been fettered by its allegiance to the demands of its intellectual and cultural environment, and in doing so freed it to be faithful to its proper object of study, the self-revelation of God in Jesus Christ. The same task of vitalizing theology and ensuring its authenticity in the face of its cultured despisers (whether they be inside or outside the Church) confronts all theologians, at the end of the twentieth century as much as at its beginning. In systematic theology this entails a two-fold responsibility: both the dethroning of idolatrous and dehumanizing modes of thought, and the unfolding of the meaning of the gospel of Jesus Christ. Likewise in Christian social thought, the search for an adequate political theology comprises both the negative undertaking of a critical analysis of political ideologies and practices and the positive task of constructing a theology of political society in the light of Jesus Christ.

Liberalism has been the dominant political ideology of modernity. If one of the primary negative responsibilities of theology in relation to the prevailing intellectual culture has been the criticism of modernity, however that is to be understood, one of the primary negative responsibilities of political theology must be the critical evaluation of liberalism. If it is true that the ascendant classes in Western societies have not seen the reality of modernity because they have seen reality with modern eyes, it is as true that they do not see the reality of liberalism because they view political reality with liberal eyes. Liberalism, especially in the form 'liberal democracy', articulates the dominant form of public self-understanding in Western societies on the North Atlantic model, and the ostensible assent granted to many of its values by those who speak for non-liberal societies suggests the degree of cogency which liberal rhetoric possesses elsewhere. When it is also added that, histori-cally, liberalism has been significantly indebted to Christianity, and that some version of the former is frequently thought to be automatically entailed by any reasonable version of the latter, the case for engaging in a theological interpretation and analysis of liberalism, as a necessary negative element in the ultimately constructive project of a general social theology, is overwhelmingly evident.

The importance of such an endeavour becomes even clearer if we attend to various other features of the contemporary world. At one level there is a range of questions which cluster around the implications for public policy of religious belief in a religiously plural society: the relation between religion and tolerance (including the possibility of participation by fundamentalist reli-gions in public debate, the content and desirability of blasphemy laws, etc.); the justification for an established church; the case for state funding of religious schools or of confessional theology departments (as contrasted with phenomenologically oriented religious studies departments) in universities; the involvement of religious bodies in politics; the debates between proponents of multi-culturalism and defenders of 'our Christian heritage'; and so on. At another level there is an array of problems connected with the process of modernization: increasing (though perhaps not inevitable) secularization, and the deposition of religion from its previous governing role both in the public commitments of society and in the recesses of personal subjectivity; the confinement of religion to private life, the realm of family and leisure; the pluralization and relativization of belief and the consequent sense that the choice of ultimate beliefs is unimportant; and, amongst these, the waning influence of the churches and their bewilderment in knowing how to respond. At a third level, there is the intellectual context of the proliferation of critiques of modernity, whether or not these adopt a self-consciously post-modern style; the mood of a profound questioning of the view of the world associated with the Enlightenment (its stress on science and the objectivity of know-ledge, on the centred self, and so on); and, along with that, the continuing problem of the cognitive status of religion and the number and types of public audiences it may claim to address.

A fully developed theological interpretation of liberal political thought would be able to take into account each of these contexts and respond to the questions which they pose. That is, it would address the issues of public policy and morality and indicate the first principles of a casuistry; it would guide the Church in the way of faithfulness amidst the cultural configurations of modernity and its aftermath; and it would contribute to an authentically theological post-modernity which neither lapses back into an uncritical pre-modernity nor indulges in a self-consuming and (despite itself) potentially conservative deconstructionism. And in doing so, it would make a contribution not only to political theology, but also, because of the mutually implicating nature of the theological enterprise, to theology itself.

Despite its importance, however, even book-length treatments of the relation of theology to liberal political theory are scarce,[1] liberalism as often as not appearing merely as one of a gallery of political ideologies to be lined up and targeted in turn.[2] If approaches of that kind are inadequate, the size of the subject ensures that the present treatment cannot pretend to comprehensiveness either. Instead of attempting a systematic approach directly, I try to explore some of the principal themes of liberalism through a series of self-standing but interrelated studies. Thus three of the central chapters proceed by taking an aspect of liberalism and then discussing how a particular twentieth-century theologian or Christian philosopher has evaluated it. This allows us, on the one hand, to build up a multi-faceted collage of images both of liberalism and of possible Christian responses to it. On the other hand, because the three theologians whom I consider are chosen largely for the complementary nature and constructive potential of their thought, we are also enabled to work in the direction of a systematic Christian theological account of political liberalism.

Of the three theologians I discuss, two wrote their most important works and enjoyed their greatest influence between the mid-1930s and the early 1960s. Reinhold Niebuhr (1892–1971), an American Protestant of German descent, was at once one of the most prominent theologians and one of the foremost political commentators of his time, whose writings both on public life and

---

[1] The collection of essays in R. Bruce Douglass and David Hollenbach (eds.), *Catholicism and Liberalism: Contributions to American Public Philosophy* (Cambridge: Cambridge University Press, 1994) form a recent exception to this.

[2] Stephen Charles Mott, *A Christian Perspective on Political Thought* (New York: Oxford University Press, 1993) is a good example of this genre.

on theology were infused with a profound sense of human possibilities and human limitations. His mature thought displayed an Augustinian tension between hope and sinfulness which enabled him to make a decisive contribution to the formation of a chastened liberalism, one that had learned from the experience of the First World War and the rise of Communist and Fascist regimes. Jacques Maritain (1882–1973), by contrast, a French Catholic convert, was primarily a philosopher who applied a supply interpreted Thomism to many areas of thought, including metaphysics, epistemology, aesthetics, science, and education as well as, latterly, to social and political theory. His version of Aquinas's philosophy made plentiful use of analogical reasoning, and his vision of the 'new Christendom'—secular and liberal rather than sacral and intolerant—inspired many Catholic thinkers and politicians, particularly of Christian Democrat persuasion, and helped advance the modernizing movement in the Roman Catholic Church which culminated in the Second Vatican Council.

The third thinker whom I discuss is less well known than Niebuhr and Maritain. George Parkin Grant (1918–88), an Anglican born into the Canadian ruling class, is a generation younger than the other two, his chief works being published in the 1960s and 1970s and addressed primarily to other Canadians rather than to an international audience. His best-known book in his native country, *Lament for a Nation: The Defeat of Canadian Nationalism* (1965), is an extended meditation on the loss of Canadian national identity and its absorption into the capitalist, progressive, spearhead of modernity that is the United States. In this and subsequent books (most notably *Technology and Empire: Perspectives on North America* (1969), *Time as History* (1969), and *English-Speaking Justice* (1974)) he interprets this establishment of American cultural hegemony as the outworking of the driving forces of modernity which lie behind both technology and liberalism. Displaying the influence of his various wrestlings with Plato, Nietzsche, Heidegger, and Simone Weil, amongst others, he powerfully evokes the idea of the modern age as fate—and of liberalism as bound up in this.

I choose these three for a variety of reasons. All were thinkers of the twentieth century, forging their theology in response to the experiences of the First World War, of Nazism and Communism, and of the forms of liberal democracy that emerged as a result. All took themselves to be critics of liberalism, even if they each believed in core features of it. Niebuhr defended constitutional liberalism in the name of 'democracy'; Grant regarded a belief in the centrality of the good of freedom as essential to sanity; and Maritain defended a form of pluralism with a codified structure of rights as part of his vision for society. All were intimately connected with the United States, the paradigm liberal state of the modern world: Niebuhr, a second-generation immigrant who became perhaps the public theologian *par excellence* of the American century; Grant, a Canadian nationalist who held a lifelong suspicion of American imperialism and the ideology that grounded it; Maritain, a European who discovered in the United States what he had dreamed of in his new Christendom. Each of them represents a different Christian tradition: Maritain the Roman Catholic, interpreting the high medieval philosophy of Thomas Aquinas; Niebuhr the Lutheran, influenced by and reacting against nineteenth-century liberal idealist theology; Grant the Anglican, drawing eclectically from various theological and philosophical traditions. Each has a distinctive preference amongst the intellectual sources of Western thought. For Grant illumination is to be found in Greek thought and a Platonic reading of the Gospels; for Niebuhr, the Hebrew prophetic tradition does most justice to the essential tension in all human perceptions of truth; for Maritain, a Thomist synthesis of classical and Christian thought provides the key to understanding. As a result of this complex series of connections and complementarities, each of them emerges as particularly appropriate for criticizing one amongst the central generating sources of liberal thought—its philosophy of history (Niebuhr), its account of the basis of value (Grant), and its understanding of human agency and political pluralism (Maritain). But it is only by putting them together that we will get a fuller picture, as we shall see.

Before we can turn to the ideas about liberalism which each of them has, however, we have to surmount one of the biggest obstacles to the enterprise as a whole: namely, the slipperiness of the notion at the centre of the debate. In Chapter 2, therefore, I present an interpretation of liberalism. In order to illustrate the history and varieties of liberalism, I include sketches of the thought of five writers often associated with the liberal tradition, as well as an outline of a loosely drawn but broadly recognizable plan of the

conceptual structure of liberal beliefs. In addition there are descriptions of what I regard as the three most important branches of the
liberal family: namely, constitutional liberalism, classical economic
liberalism, and welfare or revisionist liberalism. Although such a
picture of liberalism will unavoidably be reductive to a degree, it is
still possible to argue that there are sufficiently many family
resemblances between the different kinds of liberalism to justify
at least the initial posture of treating it as a whole. Nevertheless, it
will become clear that a theological interpretation of liberalism will
wish to distinguish between various liberal positions and arguments, rejecting some and provisionally accepting others.

This method of interpreting liberalism helps us to address the
problem of criticizing an account of liberalism which no liberal
writer has in fact held. There are opposing dangers here. On the
one hand, a composite picture of liberalism put together without
reference to particular liberals runs the risk of being an imaginary
construct which no liberal would own. On the other, engagement
with a succession of liberal writers without reference to what they
hold in common is liable to make unintelligible the description of
them as liberals at all. The mutually implicating projects of first
describing some representatives of the liberal tradition and then
drawing out some of their family resemblances should enable us to
avoid these dangers, by historically disciplining vague references to
liberalism, while allowing the imaginative discernment of typical
patterns of liberal thought.

The following three chapters form the bulk of the argument,
drawing on specific features of the analysis of liberalism by each of
the three Christian writers chosen. Any political theory has an
implicit philosophy of history. In Chapter 3 I consider Niebuhr's
criticisms of liberalism's progressivism and optimistic conceptions
of human nature and reason, together with the self-redemptive
approaches to salvation which such accounts suggest. Although the
facileness and sentimentality that Niebuhr diagnosed in early
twentieth-century liberalism do not so readily characterize contemporary liberals, it is arguable that parallel considerations to his
could be applied to the late twentieth-century obsession with, and
dependence on, economic and technological growth.

In Chapter 4 I discuss Grant's understanding of the relation
between liberalism, modernity, and technology, and the profound
civilizational contradiction to which he alleges liberalism is party—

namely, that within its own terms liberalism can provide no defence of its values which does not simultaneously legitimate the techno-logical mentality which is undermining those values. This engen-ders problems for many accounts of the basis of liberal values: the specific example taken here is that of John Rawls, particularly as his thought has been developed in his recent work *Political Liberalism* (1993). Rawls is widely—and rightly—regarded as having made a seminal contribution to Anglo-American political theory, and no serious criticism of contemporary liberalism can afford to ignore it. The criticisms I make of it arise from an attempt to bring the questions Grant puts to Rawls's earlier work to bear on these later developments in his thought.

This discussion touches on the problems of pluralism, a theme treated more fully in an account of Maritain in Chapter 5. Until relatively recently, Maritain tended to be treated in the literature as the subject of either hagiography or demonography, his social and political thought being supposed to require either mere exposition, that its light might shine forth with indisputable brilliance, or mere mention, that it might be dismissed with equally indisputable scorn. Neither approach demonstrates the critical sympathy he richly deserves. In this chapter I set his thought in the context of the current debate between 'liberals' and 'communitarians', which centres (at least in its philosophical guise) on the issue of the nature of human agency and freedom and has important ramifica-tions for questions of religious and ideological pluralism, state neutrality, and the legal enforcement of morals. Maritain's ideal of the 'new Christendom' accepts a broadly communitarian under-standing of human agency, but also endorses a quasi-neutral state by means of a Democratic Charter which would be supported by every communal tradition within a society but which would guarantee the rights of persons. In my discussion I highlight and attempt to address some of the problems, political and theological, that this combination leads to.

A number of the institutional considerations shadowed in Chap-ter 5 are taken up in Chapter 6, where I venture some theological reflections on the issues raised by the trend towards qualifying the power of elected governments in favour of the judiciary through the constitutional incorporation of Bills of Rights and the right of judicial review. The work of Ronald Dworkin and John Finnis receives special attention here, as do two different theological models of democracy. However, the argument in this chapter is more discursive than in previous chapters and does not advert to other theological treatments of this area of constitutional theory—not least because relatively little explicitly theological work has been done on it. Despite that, it is an important subject, not only because it is perhaps the central problem of current liberal constitutional theory and the occasion of an apparent conflict between the values of liberalism and democracy, but also because it is a practical issue of considerable topicality and significance.

Inevitably a book on liberalism cannot address every part of the ground liberalism covers. In particular, I make no attempt to confront the economic and social policy considerations that are connected with economic and welfare liberalism, preferring instead to concentrate on some of the underlying moral, legal, and political issues that are common to all varieties of liberalism—as well as on aspects of what might be called the liberal world-view. While the discussion is not shaped into a systematic account, and there is no continuous developing narrative between the chapters, there are a number of preoccupations which unify the book. I draw these out explicitly in the final chapter, which takes the form of a reinter-pretation of liberalism in response to the conclusions of the previous chapters. This is related to the idea of the 'turn to the subject', which is itself analysed in terms of the centrality of the will and the loss of transcendence. And from this I propose some more general conclusions for the terms of Christian engagement with political society.

2

An Interpretation of Liberalism

I INTRODUCTION

'Liberalism has been, in the last four centuries, the outstanding doctrine of Western civilization' (H. J. Laski).[1] 'To attempt to write the history of liberalism before the 1820s is . . . akin to attempting to write the history of the eighteenth-century motor car' (J. C. D. Clark).[2] Two such divergent estimates of the history of liberalism not only suggest the range of historiographical paradigms under which liberalism has been treated: they also raise suspicions that the two writers are hardly referring to the same set of phenomena at all. Similar doubts are raised by the unhesitating application of the term by different people variously to economic non-interventionism as well as welfare interventionism, to belief in natural rights as well as scepticism about a natural order of morality, to unclouded optimism and rationalism as well as more circumspect and cautious gradualism. Perhaps to talk of liberalism (in the singular) rather than liberalisms (in the plural) is to have been deceived into deducing an identity of object from an identity of name.

In response to this sceptical challenge I will argue in this chapter that, while it would be foolish to attempt a univocal definition of such a historically and conceptually complex phenomenon, nevertheless liberalism can be satisfactorily understood as defining a family of thinkers who are indeed disparate but still sufficiently close to enable us to point to a pattern of characteristic family resemblances. The most central of these resemblances are a voluntarist conception of the human subject; a constructivist meta-ethics; an abstract, universalist, and individualist mode of thought; and a broadly progressivist philosophy of history. Around these are found other features—characteristic liberal understandings of power and authority, the state, property, democracy, and

---

[1] *The Rise of European Liberalism* (London: George Allen and Unwin, 1936), 9.
[2] *Revolution and Rebellion: State and Society in England in the Seventeenth and Eighteenth Centuries* (Cambridge: Cambridge University Press, 1986), 102.

the supreme values of liberty and equality. Although such a composite portrait will inevitably be a caricature of the opinions of any individual liberal (indeed, the variety of liberal positions on many topics implies that it would not be rational for any one person to hold every view that could fairly be described as 'typically liberal'), it is still possible to claim that the liberalism thus depicted is to some extent distinct from other sets of beliefs which overlap it, such as socialism and conservatism. Moreover, this family can be distinguished from the pre-liberal thinkers of the classical and medieval periods and post-liberal writers such as Marx and Nietzsche.

After a short section on method, which lays down some of the principles of this approach to interpreting liberalism and argues for the appropriateness of the family analogy, I will introduce, by way of specific illustration, some members of the liberal family and their immediate ancestors: John Locke (constitutional liberalism), Immanuel Kant (the ethics of autonomy), John Stuart Mill (individuality), L. T. Hobhouse (welfare liberalism), and F. A. Hayek (economic liberalism). In the third section I describe some of the main varieties of liberalism—different branches of the family, as it were. Finally, I attempt an outline of some of the family resemblances.

2 ON INTERPRETING LIBERALISM: A METHODOLOGICAL PRELIMINARY

The term 'liberalism' should be understood primarily as a device within descriptive historiography. Like other similar broad category-terms, its function is to illuminate historical material, and it purports, when its content is expounded, to provide a better description of its historical object than alternatives. Its use is constrained, and so ultimately legitimated, by the historical evidence. However, the nature of history-writing demands that there be abridgement of the facts, and the requirements of generalization imply that the range of material to be subsumed under broad category-terms will be governed by the historian's purposes in writing. Thus liberalism could be taken at several levels of generalization: for example, as the creed of a particular political party (say, that descending from Gladstone); or, slightly more broadly, as a set of political beliefs whose existence cannot be presumed before the term itself was first used in a political context in the early nineteenth century; or, more broadly still, as the political aspect of a general movement of thought characteristic of 'modernity', such that nineteenth-century liberalism is one moment in that wider movement. Aside from the interpreter's interests, there is no a priori criterion for deciding the appropriate level of generalization: lower levels of generalization offer the possibility of more accurate historical detail, higher levels the possibility of greater illuminative power.

In the present case, our interest in liberalism as the subject of theological critique is guided, as was intimated in Chapter 1, by two central assertions. One is that liberalism is the dominant political ideology of the modern West, and increasingly influential outside the West. The other, whatever the nature of its connection to the first, is that liberalism is the political aspect of the Enlightenment, and thus a central and characteristic feature of modernity. Wider than a set of political values, and deeper than a range of political policies, it has affinities with Enlightenment beliefs about the nature of human agency, the nature of rationality, the basis of value, and the direction of history, as well as its own characteristic attitudes towards power, property, the state, and so on.

These guiding purposes indicate the kind of level of generalization that we should expect to find in our interpretation of liberalism. But they also suppose liberalism to be a political ideology that is both historically and contextually specific, yet also related to a broader movement of thought. And this places certain constraints on what kinds of interpretation will be appropriate for our purposes. For example, one procedure that is excluded is the one according to which liberalism is defined, ahistorically, by one or more values (such as liberty, equality, or the rights of the individual), which become the canonical standard. These values might be discovered by sieving the thought of all those who have generally been considered liberal and discovering what common values could be separated out: an example of this approach is the claim that 'the belief in freedom and the belief in conscience [are] the twin foundations of Liberal philosophy and the element of continuity in its historical development'.[3] Such an

---

[3] Alan Bullock and Maurice Shock, *The Liberal Tradition: From Fox to Keynes* (London: Adam and Charles Black, 1956), pp. liv–lv. They are referring specifically to British liberalism between 1790 and 1930.

ahistorical approach through value-definition can allow in advance no historical limits to liberalism, and might find itself acknowledging (say) Pericles or Socrates as liberals, despite the profound differences between their intellectual-historical context and that of liberalism proper. Moreover, values are not randomly thrown together, but are part of a wider world-view, and it is the relative weighting of different values as determined by these more general commitments which distinguishes liberalism from, say, socialism, which shares many of the same values.[4]

Connected with this, another approach is excluded: the attempt, based on a principle of charity, to produce the most plausible reading of liberalism as a theory. It is of course a matter of intellectual integrity for a critic of liberalism to address arguments for liberal positions presented in their most cogent form. But for those interested in criticizing liberalism as a totality of thought and practice, to separate liberalism from its history and treat it as a timeless intellectual phenomenon would be to weed out much of what is most interesting: namely, characteristic irrationalities, lapses, and hypocrisies in the historically prevalent forms of liberal thought.

A third constraint on an acceptable interpretation of liberalism for our purposes is that, for it to be meaningful to talk of liberalism as the dominant political ideology, it must be distinguishable, at least in broad terms, from rival ideologies, such as (most obviously) socialism or conservatism. Similarly, for it to be specially related to Enlightenment modernity, it must be distinguishable from pre-liberal and post-liberal patterns of political thought—those of the classical and medieval periods, on the one hand, and of (say) Marxists or Nietzscheans, on the other.

Finally, this governing interest allows us to put to one side certain non-political uses of the term 'liberal' as being of peripheral interest. The word was first used as a term of social distinction to refer to those of the class of free men; its use in 'liberal arts' derives from this, referring to those pursuits appropriate to such a class, though it was later detached from a specific class reference. It also carried from early on the sense of generosity and, conversely, of lack of restraint.[5] In modern usage it has tended to imply open-

---

[4] For these criticisms see Anthony Arblaster, *The Rise and Decline of Western Liberalism* (Oxford: Blackwell, 1984), 11–13.

[5] See Raymond Williams, 'Liberal', in *Keywords: A Vocabulary of Culture and Society* (Glasgow: Fontana, 1976), 148–9.

mindedness, tolerance, and reasonableness, central virtues of a liberal society: 'a Liberal is anyone who is perfectly sensible' (John Maynard Keynes).[6] The relation of these more general usages to the specific sense of liberalism we are addressing is interesting, and would have a place in a full treatment of the theme; but it is too broad to be useful for our purposes.[7]

However, none of these considerations address the issue of whether there might not turn out to be several things denoted by the term 'liberalism'. And this raises the question of whether it is right to be sceptical about the identity of liberalism, just as A. O. Lovejoy maintained with regard to the various movements termed 'Romanticism', that '[the] fact that the same name has been given by different scholars to all of these episodes is no evidence, and scarcely even establishes a presumption, that they are identical in essentials'.[8] Historically, more than one tradition of thought, and, conceptually, more than one structure of beliefs, have been labelled liberal. This suggests either that some arbitrary decision will have to be taken to privilege one tradition or set of beliefs, denying the title to others, or that a univocal understanding of liberalism must be rejected.

An example of the former alternative would be the designation of a particular era as exemplifying 'true' or 'pure' or 'classical' liberalism. Periods or thinkers outside this would be judged liberal to the extent that they matched up to this standard. Thus, for example, the *laissez-faire* liberalism of nineteenth-century Britain might be taken to be liberalism proper. An analysis of the ideas held by the dominant thinkers would reveal what was canonically liberal; from this it could be decided when liberalism started, whether it still exists, and so on. Such an approach has the virtue of relatively tight control over the range of legitimate meanings of liberalism, but, to the extent that it may be tempted to

---

[6] Quoted by Robert Eccleshall, 'Liberalism', in Robert Eccleshall, Vincent Geoghegan, Richard Jay, and Rick Wilford, *Political Ideologies* (London: Hutchinson, 1984), 39.

[7] On the origins of the political usage of 'liberal' and cognates, see G. de Bertier de Sauvigny, 'Liberalism, Nationalism and Socialism: The Birth of Three Words', *Review of Politics*, 32 (1970), 147–66, esp. 150–5.

[8] A. O. Lovejoy, 'On the Discrimination of Romanticisms' (1924), repr. in M. H. Abrams (ed.), *English Romantic Poets: Modern Essays in Criticism*, 2nd edn. (New York: Oxford University Press, 1975), 9. For a reply see Rene Wellek, 'Romanticism in Literature', in P. P. Wiener (ed.), *Dictionary of the History of Ideas* (5 vols., New York: Scribner's, 1973), iv. 197.

refuse the title to certain other movements widely called liberal (say, welfare liberalism), it clashes with the reasonable principle that an interpretation of liberalism should not exclude on a priori grounds those traditions which are widely called by the name.[9]

It seems more reasonable to adopt the latter approach and drop the belief that there is a 'core' or 'essence' to liberalism which can be defined through a set of necessary and sufficient conditions. Instead, the notion of a family resemblance of beliefs should be adopted, such that there is a limited number of identifiable beliefs which are liberal, a certain (though undefined) number of which it is necessary to hold in order to be counted a liberal, but none of which is individually necessary. This approach would remove the need to find a period (whether nineteenth-century Britain, or Revolutionary France or America, say) pure enough to be elevated to paradigmatic status. Its stress on the open-textured nature of liberal thought would admit the intuition that individual thinkers can hold certain liberal beliefs and yet not be liberals (and conversely); yet it would also allow room for certain permutations of beliefs to have at least a prima-facie internal consistency, and thus account for the observation that sets of liberal beliefs are often broadly accepted or rejected as a whole. And it could accept that certain positions are liberal, even if their proponents or opponents have never applied that label. This is important, inasmuch as 'liberalism' is a term with high emotive or dynamic force: it is an emblem fought over in political debate, not just a descriptive term for use by the putatively detached historian. Many liberals disown the title, while some non-liberals claim it.

For these reasons, the guiding picture in this interpretation of liberalism will be that of liberals as forming a family, sharing family resemblances in some respects, but differing sharply from one another in other respects. Not only can we describe those family resemblances; we can also describe characteristics of different branches of the family. Both of these tasks we undertake later in the chapter. But first of all, we can introduce some of the family members. The five to be discussed are representatives of different aspects of liberalism, and illustrate in their particularity some of the different political and philosophical contexts within which liberal beliefs have been defended. Not all of them are universally

---

[9] John Plamenatz, by contrast, ignores economic liberalism in his survey, 'Liberalism', in P. P. Wiener (ed.), *Dictionary of the History of Ideas*, iii. 36–61.

recognized as liberals. Nevertheless, it is precisely through the arguments for their inclusion or exclusion that it is possible to discern more clearly the nature of liberalism.

3 FIVE WRITERS FROM THE LIBERAL CANON

(a) John Locke

The traditional liberal understanding of the place of John Locke in the history of liberalism has come under significant criticism in the last twenty-five years. According to this revisionist historiography, Locke did not influence Jefferson, and thus the Declaration of Independence, as much as was formerly imagined.[10] Nor did he provide the political ideology of the alleged (and anyway not particularly liberal) Whig dominance in England: there is less evidence than might be supposed that the *Two Treatises* were used in political debate in the early eighteenth century, and he may have been known principally for the *Essay concerning Human Understanding* and the *Epistola de Tolerantia*. According to one historian, 'It seems likely that Locke's chief impact in eighteenth-century England was not to import contractarianism into politics, but Arianism into religion . . . this in itself raised formidable barriers against the acceptance of his political analysis.'[11] According to another, we must see not only the more familiar face 'that smiles benignly in anticipation of the triumph of the moderate Whiggism of the eighteenth century', but also 'the more disturbing and hidden face of Locke's radicalism'.[12] In general, it is not clear that the liberal interpretation of the *Two Treatises*, which treats the work as an exposition of the ideals of constitutionalism and good sense, makes intelligible Locke's purpose in writing it or takes account of the historical and practical context in which he wrote.[13]

[10] John Dunn, 'The Politics of Locke in England and America in the Eighteenth Century', in John W. Yolton (ed.), *John Locke: Problems and Perspectives* (Cambridge: Cambridge University Press, 1969), 45–80.

[11] J. C. D. Clark, *English Society, 1688–1832* (Cambridge: Cambridge University Press, 1985), 47; see also esp. 44–50.

[12] Richard Ashcraft, 'Revolutionary Politics and Locke's *Two Treatises of Government*: Radicalism and Lockean Political Theory', *Political Theory*, 8 (1980), 431.

[13] For the revisionist historiography, see John Locke, *Two Treatises of Government*, ed. Peter Laslett (Cambridge: Cambridge University Press, 1960); John Dunn, *The Political Thought of John Locke: An Historical Account of the Argument of the 'Two Treatises of Government'* (Cambridge: Cambridge University Press, 1969); Richard Ashcraft, *Revolutionary Politics and Locke's* Two Treatises of Government

If the unreflective liberal reading of Locke is now a matter of history, two prominent interpretations by non-liberals, which analyse his thought in the same terms as they analyse liberalism as a whole, have fared little better. C. B. Macpherson's Marxist analysis[14] places Locke within the context of seventeenth-century market society and the 'possessive individualism' espoused by the rising bourgeoisie. Thus Locke adopts the Hobbesian view of the individual as made in the image of 'market man'. However, he differs from Hobbes in that his greater sociological perception leads to a refusal to accept the reduction of all moral reasoning to market rationality: he is aware that the formal possession of equal natural rights is necessary to the justification of market society, even though the class structuring of society denies the possibility of equally effective enjoyment of those rights. The Straussian picture[15] takes Locke to be following Hobbes in subordinating natural duty to the desire for and pursuit of happiness, and thus in making natural rights the foundation of the law of nature. The rule of nature is replaced by the rule of convention, and human beings and their subjectively derived aspirations become the centre of the moral world. Both Strauss and Macpherson think that Locke attempts to justify unlimited material acquisition through his theory of property, and both see him as heralding a new understanding of the relation of human beings to the world.

However, in the light of more recent work, it is clear that neither of these interpretations is satisfactory. Neither of them takes into account the theological structure which Locke presupposed. Locke assumes an ordered cosmos in which nothing was created in vain, and in which everything must serve the purpose of God implicit in its creation. Thus, in respect of moral and political behaviour, rights are exercised in virtue of and within the limitation of this order.[16] Within this framework of natural law, Locke sets out a

(Princeton: Princeton University Press, 1986). For an overview of work on Locke's political thought, see Edward J. Harpham, 'Locke's *Two Treatises* in Perspective', in Harpham (ed.), *John Locke's* Two Treatises of Government: *New Interpretations* (Lawrence, Kan.: University Press of Kansas, 1992), 1–13.

[14] C. B. Macpherson, *The Political Theory of Possessive Individualism: Hobbes to Locke* (Oxford: Oxford University Press, 1962), esp. 1–4, 263–71; pp. 194–262 are on Locke.

[15] Leo Strauss, *Natural Right and History* (Chicago: University of Chicago Press, 1953), 202–51.

[16] Dunn, *Political Thought of John Locke*, 87–95. Locke was exercised throughout his intellectual life with the difficulty concerning the epistemology of natural law. He

claim about the limits of political right, attempting to demonstrate in theory the ultimate right to overthrow the monarch. Such a demonstration was necessary as part of the radical Whig effort in the immediate aftermath of the Exclusion crisis; its direct target was Charles II.[17] Locke's work revolves around a refutation of the 'most socially plausible, though not intellectually most rigorous' defence of absolutist theory, Filmer's *Patriarcha*, published in 1680;[18] constitutional matters were included because he believed at the time of publication (after the Revolution) that there should be incorporated into the work an understanding of the contemporary constitution and the rationale for it.[19]

The Marxist interpretation surpasses the liberal interpretation at least in explaining why Locke has inconvenient non-liberal aspects, such as his attitude to the idle poor. But it has difficulties itself: in general, it is not clear that Macpherson can explain in terms of Locke's biography why it should be he in particular that served this role of ideologist of the ascending class. In fact, many of the features that this interpretation picks out to show that Locke was fundamentally committed to justifying capitalism can be understood within the framework of his understanding of the Puritan notion of the calling.[20] His adherence to this doctrine explains his acceptance of at least some existing social structures; amongst other things, it also explains his feelings that no human authority should be allowed to interfere with individual religious belief, to treat human beings as means to its own ends, or to prevent access to the physical necessities for health in an individual's calling. Because Locke rejects the ecclesiology in which the individualism of the call was balanced by church discipline, for him the necessity

believed that although 'Our mindes are not made as large as truth nor suited to the whole extent of things', nevertheless, 'the candle that is set up in us shines bright enough for all our purposes' (quoted ibid. 94). According to Dunn, the law of nature was intended to be a conclusion of the *Essay concerning Human Understanding* which would justify his use of it as a premiss of the *Two Treatises*. He fully hoped to set out a rationalist understanding of moral obligation, and failed not for want of trying but, broadly, because of the impossibility of a knowledge of natural law within a sensationalist framework (ibid. 187–9). However, see also Ashcraft, *Locke's Two Treatises of Government* (London: Allen and Unwin, 1987), 232–44.

[17] Locke as a spokesman for the minority, radical Whig group around the Earl of Shaftesbury is the central theme of Ashcraft's work.
[18] Dunn, *Political Thought of John Locke*, 48.
[19] Ibid. 53.
[20] Ibid. 203–61, *passim*. For Locke's theology of property, see further Ashcraft, *Revolutionary Politics*, 257–85.

of individual religious knowledge becomes a postulate, and human authority comes to be treated instrumentally.[21]

Against Strauss's claim that Locke's theory is based on a right to self-preservation before any duty, there should be noted the much larger number of occasions on which self-preservation is understood as a duty to God, one which can be rationally discovered.[22] Moreover, Locke was not a Hobbist, and *Leviathan* was irrelevant to his intentions in the *Two Treatises*. Both happen to disagree with Filmer, but it is only in retrospect that they could have seemed to be part of the same movement.[23] Again (and this against Macpherson as well), wealth is a good not because Locke is trying to justify the exploitative attitudes of self-centred and happiness-oriented human beings, but because it makes available the resources which God has given for enjoyment.[24]

If the effect of Locke's political writings on the development of Whig ideology was rather more limited than has previously been supposed, and if it was not his intention to provide a detached justification of the eternal verities of constitutional liberalism, it is not clear in what sense Locke may properly be called a liberal. Strictly, he should be located in the line of neo-Thomist natural law contractarians and Calvinist revolutionaries. Nevertheless, it can still be urged that there are themes in his writings that have led to his retrospectively being appropriated as a liberal. And it is this that is interesting and relevant to present purposes. That current historiography may regard as problematic his position near the beginning of the liberal canon does not matter ultimately, for Locke *does* articulate what will later be regarded as shibboleths of constitutional liberalism: government by consent; the supreme power of the people to remove or alter the legislature when it acts contrary to their trust; the executive as subordinate and accountable to the legislature; the need for established, promulgated, and consistently applied law; private property; representation of the people; and the rights of the majority to conclude for the whole. And there are other features: his belief that coercing religion involves a category mistake,[25] his

---

[21] Dunn, *Political Thought of John Locke*, 249.

[22] Ibid. 157–64.   [23] Ibid. 218–19, 77–83.

[24] John Dunn, 'Justice and the Interpretation of Locke's Political Theory', *Political Studies*, 16 (1968), 68–87, claims that in respect of justice also, conventional human law is always subordinate to the divine demand.

[25] John Locke, *Epistola de Tolerantia* (1689), ed. Raymond Klibansky, trans. J. W. Gough (Oxford: Clarendon Press, 1968), 68–9.

granting the right to resist even to 'any single man', and the reshaping in his earlier career of the fundamental political question from what the subjects are obliged to do to what the ruler is justified in exacting, and thus to an instrumental account of political authority.[26]

(b) Immanuel Kant

That Kant's political thought verged on the radical can be seen from the historical context of his writing.[27] Unlike Britain at that time, Germany in the latter part of the eighteenth century was still largely feudal or semi-feudal. The division into little backwater principalities, the continued poverty, the tradition of absolute monarchies, and the slow growth of the bourgeoisie had not encouraged the practical, calculating empiricism of mercantilist, Calvinist England. Thus German religion had an inward, pietistic leaning, and German philosophy tended to be more abstract and remote than its English counterpart. Again, there was little room for political freedom: in Frederick the Great's Prussia, according to Lessing, freedom of speech extended only to the criticism of religion, not of government. Within political thought, the tradition which most influenced Kant—namely, the natural law school which descended from Grotius and Pufendorf—was not angled towards the justification of revolution; this was despite the radical implications that similar doctrines had had elsewhere through their stress on equality. Therefore, for Kant to celebrate in 'Theory and Practice' four years after the French Revolution the values of freedom, equality, and the independence of citizens as co-legislators was tantamount to subversion. And he allayed suspicion of this only by his deferential refusal to allow rebellion and, two years later, his ironic disclaimer to political relevance at the beginning of 'Perpetual Peace'.[28]

His political thought must be seen in the light of his philosophy

[26] Dunn, *Political Thought of John Locke*, 27–40.

[27] Kant's main political writings are collected in Hans Reiss (ed.), *Kant's Political Writings*, 2nd edn. (Cambridge: Cambridge University Press, 1991). Recent secondary literature includes Susan Meld Shell, *The Rights of Reason: A Study of Kant's Philosophy and Politics* (Toronto: University of Toronto Press, 1980); Howard Williams, *Kant's Political Philosophy* (Oxford: Blackwell, 1983); *idem* (ed.), *Essays on Kant's Political Philosophy* (Cardiff: University of Wales Press, 1992).

[28] Immanuel Kant, 'Perpetual Peace: A Philosophical Sketch' (1795), in Reiss (ed.), *Kant's Political Writings*, 93.

of history. For only if history is progressive, he claims, is it rational
to act: action has little value if there is no guarantee that it will
result in improvement. His interpretation of history also provides
an argument against rebellion: because history is advancing
towards republicanism and world peace anyway, the goals of
greater freedom and concord of humankind will be achieved in
time without violent revolution.[29] This optimistic view of history is
defended in a number of ways.[30] First, nature, which is the world
of necessity, is also the work of Providence: although the material
and phenomenal world is determined by mechanical laws, in giving
human beings the instinct for survival and self-interest it has also
worked to promote the good of the whole species. Second, human
actions are subject to patterning: though each person acts freely,
statistics over large populations of marriages or births show
predictability. Third, it would seem impertinent to suppose that
nature has assigned a function to bodily organs, but not to the
human race as a whole. World peace, he holds, will be achieved
because of the gains from international trade and universal republican freedom, and because survival will be preferred to destruction
by increasingly horrendous weapons. However, his belief in progress is ultimately governed by moral rather than theoretical
considerations: regarded empirically, history is a mechanical development; but regarded morally, to deny progress is to allow the
possibility of regress to barbarism, which is unacceptable. This
paradox is resolved in terms of his epistemology: that history *is* not
teleologically ordered does not imply that we cannot *understand* it
in teleological terms.

The specific context of Kant's political philosophy is his moral
philosophy: for him, a theory of politics amounts to a metaphysics
of justice, itself a part of the metaphysic of morals.[31] Human
beings can be seen from two standpoints, the phenomenal and the
noumenal, the worlds of nature and freedom. Corresponding to
these, there are two types of duty. First, there is duty imposed by
internal legislation, addressed to oneself as a noumenal being, and
for which the moral law is the incentive to obedience. This law
governs motives rather than actions: an action performed in

[29] Cf. Reiss (ed.), *Kant's Political Writings*, 38.
[30] Williams, *Kant's Political Philosophy*, 1–27; Reiss (ed.), *Kant's Political Writings*, 35–8.
[31] Williams, *Kant's Political Philosophy*, 52–67.

accordance with this law but with a heteronomous maxim may be moral, but the agent can only be called moral or virtuous if the motive is correct—that is, if the law is treated as in itself a sufficient incentive of the will. Second, there is duty imposed by the external legislation of the political authority, addressed to human beings considered both noumenally and phenomenally; the incentive to obey is not only the moral law but also the threat of coercion. The ideal is the 'Kingdom of Ends' outlined in the *Groundwork of the Metaphysic of Morals*; but people do not always act morally, and so the theory of right must attend to the constraints required to ensure the settlement of conflicts of interest. However, external law has jurisdiction over actions alone; though as noumenal beings people can see that positive laws are morally necessary, and therefore should be obeyed as prescribed by the moral law, they cannot be obliged by those laws to have that motive for obedience.

Morality, therefore, is concerned only with motives; politics and juridical law with actions. Further, just as maxims of the good will must be universalizable according to the categorical imperative, so actions must conform to the universal principle of right (*Recht*) to be legal: 'every action which by itself or by its maxim enables the freedom of each individual's will to co-exist with the freedom of everyone else in accordance with a universal law is *right*.'[32] Thus political freedom is the freedom from any external constraint save legal coercion: such freedom is justified because it allows the expression of autonomy, because it treats people as ends rather than means, and because we do not know the inner life of another (and therefore the motives from which they act). Although Kant's notion of moral autonomy resembles Isaiah Berlin's positive liberty, it is clear that he understands political freedom as a negative liberty.[33]

From this principle of external human right are derived a number of a priori principles which are necessary for a lawful civil state. First is the freedom of every member of the common-wealth to be happy in accordance with his own conception of happiness, 'so long as he does not infringe upon the freedom of others to pursue a similar end which can be reconciled with the

---

[32] Kant, 'The Metaphysic of Morals' (1797), in Reiss (ed.), *Kant's Political Writings*, 133.

[33] Williams, *Kant's Political Philosophy*, 67–9.

freedom of everyone else within a workable general law'.[34] Paternalism, which suspends the freedom and denies the rights of subjects, is the greatest imaginable tyranny. Nevertheless, Kant argues, a patriotic attitude is necessary, one 'where everyone in the state, not excepting its head, regards the commonwealth as a maternal womb, or the land as the paternal ground from which he himself sprang and which he must leave to his descendants as a treasured pledge'.[35] Second is the equality of all as subjects: that is, the right of coercion of each against all others, except the head of state, through whom this right is exercised on behalf of everyone. This equality is quite consistent with great inequalities of possessions: for all are equal as subjects before the law, which concerns only 'the form of right and not the material or object in relation to which I possess rights',[36] and all have equal opportunities in the sense that careers are open to 'talent, industry and good fortune'.[37] Third is the independence of members of the commonwealth as citizens and co-legislators. Not all, however, have the rights to full citizenship, even though all are obliged to obey the laws. Everyone has the right to attempt to gain property, but only those who own property and are masters of themselves, and therefore free to serve the commonwealth alone, are entitled to participate in legislation. Fourth is the principle of 'publicness'.[38] Citizens are allowed freedom of expression, to criticize the government, so long as it is exercised tactfully. This freedom does not permit outright rebellion: subjects have no right of rebellion against the head of state, since public law is derived from the a priori and infallible standard of the idea of an original contract, and is thus beyond reproach; moreover, if there were rebellion, there could be no judge to decide between the sides.[39] Nevertheless, the people have the 'freedom of the pen' as the protection of their rights, 'although

---

[34] Kant, 'On the Common Saying: "This May be True in Theory, but it Does not Apply in Practice" ' (1793), in Reiss (ed.), *Kant's Political Writings*, 74.

[35] Ibid.

[36] Ibid. 75.

[37] Ibid. 76.

[38] Williams, *Kant's Political Philosophy*, 149–57.

[39] Kant applauded the French Revolution, but disapproved of its violence. He squared it with his principles through the claim that the States-General did not usurp the Crown's authority; rather, by convoking the States-General, Louis XVI resigned his constitutional sovereignty in favour of the people. Thus Reiss, 'Postscript' to *Kant's Political Writings*, 261–3; though see Peter P. Nicholson, 'Kant, Revolutions and History', in Williams (ed.), *Essays on Kant's Political Philosophy*, 249–68.

it must not transcend the bounds of respect and devotion towards the existing constitution'.[40]

Historically, Kant's major contribution to the liberal tradition probably lies in his moral philosophy; the notion of treating people as ends rather than means is presupposed by many modern rights-based versions of liberalism. Again, his account of morality as rational willing has generated the ethics of impartiality that now often does service for objectivity.[41] But his political thought also (aside from his discountenancing of rebellion) reflects many typically liberal themes: a progressivist philosophy of history, a belief in the power of reason, a universalizing mode of thought (which for him led to an internationalism), the use of a hypothetical original contract, and the values of freedom, equality, and independence. In these, as well as in other respects (such as the limitation of active citizenship to the male and propertied), Kant is fully representative of eighteenth-century bourgeois liberalism.

(c) John Stuart Mill

By comparison with the radical liberalism of the Revolutionary era, English liberalism of the first half of the nineteenth century was a moderate political creed. Philosophically, it rejected the doctrine of natural rights and its underlying rationalist epistemology in favour of native British empiricism and associationist psychology. Socially and politically, it was sustained by a middle class whose increasingly assured position abrogated the need for violent revolution. Two overlapping intellectual traditions articulated the beliefs which served the needs of this section of society, and expressed its ideals. The political economists, notably Smith and Ricardo, had taken a stand for *laissez-faire* and free trade. Arguing from the assumption of the mutual independence of government and economy, they held that the market was self-sufficient, and, left alone, would come closer to economic equilibrium than systems of intervention.

---

[40] Kant, 'Theory and Practice', 85.

[41] 'In trying to replace speculative rationalism by a voluntaristic rationalism, Kant attempts to find a *via media* between the rationalism of Wolff and the stress on individual moral freedom of Pietism. He retains the rationalist criteria of unity, harmony, coherence and consistency; but he applies them to the will, qua practical reason, rather than to reason as a contemplative, intellectual faculty' (Keith Ward, *The Development of Kant's View of Ethics* (Oxford: Blackwell, 1972), 172). Ward argues that the conjunction is inconsistent.

State interference was pointless: those advocating poor relief or trade unions, Ricardo alleged in Malthusian vein, 'might as well attempt to regulate the tides by force'.[42] In respect of foreign trade it was believed that the mercantilist accumulation of wealth prevented the enjoyment of the gains from trade, and that restrictions should be lifted: indeed, the removal of tariffs on corn imports was the principal aim of the free-traders. The second group of theorists, the philosophical radicals, or Benthamites, also shared this goal, though they concentrated on political and judicial reform. Rejecting all sources of value other than sensation, and adopting an ontology that denied any appeal to collectivities that covertly served to resist change, Bentham used the principle of the greatest happiness and the felicific calculus to justify sweeping changes in industry, the penal system, and the constitution.

John Stuart Mill absorbed many of the ideals of his father and Jeremy Bentham: the education described in his *Autobiography* was intended for a future leader of the philosophical radical movement. His *Principles of Political Economy*, which argued for a qualified *laissez-faire*, was an update of Smith's *Wealth of Nations*; and *Considerations on Representative Government* defended a constitutional government that ensured the rights of all citizens and, through proportional representation, allowed minorities to have a role in government. However, the feature of liberalism that is especially associated with Mill, and on which attention will be focused, is his doctrine of liberty, and the theory of happiness, freedom, and human nature on which it is founded.

Perhaps the most powerful contemporary reconstruction of Mill's doctrine of liberty, that of John Gray, claims that Mill defends a theory of rights within a utilitarian framework.[43] A

---

[42] Quoted in Bullock and Shock, *Liberal Tradition*, p. xxiv.

[43] John Gray, *Mill on Liberty: A Defence* (London: Routledge and Kegan Paul, 1983): the account given here is his in all essentials. Gray's book is part of a trend towards a more generous interpretation of Mill that started with John C. Rees ('A Re-reading of Mill on Liberty', *Political Studies*, 8 (1960), 113–29) and was developed in, for example, Alan Ryan, *The Philosophy of John Stuart Mill*, 2nd edn. (London: Macmillan, 1987); the older interpretations (e.g. Isaiah Berlin, 'John Stuart Mill and the Ends of Life', in *Four Essays on Liberty* (Oxford: Oxford University Press, 1969), 173–206) usually took him to be guilty of massive inconsistencies between *On Liberty* and *Utilitarianism*; for these see Gray, *Mill on Liberty*, 1–9. For an important restatement of the older view, see C. L. Ten, 'Mill's Defence of Liberty', in John Gray and G. W. Smith (eds.), *John Stuart Mill's On Liberty in Focus* (London and New York: Routledge, 1991), 212–38.

chapter in *A System of Logic*[44] is the starting-point for this reconciliation of *Utilitarianism* and *On Liberty*: according to this, the several principles and conclusions of the practical arts form a body of doctrine called the 'art of life', which governs all conduct. The supreme principle of the 'art of life', the one which judges all others if they conflict, is the principle of utility: this is not practical, but axiological, and states that happiness (understood in terms of pleasure and pain) is the only valuable end. This principle can only become action-guiding if it is complemented by the (not always explicit) principle of expediency; according to this, an expedient act is one which produces a net increase in utility, and a maximally expedient act is one which produces as much utility as any other. However, direct recourse to utility, whether to decide social rules or particular acts, is liable to be self-defeating. There are three reasons for this. First, there is only limited information concerning probable consequences. Second, happiness cannot be directly aimed at, but is epiphenomenal to participation in activities which are chosen for themselves. Third, happiness can only be achieved within a stable set of social and political conditions and the reliable expectations that these provide—they should not be defeasible by particular utilitarian calculations. Utility maximization is more likely to be served, not by continually allowing direct appeals to utility, but by adopting side-constraint principles that prevent such direct appeals. Though the principle of utility is useful for judging codes of conduct as a whole (that is, for critical morality), it will tend to be self-defeating in settling questions of practical morality, and should only be consulted if the precepts of the 'art of life' conflict. Mill thus has neither an act- nor a rule-utilitarianism, but rather an indirect utilitarianism.[45]

The side-constraint principle which performs this function of protecting rights against the ravages of unfettered utility is the principle of liberty. This is expressed in the two maxims which 'form the entire doctrine' of *On Liberty*: that 'the individual is not accountable to society for his actions, in so far as these concern the interests of no person but himself', but only for 'such actions as

---

[44] VI. xii. 6 (in *The Collected Works of John Stuart Mill*, vii–viii: *A System of Logic Ratiocinative and Inductive*, ed. J. M. Robson (Toronto: University of Toronto Press, and London: Routledge and Kegan Paul, 1973–4), viii. 943–52).

[45] Gray, *Mill on Liberty*, 19–47.

are prejudicial to the interests of others'.[46] Not all interests, however, seem to give rise to rights (otherwise any whimsical desire could be claimed to be an interest),[47] but only the 'vital' or 'essential' interests of security and autonomy. Security—that is, the freedom from arbitrary government, the right to have promises and contracts kept, and the other conditions of stable society—is necessary, 'since nothing but the gratification of the instant could be of any worth to us, if we could be deprived of anything the next instant by whoever was momentarily stronger than ourselves'.[48] Autonomy (which is autarchy—the possession of negative freedom and rational self-direction—plus the freedom of an agent to be detached from social habits and conventions and from the pressure to conform) is a vital interest because it is a necessary ingredient of, and not just a means to, happiness. Harm to these two interests alone justifies limiting liberty.[49]

Mill's general doctrine of liberty, then, including the principles of utility, expediency, and liberty, and also an implicit principle of equity, is characterized by its separation of critical and practical morality, its sophisticated justification of rights from utilitarian premises, and its granting of special status to the interests of autonomy and security. His defence of security as a vital interest is reasonable, but that of autonomy requires further justification. For this it is necessary to turn to his theory of human nature and happiness.

Mill's theory of human nature is radically historicist: though he believes that the only way to make human behaviour intelligible is to subsume it under law-like principles, he does not think that human nature is constant. Rather, it is susceptible of indefinite change and improvement, because of the indeterminacy engendered by the faculty of choice. However, although Mill has this basically non-essentialist conception of human nature, he does share the Romantic belief that each individual has his or her own unique nature, difficult though this may be to square with his official empiricism. Discovery of this nature is a matter of self-knowledge, and may be assisted by the 'experiments in living' he

[46] Mill, *On Liberty* (1859), in Mary Warnock (ed.), *Utilitarianism* (London: Collins, 1962), 226.
[47] Rees, 'A Re-reading of Mill', had come to a similar conclusion.
[48] Mill, *Utilitarianism*, in Warnock (ed.), *Utilitarianism*, 310.
[49] Gray, *Mill on Liberty*, 48–69. It is debated whether the principle of liberty is to be interpreted as preventing harm or harmful conduct.

advocates. Connected with this notion of individual human nature is a pluralistic conception of happiness: pleasures will differ between people. Happiness is also hierarchical. There are higher pleasures, which express the individual nature of the person experiencing the pleasure. However, they must be chosen after trying out a selection of alternatives appropriate to that particular nature. This is because for Mill the making of choices is central to the good life: those who have experienced the freedom to choose always prefer having it, *ceteris paribus*, to not having it. It is this capacity to make choices between the alternative ways of life compatible with the individual nature of each that constitutes autonomy. Such a conception of autonomy is not to be taken to imply that Mill has an ideal-regarding moral theory: it is as much because the presence of autonomy is very widely regarded as preferable to its absence that it is treated as an essential interest, as it is that Mill thinks that all should prefer the freedom of choice. Similarly, liberty is not defended by him because it will lead to a free society, but rather because autonomy is possible only if there is liberty.[50]

'If anyone has ever been a true liberal, it was John Stuart Mill' (Gray).[51] Such a sentiment goes virtually unchallenged, at least among English-speaking writers. For Gray, Mill's liberalism is most prominent in two areas. First is his commitment to a regulative neutrality between different understandings of the human good; Mill, it is claimed, may have preferred self-chosen to conventional lives, 'but this is a procedural perfectionism rather than a full theory of the good life'.[52] Second, Gray points to Mill's belief in the near irreversibility of the condition of freedom. This is not merely the claim that those who have tasted liberty and non-liberty will always prefer the former, but also that, were democracy to stop increasing in influence (about which Mill is doubtful), human history would progress towards increasing freedom for individuals. In addition to these aspects named by Gray, two other characteristically liberal features are to be found. The first is Mill's belief in the role of reason in the discovery of truth and the settling of disputes. The second centres around his concern for the individual: not only did he defend the individual against social coercion and demand a private realm free from social interference,

---

[50] Ibid. 70–89.   [51] Ibid. 119.   [52] Ibid. 88.

which was his purpose in writing *On Liberty*; he also recognized the contribution of individuals to the progress of society—a liberal-romantic appreciation of individual genius. In all of these respects Mill's claim to inclusion in the liberal canon must remain undisputed.

(d) L. T. Hobhouse

Towards the end of the nineteenth century, many of the traditional liberal ideals—constitutional government, universal suffrage (at least for male ratepayers), freedom of opinion and expression, and others—had been realized in Britain. Liberalism seemed to have served its purpose, and was destined to be a fading political force for the very reason of its success. Political attention had turned to the need for social reform, to rectify injustices perceived to stem largely from inhumane industrial practices and the economic liberalism which in effect legitimated them. If liberalism was to remain the dominant political movement, it would have to find a rationale for greater government intervention, so that it could justify industrial and sanitary reform, state education and health provision, unemployment benefit and free labour exchanges. That it was made relevant again to the mood of the age was the work of a group of intellectuals who, during the four decades that straddled the turn of the century, fashioned a political theory which significantly influenced policy and which (although it failed to revive the Liberal Party) still—to many minds—represents a viable and attractive set of beliefs.

Like other contemporary doctrines, the New Liberalism was heir to many intellectual movements of the nineteenth century.[53] Political economy was no longer regarded as supreme amongst human sciences, a theoretical enterprise devoted to the abstract structure of a perfectly functioning society. As a result of those prophets who protested against unfeeling industrialization that there is no wealth but life, economics began to be treated instead as a means to relieving suffering; likewise, the role of community displaced the ideal of competition. Utilitarianism continued to provide the motivation for social reform, and encouraged liberals to drop their traditional hostility to the state. It too had changed, relinquishing the greatest happiness principle, the felicific calculus,

[53] Michael Freeden, *The New Liberalism: An Ideology of Social Reform* (Oxford: Clarendon Press, 1978), 7–21.

and the aggregative approach to society, and adopting instead a social conception of utility and the goals of liberty and welfare. From positivism the New Liberals took the evolutionary outlook, the sense that the whole social system was worthy of attention, and the beliefs that there could be a unified social science and that the environment could be controlled rationally; however, they rejected the value-free approach to the human sciences, the quantificational analyses of behaviour, and the reduction of ethics to science that positivism had espoused. The influence of idealism was less than some accounts have suggested, and was only one element in the general progressive movement: '[had T. H.] Green not existed, liberalism would still have become collectivist and favourably oriented to progressive social reform.'[54] Similarly in the case of biology, which was the dominant scientific influence on contemporary social thought, the organicist conception of society was more influential than the better-known social Darwinism. Again, the role of evangelicalism should not be exaggerated: by the time of the New Liberals, Non-conformist moral vigour probably provided little more than the 'ethical overtones of reform'.[55]

Perhaps the most important of the New Liberals was L. T. Hobhouse, who attempted to refashion liberalism by changing its conceptions of freedom and of the relation of the individual to society. Against the Manchester school, he pointed up the hypocrisy of supporting unlimited freedom and opposition to coercion: while traditional economic liberalism had defended the right to complete freedom from force in (for example) the making of contracts, it had neglected to note that not all consent is free, or all coercion overt and physical. True consent, he argued with Green,[56] requires equality of both parties to the transaction, unlike forced bargains in which '[the] weaker man consents as one slipping over a precipice might consent to give all his fortune to one who will throw him a rope on no other terms'.[57] Freedom

---

[54] Ibid. 17.   [55] Ibid. 16.

[56] Cf. T. H. Green, 'Lecture on "Liberal Legislation and Freedom of Contract"', in R. L. Nettleship (ed.), *Works*, 3 vols. (London: Longmans, Green & Co., 1885–8), iii. 382: 'To uphold the sanctity of contract is doubtless a prime business of government, but it is no less its business to provide against contracts being made, which, from the helplessness of one of the parties to them, instead of being a security for freedom, become an instrument of disguised oppression.'

[57] L. T. Hobhouse, *Liberalism* (1911) (repr. New York: Oxford University Press, 1964), 50.

always depends on the restraint of those who threaten it, and is thus complemented by, rather than opposed to, coercion.

Behind this lies a rejection of the traditional liberal conception of the individual person separate from society, with unassailable rights over life, liberty, and estate, who enters into society by contract. By the time of Hobhouse's *Liberalism*, the organic conception of society, derived from biology and idealism, had become commonplace. Hobhouse's version of it holds that something is called 'organic' when 'it is made up of parts which are quite distinct from one another, but which are destroyed or vitally altered when they are removed from the whole'.[58] Human beings are much more than their opinions and actions: '[the] real man is something more than is ever adequately expressed in terms which his fellows can understand'. It is the sense of ultimate oneness which is the 'real meaning of equality' and the 'foundation of social solidarity'.[59] From this notion of society as an organic unity it follows that the individual would be 'something utterly different if he could be separated from society . . . By language, by training, by simply living with others, each of us absorbs into his system the social atmosphere that surrounds us.'[60] The individual, that is, is by nature social. This results in a fundamental recasting of the notion of a right: it is not something which cannot be overridden by considerations of the common good; indeed, for Hobhouse it cannot conflict with or exist apart from the common good. For a right must be grounded not merely in a claim, but in a claim that is reasonable to an impartial observer; and such an observer will consider not only the good of particular individuals but also the common good: thus rights and the common good cannot ultimately be opposed to each other. Moreover, since (on this understanding of the common good) the good of each is part of the good of all, it seems that each has a concern for the interests of all others. Hobhouse agrees with Mill that the correct response to error is not indifference but argument for the truth. Again, '[if] we refrain from coercing a man for his own good, it is not because his good is indifferent to us, but because it cannot be furthered by coercion.'[61]

This raises the question of the role that Hobhouse allots to the individual. Individuals do not remain unaffected by association. Yet this does not imply that society is in itself a whole which is

[58] Hobhouse, *Liberalism*, 67.   [59] Ibid. 65.
[60] Ibid. 67–8.   [61] Ibid. 76.

opposed to the sum of individuals, or in which the identity of individuals is lost.[62] Hobhouse therefore rejects the ideas of a 'real will' of society and of a concrete universalism in which every particular is a moment in the systematic totality that is the state. He could never have countenanced the kind of coercion that some have detected in Hegel or in parts of Rousseau, where freedom is compulsion to do the good. Nevertheless, Hobhouse does adopt a notion of freedom as rational self-direction that resembles superficially that of Mill, but which denies the want-regarding elements in Mill's conception. For 'liberty is necessary to the development of personality. And since personality consists in rational determination by clear-sighted purpose as against the role of impulse on the one side or external compulsion on the other, it follows that liberty of choice is the condition of its development.'[63] For Mill, autonomy was a good because people preferred it to its absence, but for Hobhouse, it is itself a good, since it contributes to the growth of personality which is the human ideal.[64]

Hobhouse's organic conception of society is ultimately justified by his doctrine of progress. He believes, indeed, that '[every] constructive social doctrine rests on the conception of social progress'.[65] Although such a process depends on choosing the course that makes for social harmony out of the possible forms of disorder, it seems likely that he would only have been as optimistic as he was (and as disillusioned by the First World War[66]) if he had believed that progress was likely. And indeed, the metaphysical ground for such a belief is to be found in the quasi-idealism and teleological conception of reality, with its concentration on potential harmony rather than actual conflict, that he absorbed from the British idealists[67] and his Oxford Greats lectures on Aristotle.

Was Hobhouse a liberal? Or is he better termed a social democrat or even a socialist? In the usage of the time 'socialism'

---

[62] Cf. Hobhouse, *The Metaphysical Theory of the State* (London: George Allen and Unwin, 1918), 32–3, on the relation of parts to the whole.

[63] Hobhouse, *Social Evolution and Political Theory* (New York: Columbia University Press, 1911), quoted in Stefan Collini, *Liberalism and Sociology: L. T. Hobhouse and Political Argument in England, 1880–1914* (Cambridge: Cambridge University Press, 1979), 123.

[64] Collini, *Liberalism and Sociology*, 123–4. In fact, this contrast is too schematic: Mill would never have denied that autonomy was a good in itself. Mill does not come out clearly on one side of the want-regarding/ideal-regarding distinction.

[65] Hobhouse, *Liberalism*, 57.

[66] Collini, *Liberalism and Sociology*, 245–53.   [67] Ibid. 235–44.

could refer to several things: a new society without the family, religion, etc.; a society based on co-operation, not competition; proletarian revolution; nationalization of basic industries; and distributive justice.[68] Of these, only the last is plausibly ascribed to Hobhouse. But such a doctrine about redistribution is compatible with a wide range of liberal beliefs: indeed, much of this kind of socialist thinking—that which had descended from heaven to political relevance—took place within the Liberal movement. Hobhouse could find the Labour Party too sectional;[69] he could condemn mechanical socialism—that is, the various Marxisms—and official socialism—that is, the élitist, eugenist, standardizing Fabianism. Yet he could toy with the idea of a liberal socialism which would be democratic (expressive of and responsive to the desires of the people) and protective of individual liberty as necessary to the development of personality.[70] It is best to perceive him (as in practice it is best to perceive Mill) as a liberal with socialist, or at least social democratic, tendencies.[71]

(e) F. A. Hayek

The interest of Hayek for the historian of liberalism lies in two areas: first, through his *The Road to Serfdom* he helped create the post-war climate of liberal consensus, fuelling the cautious gradualism and opposition to 'totalitarianism' that characterized the time of the Cold War and beyond. Second, he was the most important defender of the revived classical economics adopted by several right-wing governments during the 1980s. Both his brand of conservative liberalism and his advocacy of *laissez-faire* are grounded in a distinctive epistemology and theory of society, and it is from these that we start.

Hayek's epistemology is a modified Kantianism.[72] From Kant he

---

[68] Collini, *Liberalism and Sociology*, 34–5.

[69] Peter Clarke, *Liberals and Social Democrats* (Cambridge: Cambridge University Press, 1978), 237–8.

[70] Hobhouse, *Liberalism*, 87, 88–91.

[71] There was also a difference between liberal and socialist social reform (Freeden, *New Liberalism*, 158–60): liberals retained competition, were concerned to avoid sacrificing liberty to equality, preferred equality of human dignity to economic equality. Cf. also Green's liberal proposal that the law should prevent sale of labour on terms below certain standards, compared with the socialists' general concern for different economic conditions (Melvin Richter, *The Politics of Conscience: T. H. Green and his Age* (London: Weidenfeld and Nicolson, 1964), 285).

[72] John Gray, *Hayek on Liberty* (Oxford: Blackwell, 1984), 4–8, 10–16, 21–6.

derives a scepticism with regard to knowledge that claims to be independent of the structures of the mind, maintaining that there are no discernible essences and that all experience is theory-laden. To this he adds several features. From Michael Polanyi he accepts that tacit knowledge is central and that practical knowledge is prior to theoretical knowledge. He anticipates Popper's later work in adopting an evolutionary epistemology, and agrees with the later Wittgenstein about the shaping role of language on thought and the function of social rules in the communication of practical knowledge. This generally cautious view of knowledge is reinforced by the belief that there are meta-conscious rules of the mind which are in principle unidentifiable: although the mind is governed by rules, the most fundamental of these can never be known, so there can be rule-following without fully articulated knowledge.

Because we know more than we can say, the social order cannot be the result of a directing intelligence. The problem with economic or social planning is not just that the information required to plan successfully is too vast and too complex, but that the mind responsible for planning is itself governed by rules to which it has no access. Therefore, if there is apparent order in society, this cannot be due to design (to claim which would be to commit what Hayek calls the 'constructivist' fallacy), but to the ability of a spontaneous order to solve the problem of knowledge involved in achieving a satisfactory and balanced society or economy. Such a balance is attained through the rules developed in the natural self-regulation of the evolutionary process. Thus Hayek attacks the dichotomy, found in some traditional explanations of social phenomena, of unchangeable instinct (the Sophists' *phusis*) and intentional contrivance (*nomos*).[73]

This notion of a spontaneous social order (which he calls a 'catallaxy') therefore comprises three elements: first, the 'invisible hand' thesis, that social arrangements are due to human action, but not ultimately to human rational design; second, the belief in the priority of tacit knowledge; and third, the thesis that cultures evolve through the natural selection of conflicting traditions.[74] The general conception is applied in most detail to the economic order, with the conclusion that unrestrained economic activity will lead to equilibrium. The market solves the basic epistemological problem implicit in distributing a limited quantity of resources

[73] Ibid. 27–30.   [74] Ibid. 33–4.

among an indefinitely large number of agents: the problem, that is, of gathering up data, widely scattered and constantly changing, about individual preferences and demands for goods, on the one hand, and about available supplies, on the other. Complete knowledge of this sort is unavailable either to individuals or to groups of economic agents, but is embodied in the fluctuations of prices in the open market. Thus no rationally planned economy will achieve the same economic use of resources and satisfaction of consumers as an unfettered price system.[75] Moreover, because of this problem of knowledge, it is inappropriate to criticize economic systems on moral grounds. Rather, they should be judged in terms of their ability to solve a central economic question: namely, that of the efficient distribution of scarce resources.[76]

Hayek's claims about the limited role of reason lead to some conservative tendencies in his thought. He holds that conservatives correctly emphasize the spontaneous development of phenomena such as language, law, and morality.[77] And he criticizes those who think that a rich cult of individuality is viable without strong moral conventions, as well as those who fail to see that individuality is a historical growth and not a timeless natural given.[78] Traditional morality must be accepted, because morality evolves and is thus relative to an age; however, because nobody knows to which aspects of an age morality is relative, nobody can safely tamper with it. Nor can its future be predicted; so arguments which appeal to future trends cannot be used to defend deliberate moral innovations.[79]

But Hayek is not a conservative. Among the reasons he lists in his celebrated piece 'Why I Am Not a Conservative',[80] he mentions that conservatives are afraid of the future, whereas he believes that it should be faced with courage and confidence. Moreover, they are fond of authority in a way incompatible with liberty; they do

---

[75] Hayek, 'The Use of Knowledge in Society', 'Socialist Calculation I', and 'Socialist Calculation II', in *Individualism and Economic Order* (London: Routledge and Kegan Paul, 1949), 77–91, 119–47, 148–80 respectively. These papers lack the (Michael) Polanyian twist found later.

[76] Gray, *Hayek on Liberty*, 41.

[77] Hayek, *The Constitution of Liberty* (London: Routledge and Kegan Paul, 1960), 399–400.

[78] Gray, *Hayek on Liberty*, 99–101. This of course need not have only conservative implications.

[79] Ibid. 56–8; Hayek, *Constitution of Liberty*, 35–6, 65–7.

[80] In Hayek, *Constitution of Liberty*, 397–411.

not understand economic forces; they have no principles by which they can work together politically with those who disagree, and so build a peaceful society with the minimum of coercion; and they tend towards regarding moral and religious beliefs as the proper objects of coercion. Although he holds to the doctrine of tacit knowledge, he is opposed to mystification: 'I am simply an unrepentant Old Whig—with the stress on the "Old"'.[81]

His liberalism extends much further than opposition to economic interventionism. For there are also limitations on the knowledge of how civilization grows. Since innovation cannot be predicted, progress cannot be planned, but rather happens through the independent and anonymous workings of lots of individuals. This requires freedom for all, so that opportunity is provided at least for the unknown few to make beneficial contributions to society.[82] This freedom he interprets in a traditional liberal manner: the state of liberty is 'that condition of men in which coercion of some by others is reduced as much as is possible in society',[83] and coercion is 'such control of the environment or circumstances of a person by another that, in order to avoid greater evil, he is forced to act not according to a coherent plan of his own but to serve the ends of another'.[84]

This stress on liberty has two implications for Hayek. First, it justifies equality before the law and equality in the rules that govern moral and social conduct, for these genuinely extend freedom. No other kinds of equality are similarly compatible with liberty: resources egalitarianism is anti-liberal (as well as being necessarily inaccurate in its results because of the inherent epistemological problem), since it requires differential treatment of people, and this conflicts with the prior liberal principle of equality before the law. Moreover, such distributivism requires the imposition of an allocative pattern chosen because of a particular theory of individual merit; such a theory is in principle unjustifiable, because nobody has 'the capacity to determine conclusively the potentialities of other human beings'.[85] People should enjoy advantages in proportion to the benefits (as evaluated by the market) which accrue from their activities, rather than in proportion to other people's opinions of the moral character of their actions.[86]

[81] Ibid. 409.　　　　　[82] Ibid. 22–32.　　　　　[83] Ibid. 11.
[84] Ibid. 20–1.　　　　　　　　　　　　　　　　　　　[85] Ibid. 88.
[86] Ibid. 85–102. He has an ostensibly voluntarist justification of equality:

Second, Hayek's emphasis on liberty has consequences for legislation. If legislation is not limited by more general principles, freedom is likely to be eroded by piecemeal legislation enacted in response to the immediate demands of expediency.[87] These principles Hayek finds in a Kantian universalizability. Like R. M. Hare, he holds that this will lead to the formal criterion of consistency, yet also to impartiality between agents and moral neutrality between versions of the good life, and thus to a concern for the general welfare. Therefore, when he accepts from Hume that certain rules of justice are indispensable to human welfare (namely, the artificial but not arbitrary principles of the rights of property, of transfer by consent and of promise-keeping), his ultimate ground is not utilitarianism but Kantianism. Moreover (though this is arguably not Kantian), this test of universalizability shows, he thinks, that law is not ultimately positive but a matter of rational discovery—a claim which he holds in tension with his beliefs about the importance of tradition.[88]

Freedom is important, Hayek says, because it promotes progress. But progress is not a good because of the goal it leads to; indeed, '[the] question whether, if we had to stop at our present stage of development, we would in any significant sense be better off or happier than if we had stopped a hundred or a thousand years ago is probably unanswerable'.[89] Rather, the process itself is valuable, the 'successful striving for what at each moment seems attainable . . . movement for movement's sake'.[90] Nevertheless, its value seems to be at least ambiguous. Since a significant part of the world's population has become accustomed to the expectation of increase in material possessions, failure to satisfy this would probably lead to international war, since human beings are 'not only the creatures but also the captives of progress'. Freedom is a

'Nothing . . . is more damaging to the demand for equal treatment than to base it on so obviously untrue an assumption as that of the factual equality of all men. To rest the case for equal treatment of national or racial minorities on the assertion that they do not differ from other men is implicitly to admit that factual inequality would justify unequal treatment; and the proof that some differences do, in fact, exist would not be long in forthcoming. It is of the essence of the demand for equality before the law that people should be treated alike in spite of the fact that they are different' (p. 86).

[87] Hayek, *Constitution of Liberty*, 67–8.
[88] Gray, *Hayek on Liberty*, 58–70.
[89] Hayek, *Constitution of Liberty*, 41.
[90] Ibid.

necessity, for it fuels progress; progress is a necessity, for 'even a small decline in our rate of advance might be fatal to us'.[91]

4 SOME VARIETIES OF LIBERALISM

These five writers illustrate some of the diversity of philosophical styles and political concerns, as well as more obvious differences of belief, that may be found within the liberal tradition. Nevertheless, their distinctive emphases and downright disagreements should not obscure their similarities or proscribe the attempt to elaborate an account of liberal family resemblances. Before proceeding to this task, however, we should sketch some of the more prominent branches of the family.

The first, and chronologically the earliest, is the one retrospectively titled 'constitutional liberalism'. This was discussed above, particularly in connection with Locke and Kant. It is the supposed liberalism of the American and French revolutions, and its characteristic suppositions are traditionally associated with seventeenth- and eighteenth-century contractarianism, as well as with political and constitutional theorists such as Montesquieu and the authors of *The Federalist*. It is rooted in opposition to arbitrary, personal, or unlimited power, to the possession of privileges by the few, and to the cramping demands of the feudal order. In general, it attempts to provide a theoretical justification for a set of practices clustered around the principle of limited government, including most or all of the following: effective restraints on the arbitrary or tyrannical exercise of power, constitutional definition of governmental powers, the rule of law, government legitimated by consent of the people, maintenance of the rights of individuals, especially their civil and political rights, official toleration of a plurality of religions and moral codes, and the legal protection of private property.

Constitutional liberalism is not the only defence of limited government: the particular complexion it has given that notion is illustrated by perhaps its most characteristic form of argument, the idea of the possession by individuals of natural rights independent of society and the justification of social and political relations on that basis by means of a social contract and contract

---

[91] Ibid. 40–1.

of government.[92] Nevertheless, it includes the most prominent modern defences of limited government, and the status in the West of the political values of this liberalism may fairly be described as hegemonic.[93]

The second variety of liberalism, *laissez-faire* or classical economic liberalism, was discussed above, especially in connection with Hayek, though Mill's political economy exemplifies it as well. It is primarily a set of economic rather than political doctrines, given theoretical underpinning in the last quarter of the eighteenth century by the classical political economists, but never uncompromisingly practised. Nineteenth-century Britain arguably came the closest to practising it, though it was revived in the 1980s in a number of Western countries. In this century it has been resuscitated under Hayek and others, with some important changes, notably the introduction of the Austrian subjective theory of economic value, while philosophers such as Robert Nozick have explored related issues within political theory. This kind of liberalism typically advocates *laissez-faire* in economics, freedom of trade internationally and minimal government intervention domestically, the right of individuals to freedom of contract, and the justice of any distributions of wealth which result from free exchange.

The third variety, welfare or revisionist liberalism, was discussed above in connection with Hobhouse and the New Liberals. Inspired to social and economic reform by the evident ills that had accompanied the growth of eighteenth- and nineteenth-century industrial capitalism, it is critical of classical economic liberalism while sharing a number of its more general commitments. Thus it stresses the importance of social justice and equitable material distribution, but also the need for a framework which guarantees civil liberties and the rights of the individual. Instrumental in bringing about the New Deal in the United States and the post-war welfare state in Britain, this is the liberalism of Beveridge and Keynes, the received wisdom of the left-liberal intellectual classes of the 1960s and 1970s, and has been given sophisticated theoretical elaboration in the political philosophy of

---

[92] J. W. Gough, *The Social Contract: A Critical Study of its Development*, 2nd edn. (Oxford: Clarendon Press, 1957).

[93] Those who wish to hold on to the principle of limited government but prefer not to be regarded as liberals may like to distinguish liberal constitutionalism (i.e. the doctrine of limited government) from constitutional liberalism (i.e. one approach amongst others to interpreting and defending limited government).

John Rawls. Especially in North America, this branch of liberalism has come to be associated not only with redistributionist economic policies and welfarist social policies, but also with, for example, support for the civil rights movement and the rights of minorities in general, suspicion of the influence of big business on government, opposition to fundamentalism and moral dogmatism, a preference for non-coercive to coercive measures, and the like.

These are the three most important varieties of liberalism. While they scarcely constitute an exhaustive listing, they may help as a rule-of-thumb guide, and make clearer some of the tensions within liberalism, of which any interpretation of the tradition must take account. They are not all exclusive alternatives: although disputes between economic liberals and welfare liberals are a regular feature of contemporary political life, those on both sides of the argument will invariably be found to be committed to limited government, and, almost as frequently, to some form of constitutional liberalism. Moreover, it can be argued that there is an overlapping range of commitments among all these varieties of liberalism, which can be interpreted in terms of family resemblances. It is these that we will now attempt to pick out.[94]

[94] The distinctive national traditions of liberalism should be noted here: different political, cultural, and philosophical traditions lead to emphases on different aspects of liberalism. In Britain the prevailing empiricist spirit has led to a greater particularism than is generally found in France, where rationalist philosophies have generated a commitment to more abstract values. 'English liberalism, unlike certain foreign sorts of liberalism, looks for "the positive" not in freedom, but in the qualities of individual persons' (Maurice Cranston, *Freedom: A New Analysis* (London: Longmans, Green & Co., 1953), 71). This empiricism has led it to stress satisfaction of felt wants rather than of externally determined needs, and to dismiss notions of a rational self superior to the empirical self. Freedom therefore is primarily negative: '[the] English liberal has demanded freedom for the individual from the constraints of the state because he has regarded the individual person as an ethical end, and the state as an instrument, of value only in so far as it could serve the interests of the individual person' (ibid. 71–2). By contrast, French liberalism of the revolutionary period, apart from being strongly progressivist, tends to be *étatiste* and Rousseauesque; yet in the nineteenth century, its moderate leaders—Constant, Guizot, and others—tried to forget the excesses of the Revolution and to establish what they saw (like Voltaire and Montesquieu) as the balance and sanity of the English constitution. In Germany a peculiar development is the relation of liberalism to the movement for national unity: liberty is related to submission to a strong nation-state, and the result of German liberalism in 1848 was the Declaration of the Rights of the German People. Likewise in Italy, liberalism signalled the self-determination of the united people against Austria, the several petty despots, and especially (reflecting the wholesale anticlericalism of liberalism in Catholic countries) the Papal estates (ibid. and Cranston, 'Liberalism', in Paul Edwards (ed.), *The Encyclopaedia of Philosophy* (8 vols., New York: Macmillan and Free Press, 1967), iv.

5 LIBERALISM'S FAMILY RESEMBLANCES

I argued earlier that there is no common or unitary core of doctrine, indeed, arguably, no single (relevant and sufficiently specified) doctrine which anybody who wishes to qualify as a liberal must hold. It is better to think in terms of an overlapping range of beliefs, none of which individually a liberal must hold, but to some interpretation of which, when taken together, a liberal must subscribe. This is not to say that the range of liberal beliefs is indefinitely diffuse, however, and in the outline of liberalism's family resemblances that follows I attempt to delineate, in relation to each of a number of issues, the breadth of responses liberals have made.[95]

At the heart of liberalism lies a conception of the human agent. This has two aspects. The first concerns the relation of individuals to their ends and obligations. The self is fundamentally detached from contingencies, being related to them (if at all) through choice or consent: whether or not this is raised to an explicit metaphysical claim, it generally implies that individuals are taken to be sovereign choosers, free to revise their ends as they wish, bound by nothing to which they have not consented, the ultimate authorities on how they should lead their lives. In one form this may simply be the claim that every individual must answer to God, and therefore that each has the responsibility to decide his or her religion; in another form it may be a claim about the value of self-chosen lives; in a strong form, it may engender the belief that it is reasonable and possible to give satisfactory value to one's own life, and thus that meaning in life does not require extrinsic support.[96]

The second aspect of the liberal conception of the human agent concerns its necessarily irreducible individuality. Every major strand of liberalism assumes (i) that there are criteria by which individuals can be distinguished from each other. The individual has usually been identified, by appeal to common sense, as the possessor of an individual body. However, the empiricist failure to

458–61; Irene Collins, *Liberalism in Nineteenth-Century Europe* (London: The Historical Association, 1957).

[95] The following analysis develops ideas owed in part to Steven Lukes.

[96] For one contemporary, liberalism 'is itself an answer to the unanswerable but irrepressible question: "What is the meaning of life?"'' (Brian Barry, *The Liberal Theory of Justice: A Critical Examination of the Principal Doctrines in 'A Theory of Justice' by John Rawls* (Oxford: Clarendon Press, 1973), 127).

provide a theoretical justification for this raises significant questions about the philosophical basis for the liberal notion of individuality. Liberalism also requires (ii) that the individual can be distinguished from an unindividuated whole. The individual cannot properly be wholly explained in supra- or extra-individualistic terms, as an expression of the *Zeitgeist* or of the stage of the development in productive forces, as reducible to structural relations or functional roles, or in general as the product of any cultural, linguistic, or social determinism. Liberalism is therefore often associated with methodological individualism in social and economic explanation.

Second, at the level of meta-ethics, liberalism has been dominated by acceptance of the so-called fact–value distinction and the human self-understanding implied in this. Though this distinction does not itself imply an individualistic ethic, the circumstances in which it arose (Protestantism, capitalism, the breakdown of traditional forms of authority, increased social mobility, the rise of affective individualism, and so on) ensured that within the liberal tradition the distinction would be construed in terms of individual moral autonomy. This autonomy is asserted (i) against any possible description of 'the facts': thus liberalism has often been regarded as a most eligible partner for value-free natural and social science. It is also asserted (ii) against institutional or collective attempts to control individual decision-making. From this comes the rejection of coercion in matters of belief or behaviour, which may be justified on the grounds of scepticism about there being correct ways to act beyond adherence to 'formal' rules, or (non-sceptically) on the grounds that it can be no part of the best life that individuals be forced to live it.

Third, the typically liberal mode of thought is individualist, universalist, and abstract. Its individualism[97] includes ethical individualism, individualism in the choice of religion and the good life, in equal and non-corporate consent to government and political representation, and in economic arrangements. But it has often also been associated with epistemological individualism, with its characteristic root problem of arguing itself out of solipsism, its attempt to discover knowledge by reducing wholes to parts, and its dispositional opposition to claims about the social construction of

[97] See in general Steven Lukes, *Individualism* (Oxford: Blackwell, 1973).

experience; and to metaphysical individualism, with its stress on substances rather than relations and its atomistic or monadic understanding of matter. The universalism of the liberal mode of thought is shown, first, in the broadening scope of the features of persons that it counts as morally irrelevant: hence doctrines of equality before the law and the rejection of discrimination on grounds of class, property ownership, race or gender, as well as equality of resource distribution, and, more radically, of equality of welfare or of want-satisfaction. Its universalism is shown, secondly, in the belief that its generalizations hold for all times and places regardless of historical or cultural contingencies: this has led to the charge, for example, that it rationalizes the pressures towards the levelling conformities created by, and suited to, mass production and economies of scale. The abstractness of the typical liberal mode of thought is one aspect of its universalism. Seized on by Marxists, feminists, and others, this is usually taken to refer to a narrow-sighted tendency to universalize conditions that are merely temporary or local, by attending only to the political rights of male heads of households, for example, or deriving general truths from the capitalist phase of social evolution.

Fourth, from the characteristic liberal mode of thought and from its meta-ethics come the two facets of its approach to rationality. Reason is widely taken, first, to be the appropriate instrument for the discovery of truth and for the settlement of disputes. This does not commit liberalism to philosophical rationalism, but it does signal its dispositional preference for diplomacy to war and its opposition to special or privileged knowledge, revelation to initiates, and appeals to tradition. Liberals may be prone, therefore, to underestimate irrational factors in knowledge, to disregard the sociology of knowledge, or to be rationalist in politics, and to talk of ignorance rather than false consciousness. Second, reason is also often construed as the calculation of individual advantage, instrumental in the pursuit of goals generated by the passions, not as a speculative faculty fitted for scanning the world order for guidance concerning the good life. Moral rationality in contemporary thought is therefore often taken to be the combination of self-interest and technological means–end reasoning—that is, the maximization of individual utility. It is worth noting that these two understandings of reason do to some extent conflict: the first allows moral truth to be discoverable by reason, the second denies this. This is a genuine tension in the liberal tradition: for some, moral value will be found (if at all) by reason, not by submission to tradition or institution; for others, it will not be found outside the individual agent.

Finally, the liberal philosophy of history should be noted. Some doctrine of progress was indicated earlier as being central, even essential, to the theories of Kant, Hobhouse, Hayek, and perhaps Mill. Indeed, it is plausible that some notion of improvement in moral and political understanding and behaviour is fundamental to any form of liberalism.[98] By no means all agree with Condorcet that '[the] real advantages that should result from this progress, of which we can entertain a hope that is almost a certainty, can have no other term than that of the absolute perfection of the human race'.[99] Neither Condorcet's certainty nor his belief in perfectibility have been shared by most liberals. Moreover, although perfectionist liberals can readily be found, the liberal ideal more usually takes the form of a pluralistic 'meta-utopia' which co-ordinates the optimized wants of individuals severally, not as the achievement of some externally defined human perfection.

From these five central features of liberal thought may be derived most liberal political beliefs. Towards the state, for example, most liberals (until this century) were hostile or suspicious, regarding it as at best a necessary evil. Nevertheless, it has always been regarded as the proper political authority, a governmental apparatus separate from the persons of the office-holders. The state has more often been regarded as held in trust for, or delegated by, the people (Locke and the republican tradition), rather than as separate from them also, as a consequence of transferral or alienation of rights (Hobbes). As regards the extent of state activity, liberal economists and most of the tradition have advocated limited government and not the minimum 'night-watchman' state, in recognition of the importance of the service functions provided by the state. The New Liberals stressed most the positive role of the state, although (it was hoped) never at the expense of individual freedom: '[the] only

[98] Gray, *Liberalism* (Milton Keynes: Open University Press, 1986), p. x, makes meliorism one of his four essential constituents of liberalism, the others being individualism, universalism, and egalitarianism. For a more extended account of the liberal belief in progress, see Ch. 3 below.

[99] In E. K. Bramsted and K. J. Melhuish, *Western Liberalism: A History in Documents from Locke to Croce* (London: Longman, 1978), 235.

rational liberty was that conducive to the welfare of all; the only true welfare was the one that acknowledged individual liberty as its indispensable ingredient'.[100] Mill, by contrast, illustrates liberal anti-paternalism in arguing that the purpose of sanitary laws (for example) is not to make individuals into better people, but to protect others from disease.[101]

The liberal suspicion of the state is reflected in its attitudes towards power and authority. The dominant liberal view from all periods is that authority is based on convention derived from consent, and is exercised over conduct alone, never over belief. It is not maintained by an illusory legitimacy that depends on cloaking the use of power; nor is it derived from tradition, special knowledge, superior ability, or power of personality. Power is regarded as asymmetric and coercive, rather than as a function of the collective will of the community.[102] Liberals tend to avoid the topic of power, either ignoring it or regarding its exercise as a necessary evil. In line with their optimism about rationality, they have often seen coercion as physical; again, it was the New Liberals who were alert to this short-sightedness.

Concerning property, the dominant strand of opinion is that absolute private property is necessary to individual freedom. This is argued (especially in classical liberalism) from the right of every individual to self-ownership (that is, the right to control the use of his or her talents) to ensure liberty. By extension, it is usually claimed that the effective exercise of self-possession requires private property, since under communal ownership the veto of other members of the community would inevitably hamper individual self-directed development. In the Whig tradition it was often taken as a corollary of this that the vote should be limited to those with property, since only they could be guaranteed to be independent and responsible solely to the nation. Such an assignment of political rights to property rather than to human beings was (in democratic hindsight) one of the blind spots of English Whiggery.

This last point raises the question of the relation of liberalism and democracy. Some distinguish the two by definition: 'Liberalism is a doctrine about what the law ought to be, demo-

---

[100] Freeden, *New Liberalism*, 258.

[101] Ryan, *J. S. Mill* (London: Routledge and Kegan Paul, 1974), 147.

[102] See Lukes, 'Power and Authority', in Tom Bottomore and Robert Nisbet (eds.), *A History of Sociological Analysis* (London: Heinemann, 1979), 633–76.

cracy a doctrine about the manner of determining what will be the law.'[103] Nevertheless, political history has ensured that the two are connected as a matter of reflex: 'democratic theory is the unthinking normative political theory of the modern West and . . . liberalism is its painfully precarious reflective normative theory.'[104] Historically, liberalism has usually been suspicious of democracy (revealing here as clearly as anywhere its middle-class associations), in the belief that majority rule would compromise the rights of minorities, that the mob would interfere with privacy, and that popular sovereignty usually degenerates quickly into popular tyranny. Thus, although liberal democracy has become a closely intertwined unity in Western self-understanding, it is evident that the nature of the relationship between them is such that 'the adjective Liberal has the force of a qualification'.[105]

Finally, grounded on these foundations are the two central values of liberalism: equality and liberty. Equality as a liberal value can be derived (in terms of the structure of liberal beliefs) from the liberal respect for human beings and the commitment to universalism in liberal individualism; these may be derived in turn (in terms of the history of ideas) from the Christian and natural law traditions. As regards the relation of equality and liberty, liberals have often been criticized, most naturally by Marxists and other socialists, for emphasizing the latter at the expense of the former. However, equality has always been a feature of the liberal tradition, at least at the level of its formal commitments:[106] contractarianism posits that individuals are equal in the state of nature, and utilitarianism assumes that each counts for one, and nobody for more than one, in its calculation of utilities. Nevertheless, it is the case, historically, that liberals have been more

---

[103] Hayek, *Constitution of Liberty*, 103.

[104] John Dunn, *Western Political Theory in the Face of the Future* (Cambridge: Cambridge University Press, 1979), 80.

[105] Guido de Ruggiero, *The History of European Liberalism* (Oxford: Oxford University Press, 1927), 379.

[106] Larry Siedentop ('Two Liberal Traditions', in Alan Ryan (ed.), *The Idea of Freedom* (Oxford: Oxford University Press, 1979), 153) claims that 'the fundamental or root concept of liberalism is equality, and its commitment to liberty springs from that'. The most prominent exponent of this account of liberalism is Ronald Dworkin (*TRS* and *MP*, esp. 181–213), for whom equality of concern and respect is the fundamental liberal value; though, arguably, equality of respect itself can only be understood at least in part in terms of liberty (cf. Jeremy Waldron, 'Theoretical Foundations of Liberalism', *Philosophical Quarterly*, 37 (1987), 130).

willing to advance liberty than equality, pressing (for example) for equality of rights long before they were willing to give substance to such equality, and similarly with equality of opportunity. Moreover, it is possible (granted the framework of liberal constitutional rights) for a liberal to recommend inequalities, for the reason, for example, that they are necessary to economic growth. But the converse is rather less likely, that a liberal would urge egalitarian measures without any regard for the loss in liberty involved.

Liberty is the principal value of liberalism. The contentless ideals of happiness and democracy left aside, freedom is plausibly regarded as the supreme value available to the moral and political vocabulary of the modern West. As Iris Murdoch puts it, 'Our central conception is still a debilitated form of Mill's equation: happiness equals freedom equals personality.'[107] The quest for the enlargement of liberty has been extended by liberals to every department of social existence: Hobhouse lists civil liberty, fiscal liberty (that is, no taxation without representation), personal liberty, social liberty (that is, no class restraints), economic liberty, domestic liberty (that is, rights for women and for children, and contract as a sufficient legal basis for marriage), local, racial, and national liberty, international liberty, and political liberty.[108]

If the distinction between positive and negative aspects of liberty is helpful, most of these applications of liberty seem to stress its negative aspect: that is, as a private space of free action in which non-interference by the state or others is guaranteed. Indeed, many interpretations of its positive aspect are unacceptable to liberals. Thus, (i) if it means a right to joint participation in decision-making, whether directly or by representation, not all liberals have assented to it, as was said above in connection with democracy. Again, (ii) liberals have widely rejected any identification of freedom with self-realization or the fulfilment of a 'real will' detachable from the 'empirical self', on the grounds of the possibility of forced freedom. Isaiah Berlin attempts to distinguish illegitimate and legitimate government intervention by noting that it is one thing 'to say that I may be coerced for my own good which I am too

---

[107] Iris Murdoch, 'Against Dryness; A Polemical Sketch' (1961), in Stanley Hauerwas and Alasdair MacIntyre (eds.), *Revisions: Changing Perspectives in Moral Philosophy* (Notre Dame, Ind.: University of Notre Dame Press, 1983), 46.

[108] Hobhouse, *Liberalism*, 16–28.

blind to see', but another 'to say that if it is my good, then I am not being coerced, for I have willed it, whether I know this or not'.[109] However, (iii) there is a sense of the positive aspect of freedom which, given that it can be distinguished from that in (ii), certainly is not incompatible with liberalism: namely, freedom as self-control and the ability to pursue long-term goals unhindered by the passions. Indeed, this is one of the three elements in the ideal of autonomy as Mill seems to have understood that notion, the others being negative freedom and detachment from circumstances. Concerning this, two questions are debated among liberals. The first concerns the extent to which it justifies the demand for public provision of the resources necessary for the attainment of the autonomy which is a pre-condition of the pursuit of the individual's understanding of the good life. The second concerns the extent to which the ground of the value of autonomy is want-regarding or ideal-regarding: schematically, and slightly inaccurately, Mill took it to be the former, Hobhouse the latter. Though Mill is perhaps nearer to the heart of liberalism in this respect, the liberal tradition has not always carefully distinguished the two defences of the value of individual rational autonomy.

This, then, is how I propose to interpret liberalism: as a diffuse phenomenon, certainly, but one which is sufficiently coherent to warrant talk of family resemblances. This account, it should be noted, also shows that the diffuseness occurs in two dimensions. It is not just that a liberal could hold 'typically liberal' views in relation to some issues but views that are not typically liberal in relation to others, but that in relation to many issues there is in fact a range of typically liberal views. This has the somewhat unsettling implication that, at an extreme, two people could conceivably hold no (relevant and sufficiently specified) doctrine in common, and yet still both be liberals. Despite this, the principle mentioned at the beginning of the previous section should still be followed: namely, that the extent to which any individual should properly be called a liberal turns on a judgement concerning the extent to which he or she could subscribe to some interpretation of the above account. Such a judgement will at times be difficult—which, after all, witnesses to a faithful rendering of the subject-matter. And it will

[109] Berlin, 'Two Concepts of Liberty', in *Four Essays on Liberty*, 134.

be clouded by liberals who for extraneous reasons reject the designation, and conversely. But further, by separating the central themes of liberal views regarding the human agent, the basis of moral value, and so on, on the one hand, from its range of attitudes to political matters, on the other, this account allows the critic of liberalism to concentrate on some of the generating forces of liberalism, rather than just on their outworkings. It is these generating forces which in different ways form the subjects of the following chapters.

3
Reinhold Niebuhr and the Liberal Philosophy of History

I INTRODUCTION

One of the first questions any political theory needs to address concerns what politics may hope to achieve. Is an ideal social order possible in this world? If so, can it be achieved through means which are in the broadest sense political? Or is such an order possible only, if at all, beyond this world in some sense? These questions are in turn closely connected to others. Does history somehow of itself guarantee, or even make probable, any kind of future outcome, ideal or otherwise? Can lineaments of meaning be found in history? Indeed, what is the meaning of the phrase 'the meaning of history'? And what difference do the answers to these questions make to the motivation towards, and prospects for, social and political action?

It follows that a central issue for a theological critique of liberalism is the liberal philosophy of history. As mentioned in the previous chapter, liberalism has often been associated with doctrines of progress towards wider moral understanding and more rational human behaviour. This was strikingly true of nineteenth-century liberalism, but even in this century a meliorist ambience has regularly surrounded liberalisms of both left and right. As a result of the anguished central experiences of the twentieth century, progress itself has come to be interpreted less in terms of moral and political aspirations for a definitively transformed world order, and more in relation to the consumer-driven consolations of economic and technological growth. Yet the nineteenth-century ideal has not wholly died: when, around the time of the fall of the Berlin Wall, Francis Fukuyama boldly proclaimed the 'end of history', it came as a surprise to nobody to learn that he had managed to associate this evidently happy event with the coming-to-be of Western liberal democracy.[1]

[1] Francis Fukuyama, 'The End of History?', *The National Interest*, 16 (Summer

Reinhold Niebuhr is a particularly suitable discussion partner in connection with this aspect of liberalism, partly because he was initially a strong progressivist, but subsequently became disillusioned; and partly because he was one of the most influential mid-century figures in helping to reform American self-understanding after the demise of progressivism. More importantly for a theological understanding of liberalism, he was also able to recognize the connection of progressivism with Pelagianism: that is, of the liberal philosophy of history with a characteristically liberal understanding of human nature. In liberalism, in common with all modern culture, he claimed, it is believed that history is itself the Christ, the locus, but also the means, of redemption. And it is this sense of liberalism as comprising an alternative, disastrously false attempt to secure salvation—ultimately through human virtue—which explains much of the pungency and incisiveness of his criticism.

His wrestle with liberalism was amongst the most prominent features of his intellectual career. Indeed, the changing phases of his thought can be characterized precisely in terms of the varying positions he took up in relation to liberalism. In his mature writings, extending from the mid-1930s, which are the principal focus of this chapter, his attitude was largely critical; though in his later writings of the 1950s and 1960s he began to recognize some of the inordinacy of his earlier posturing and to admit to himself how much of liberalism he owned, albeit under the name of democracy. In fact, to use the categories outlined in the previous chapter, he became, broadly, a chastened welfare liberal with a strong commitment to liberal constitutionalism, who, despite his strictures, was well aware of the virtues of the general liberal movement in history.[2] Thus, for example, he noted how modern

---

1989), *idem*, 3–18; *The End of History and the Last Man* (London: Hamish Hamilton, 1992).

[2] His mature writings are certainly taken to include *BT*. It is assumed here that what Ronald H. Stone calls Niebuhr's fourth stage, his 'pragmatic-liberal synthesis', was a change more in the presentation than the structure of his thought (*Reinhold Niebuhr: Prophet to Politicians* (Nashville: Abingdon Press, 1972)). Stone is sometimes more alert to the ambiguities in Niebuhr's development than Richard Wightman Fox admits ('Reinhold Niebuhr and the Emergence of the Liberal Realist Faith, 1939–45', *Review of Politics*, 38 (1976), 244–65: cf. Stone, *Reinhold Niebuhr*, 10). In general, the changes in direction in Niebuhr's intellectual biography should be cast in much more moderate and nuanced terms than is customary: he was less of a liberal in his earliest works, and more of a liberal in his mature works, than he admitted in mid-career. *MNHC* 9–20, should be given prominence in accounts of his develop-

society had served to free the Church from the civilization which it had fostered and with which it had become identified: in its opposition to literalism and its demand for tolerance, it had released society from the ecclesiastical dogmatism and obscurantism that had sacralized injustice.[3] Again, just as the Christian faith had been used in the Middle Ages to sanctify oppression, so the Age of Reason had recognized the need for critical intelligence to provide just arbitration between conflicting interests.[4] And the great virtue of the Social Gospel (as a species of liberalism) was its belief that the law of love was relevant to economics and politics.[5] But, above all, 'the great achievement' of liberalism was democracy: it was this that Niebuhr sought to vindicate against its traditional liberal defenders.[6]

In spite of his awareness of the achievements of liberalism, however, he is better known for his criticisms of it. In this chapter I will argue that his diagnosis of progressivism is astute, but that both his account of liberalism and the theological basis of his criticisms of it are misplaced. I connect these failings to aspects of the apologetic nature of his work; while it is glib to regard them as the result of a simple 'theology-by-apologetics' approach, as neo-orthodox critics charge, there is an element of truth in this notion that is worth attention.[7] However, to provide the background for these criticisms, we must first look at his theological method and, second, at his understanding of liberalism.

2 NIEBUHR'S THEOLOGICAL METHOD

The structure of Niebuhr's thought turns formally on his understanding of the 'circular relation between faith and experience'.[8]

ment; this also makes it clear that Niebuhr's anti-utopianism was never intended to be put to the service of political conservatism.

[3] *MNHC* 13; 'Ten Years That Shook My World', *Christian Century*, 56/17 (26 Apr. 1939), 543; *BT* 232–3; *ICE* 173–5; *FH* 231.
[4] *ICE* 174–5. [5] Cf. *ICE* 181. [6] 'Ten Years', 545.
[7] The distinction between theology and apologetics was not one that interested him ('Intellectual Autobiography', in Charles W. Kegley and Robert W. Bretall (eds.), *Reinhold Niebuhr: His Religious, Social and Political Thought* (New York: Macmillan, 1956), 3). Niebuhr 'refused to study Barth' (Richard Wightman Fox, *Reinhold Niebuhr: A Biography* (New York: Pantheon, 1985), 258).
[8] 'Intellectual Autobiography', 15–17. See further 'Coherence, Incoherence, and Christian Faith', in Robert McAfee Brown (ed.), *The Essential Reinhold Niebuhr: Selected Essays and Addresses* (New Haven and London: Yale University Press, 1986), 218–36; and Robert H. Ayers, 'Methodological, Epistemological, and

According to this, no empirical enquiry is possible without a framework of controlling presuppositions which are not themselves derived from experience. Although these presuppositions partly shape the evidence gained from experience, the evidence is not merely a projection of them: in principle, therefore, a piece of evidence might emerge which showed them to be untenable. Such a set of presuppositions may thus be corroborated by, though not derived from, experience. If taken with a principle of procedure by the exclusion of alternatives and an implicit belief in the limited number of those alternatives, it is possible for this understanding of the relation between form and content to serve as the epistemological ground of an apologetic. For, on the one hand, a system of meaning can be refuted by the facts. Yet, on the other, every conceptual framework with which experience is approached, inasmuch as it points beyond itself to a level of meaning 'which cannot be simply identified with rational coherence', requires faith: natural science, for example, presumes the orderliness of the universe.[9] This approach is sufficiently realist to allow conversation between different frameworks, yet relativist enough to ground an attack on rationalism and to reveal the place of 'mystery' in any system of meaning. The role of faith, and indeed repentance, traditionally demanded by Christianity is thereby assured.

Niebuhr came to his own position through such an approach.[10] He had, for example, found the presuppositions of liberalism and Marxism to be incapable of explaining the facts of twentieth-century history. Christianity, however, while undeniably and inescapably an interpretation of the evidence, was nevertheless the best explanation of that evidence, and did not, he believed, face similar counter-evidence. A faithfulness to the facts supported an understanding of human nature and history which dovetailed with the findings of biblical faith. Because of this correlation, it was possible for Niebuhr to reach conclusions argued either from a consideration of the facts or from the premises of theology. Thus, to continue the previous example, it was possible for him later to

Ontological Motifs in the Thought of Reinhold Niebuhr', *Modern Theology*, 7 (1991), 153–73.

[9] 'Intellectual Autobiography', 14.

[10] Cf. Donald B. Meyer, *The Protestant Search for Political Realism, 1919–41* (Berkeley and Los Angeles: University of California Press, 1960), 256–7, who also mentions Niebuhr's rejection of social science and conservatism by a similar method.

wonder whether it had been his better understanding of the Christian faith or the evidence of the totalitarianisms and world wars which had led him to reject liberalism and Marxism.[11] Viewed from one standpoint, this dovetailing could serve as the basis for an apologetic; viewed from another, as the foundation of a theological critique of other frameworks of meaning.

Provided the epistemology can be substantiated, it is clearly a powerful method. Nevertheless, it holds dangers for an authentically theological approach which, I will argue, Niebuhr (who moved biographically from social imperatives to their theological basis and whose 'mythical' treatment of theological doctrines allowed him significant latitude in his interpretation of them) did not wholly avoid.

Such dangers were compounded by his manner of treating theological material. For Niebuhr, the subject-matter of theology is traditional Christian doctrine interpreted 'mythically' or 'symbolically'. Although it is not always easy to discern what he means by these terms, he seems to be saying the following. It is the value of myth to 'suggest the dimension of depth in reality and to point to a realm of essence which transcends the surface of history';[12] that is, an ultimate ground of the meaning of existence. Myth is thus 'supra-scientific', and points to a realm of mystery which precludes approaches that are too simple and lead to pantheism or dualism.[13] Myths must therefore be treated 'seriously but not literally'; their primitive elements, which have been disproved by science, must be weeded out from their permanent elements, which are necessary for a complete understanding of reality. They must not, with Christian orthodoxy, be taken literally, because obscurantism results. But neither, with Bultmann, must they be 'demythologized', since they incorporate permanently valid symbols: deliteralization is necessary, but not demythologization.[14] Nor, as non-cognitivists

---

[11] 'Intellectual Autobiography', 9.

[12] *ICE* 22. Sources for his use of myth include 'The Truth in Myths', in Ronald H. Stone (ed.), *Faith in Politics* (New York: George Braziller, 1968), 15–32; 'As Deceivers, Yet True' in *BT* 1–24; 'Mystery and Meaning', in *DST* 132–49; and 'Mystery and Meaning', in *The Godly and the Ungodly: Essays on the Religious and Secular Dimensions of Modern Life* (London: Faber and Faber, 1959; originally published as *Pious and Secular America*), 123–45. See also Dennis P. McCann, *Christian Realism and Liberation Theology: Practical Theologies in Creative Conflict* (Maryknoll, NY: Orbis Books, 1981) 33–51.

[13] *ICE* 23; *FH* 46; *BT* 4.

[14] *ICE* 23; 'Reply to Interpretation and Criticism', in Kegley and Bretall (eds.), *Reinhold Niebuhr*, 431–51, at 446.

argue, must they be assumed to be content-free: there has been revelation, and faith expects that 'ultimately all mystery will be resolved in the perfect knowledge of God';[15] though we see through a glass darkly, we do see. Nor, finally, with rationalism, can their content be analysed out without destroying religion.[16] Niebuhr offers here, clearly, the groundwork for an important approach to questions concerning the nature of doctrine and of religious language. But the potential danger of founding it on an understanding of religion as the dimension of depth in human existence is that the symbols may gain existential or experiential purchase at the expense of referential content: the content may become subordinated to (say) social or political requirements, which may themselves be interpreted in a way that is insufficiently rooted theologically.

None of this of course implies that Niebuhr denies a role to revelation. Indeed, for him revelation is necessary, since sinful human beings are unable to direct their wills aright, so cannot save themselves. Revelation, he argues, is of two kinds: general and special. General, or private, revelation is necessary to give credence to special revelation: it is obtained from an examination of experience, and comprises those experiences which defy immanent explanation in that they point to a reality beyond the empirical, namely, i), the sense of reverence and dependence, ii), the sense of moral obligation, and iii), the longing for forgiveness.[17] Special revelation is in turn necessary to clarify the content of general revelation. Thus, correlated with each of the three elements of general revelation are forms of special revelation. To the sense of moral obligation corresponds the covenant relation between God and Israel, and to the longing for forgiveness corresponds the life and death of Christ. These are derived from social-historical experience, and define God as, respectively, Judge and Redeemer.[18] Related to the first element of general revelation, the experienced sense of dependence, is the biblical idea of God as Creator; this occupies an anomalous position in that, on the one hand, it is only available to faith, but, on the other, unlike the history of Israel and of Jesus, it is not one of 'those events in *history* in which faith discerns the self-disclosure of God'.[19] It is these

[15] *DST* 148.
[16] *ICE* 22.
[17] *NDM* i. 141.
[18] *NDM* i. 142, 146–60.
[19] *NDM* i. 146, my emphasis.

events that take place in history which are the clue to the meaning of history, with their culmination in 'the climax of revelation in the life, death, and resurrection of Christ'.[20]

For Niebuhr, therefore, there is revelation; and above all, the Christ-event serves as the final disclosure of the whole meaning of history: 'the atoning death of Christ is the revelation of ultimate reality which may become the principle of interpretation for all human experience'.[21] Because of his commitment in this way to the language of disclosure and revelation, it would be a mistake to charge Niebuhr with simply deriving his theology from anthropology.[22] Moreover, he is a theological realist; his symbolic approach to talk about God should be seen as his attempt to preserve a basic realism against the assumed background of a theory of language which associated truth with empirical demonstrability and did not readily see metaphorical language as capable of depicting reality. Even so, the danger remains that the generating source of theology will be found not in what is theologically given, but in some potentially capricious interpretation of human need.

3 NIEBUHR'S UNDERSTANDING OF LIBERALISM

Niebuhr's typological method of characterizing and criticizing broad historical movements leads him often to describe aspects of, but rarely to define, those movements. It affords him a looseness in his treatment of historical material that sometimes borders on the outrageous, but also an acuity in his perception of common

---

[20] *FH* 27.

[21] *BT* 19–20. This Christological orientation is not worked through monomaniacally in his theology; he is quite prepared to use other doctrines, such as creation or eschatology, as sources for the meaning of history without any conspicuous assertion of their Christological connection. Against Paul Lehmann ('The Christology of Reinhold Niebuhr', in Kegley and Bretall (eds.), *Reinhold Niebuhr*, 251–80), who sees Christology as the controlling concern in every phase of Niebuhr's theology, Kenneth Durkin (*Reinhold Niebuhr* (London: Geoffrey Chapman, 1989), 175–9) argues cogently that Niebuhr's theology appeals more widely to the four primary myths of creation, fall, atonement, and parousia; though out of these, one might add, atonement has clear primacy.

[22] Paul Ramsey, *Speak Up for Just War or Pacifism: A Critique of the United Methodist Bishops' Pastoral Letter 'In Defense of Creation'* (University Park, Pa.: Pennsylvania State University Press, 1988), 114.

features that is possible only by adopting a synoptic approach.[23] Broadness in the use of terms cannot be equated with emptiness of content, however, and on at least one occasion he takes care to elucidate his understanding of liberalism.[24]

In its most general sense, secular liberalism for Niebuhr may be associated with the growth of political and economic institutions that opposed medieval aristocratic feudalism. Thus it seeks the freedom of the individual from restrictions of traditional authority, the establishment of government by popular consent, the abolition of privilege, and the social mobility and freedom of opportunity that characterize liberal society. 'Liberalism in the broadest sense is therefore synonymous with democracy.'[25] However, the term has two narrower usages also. First, it denotes two opposed streams of specifically political thought deriving from the history of the middle classes. On the one hand, it refers to the philosophy that calls for the elimination of economic constraints in the belief that natural balances will ensure the general welfare: such ideas were held by those with sufficient personal power or wit to have reason to prefer liberty to security. On the other hand, liberalism is the political programme that tries in the name of social justice to ensure governmental control of the economic process for the sake of guaranteed welfare for all.[26] Second, the word signifies a 'total philosophy of life' that was rooted in the Renaissance and flowered in the French Enlightenment. Typically, it is optimistic about human nature, believes in historical progress, and is utopian in its social and moral expectations.[27]

Liberal Christianity is taken to be a historical outgrowth of

---

[23] For apposite comments on Niebuhr's typological method, see D. D. Williams, 'Niebuhr and Liberalism', in Kegley and Bretall (eds.), *Reinhold Niebuhr*, 195–7 (and Niebuhr, 'Reply', 441); Golo Mann, 'Reinhold Niebuhr und die Kritik der Liberalismus', *Merkur*, 12 (1958), 131–2.

[24] See Harry R. Davis and Robert C. Good (eds.), *Reinhold Niebuhr on Politics* (New York: Scribner's, 1960), 13–14, quoted from 'Liberalism: Illusions and Realities', *Nation*, 133 (1955), 11–12.

[25] Ibid. 13. In general, the aspects of liberalism that appeal to him are defended under the heading 'democracy'; those that do not are dismissed as 'liberalism'.

[26] Ibid. 13–14.

[27] Ibid. 14. Note the closeness of this categorization to that outlined in Ch. 2. Niebuhr also refers (*NDM* ii. 286) to varieties of liberalism in which 'the power of government is regarded as a simple rational authority over rational men, which will become more just and more universal as reason is extended'. These varieties evidently combine liberalism 'in the broadest sense' and liberalism as a 'total philosophy of life'.

secular liberalism. It adds sentimentality to optimism, replaces the truth of the Gospel with the doctrine of progress, and invests the relative moral standards of a commercial age with an aura of sanctity and ultimacy.[28] Such modernizing reinterpretation of Christianity is found in, for example, Herder, Ritschl, Lessing, Hegel, Wellhausen,[29] and Schleiermacher.[30] However, for Niebuhr it was represented most relevantly in the moralizing rationalism of American liberal Protestantism that culminated in the social gospel of, for example, Walter Rauschenbusch, Washington Gladden, Francis Peabody, and Shailer Mathews. While ostensibly an effort to reunite the Renaissance and Reformation elements of the medieval synthesis,[31] in effect it had become a degenerate belief that redemption was possible through combining secular intelligence with Christian piety. It was beguiled by its rationalism into thinking that recognition of sins would lead to their elimination, and by its naïvety into regarding transcendent love as a simple possibility for politics. Thus it treated love as the force in history that would overcome evil.[32] Typically, it expressed this belief in terms of pacifism, though Niebuhr concedes that 'it was usually realistic enough to know that justice in the social order could only be achieved by political means'.[33]

Although Niebuhr is able to distinguish these variants of liberalism, he believes that all of them—secular and religious liberalism, liberal political and economic thought, and the wider liberal philosophy of life—share essential features. Thus there is 'a pretty sharply defined credo which holds all liberalism together'; amongst its articles are:

a. That injustice is caused by ignorance and will yield to education and greater intelligence.
b. That civilization is becoming gradually more moral and that it is a sin to challenge either the inevitability or the efficacy of gradualness.
c. That the character of individuals rather than social systems and arrangements is the guarantee of justice in society.

---

[28] See e.g. *MMIS* 78–9; *ICE* 13–15, 20, 25–6; 'Ten Years', 542; *FH* 31–2, 207.
[29] *FH* 31.　　　　　　　　　　　　　　　　　[30] *NDM* ii. 76.
[31] *NDM* i. 5.　　　　　　　　　　　　　　　　[32] *NDM* ii. 47.
[33] *ICE* 182. For definitions of liberalism and modernism as general theological movements, see Stone, *Reinhold Niebuhr*, 35–6; William R. Hutchison, *The Modernist Impulse in American Protestantism* (Oxford: Oxford University Press, 1976), 2–4.

    d. That appeals to love, justice, good-will and brotherhood are bound to be efficacious in the end. If they have not been so to date we must have more appeals to love, justice, good-will and brotherhood.

    e. That goodness makes for happiness and that the increasing knowledge of this fact will overcome human selfishness and greed.

    f. That wars are stupid and can therefore only be caused by people who are more stupid than those who recognize the stupidity of war.[34]

Underlying all these claims are beliefs about the nature of humankind and of history. 'The faith of modern man contains two related articles: the idea of progress and the idea of the perfectibility of man.'[35] Perhaps the central feature of liberal anthropology is the denial of sin. Human deviancy is ascribed to factors such as ignorance, finiteness, residual entanglement in nature, or social institutions, which are external to the reasoning, willing self.[36] Reason can transcend nature, and therefore subdue it: this nature includes human nature, and so it is thought possible to model the human sciences on the natural sciences.[37] Whether the essential goodness of human beings is to be realized by a romantic return to nature or by escape into the life of reason, liberalism sees them fundamentally as harmless individuals.[38]

    Optimism about human nature is naturally connected to optimism about history. Liberalism here is typical of modernity as a whole. From the observation that there is not cyclical repetition, as was believed by adherents of classical conceptions of time and history, but rather historical novelty and indeed progress in, for example, scientific knowledge or social organization, modernity has inferred that all problems and insecurities will be resolved by history.[39] No longer (as for classical thought) the thing to be

---

[34] Quoted in Davis and Good (eds.), *Niebuhr on Politics*, 15, from 'The Blindness of Liberalism', *Radical Religion*, 1 (1936), 4–5. Although this appeared before his fully mature period, it represents fairly, if brusquely, what he takes himself to be attacking. Certainly he admitted later that many of his attacks on utopianism were overdone (e.g. *MNHC* 13), but he never recanted on the thrust of his criticism.

[35] Niebuhr, 'Intellectual Autobiography', 15.

[36] See e.g. *BT* 141; *FH* 47; 'The Sickness of American Culture', *Nation*, 166 (6 Mar. 1948), 268; *NDM* i. 289–90 n. 3.

[37] *FH* 5, 11–13.   [38] 'Ten Years', 543; *CLCD* 20.

[39] *FH* 1–2, 29–30, 33–4, 41; 'A Faith for History's Greatest Crisis', *Fortune*, 26/1 (July 1942), 126.

explained, history has become the explanation.[40] 'Though there are minor dissonances the whole chorus of modern culture learned to sing the new song of hope in remarkable harmony. The redemption of mankind, by whatever means, was assured for the future. It was, in fact, assured by the future.'[41]

In this chorus Niebuhr includes the early Italian Renaissance, Cartesian rationalism, the French Enlightenment, liberal progressivism, Marxist catastrophism, sectarian perfectionism, and secular utopianism.[42] While he rarely troubles to distinguish liberalism from other elements of modernity, Marxism as 'hard utopianism' (claiming to embody perfection and thus justified in eliminating imperfection) is separated from liberal 'soft utopianism', which merely believes that perfection will evolve from the process of history.[43] Again, while liberalism is divided between naturalists who believe that nature guarantees progress and rationalists whose faith lies in disengagement from the partial impulses of nature, it still shares with all modern culture a belief in an indefinite increase in human power and freedom, and thus in mastery over human destiny.[44]

4 NIEBUHR'S CRITICISMS OF THE LIBERAL CONCEPTION OF HISTORY

With this account of Niebuhr's understanding of liberalism, we are now in a position to turn to his criticisms of its conception of history. The fundamental structure of Niebuhr's attack on the liberal idea of history was in place by the time of his exposition of the mythical conception of religion in *An Interpretation of Christian Ethics*.[45] He held that this conception of religion and of theological doctrine was embodied in the world-view of the Hebrew prophetic tradition, and enabled it to 'enjoy the pleasures of this life without becoming engrossed in them, and to affirm the significance of human history without undue reverence for the merely human'.[46]

---

[40] *FH* 37–8.   [41] *FH* 6.   [42] *NDM* ii. 166.

[43] See Davis and Good (eds.), *Niebuhr on Politics*, 12–13, quoted from 'Two Forms of Utopianism', *Christianity and Society*, 12 (1947), 6–7.

[44] 'Ten Years', 543; *FH* 1–2, 14–16, 30.

[45] See esp. *ICE* 21–6, 32–44 (lectures delivered in Spring 1934). For Niebuhr's understanding of irony—which is irrelevant to the present discussion—as a key to the prophetic interpretation of history, see Gordon Harland, *The Thought of Reinhold Niebuhr* (New York: Oxford University Press, 1960), ch. 5, s. 3.

[46] *ICE* 38.

The mystical conception of religion, with which he contrasts the mythical conception, is inferior, in that it degenerates either into a pessimistic other-worldly dualism, or, in some more rationalistic forms, into an optimistic philosophical monism, in each case destroying the essential tension between the historical and the eternal.

In his approach to these two contrasting conceptions it is possible to discern the two movements of his dialectical understanding of the nature of history. On the one hand, he opposes naturalistic philosophies to the extent that they regard the temporal process as self-explanatory and self-fulfilling; on the other, paradoxically, he affirms the meaningfulness of history. The weight of Niebuhr's criticism of the liberal conception of history falls under the former movement; nevertheless the latter is necessary for a full understanding of his position. We will look at each in turn.

(a) Against progress as a belief in the immanent meaningfulness of history

Niebuhr never makes explicit a distinction which is essential for understanding his theology of history. For him, the question 'Is there meaning in history?' has two different meanings. First, it is the question of whether there exists a story which can be drawn out of the historical process, in terms of (for example) laws of development or stages of progress. Second, it is the question of whether human fulfilment in history is possible. Liberalism believed in meaning in history in both senses. Niebuhr, it will transpire, also believed in at least the possibility of meaning in history in each of these senses (and indeed, this is connected below with a third meaning of 'meaning in history'): what he denied was that either could be derived immanently.

Corresponding to each of these senses, Niebuhr's attack on the beliefs that the meaning of history can be discerned without reference to a transcendent order of being and that progress to historical perfection is possible falls into two parts. First, epistemologically, human finiteness implies that the pattern of the whole of history is inscrutable. Second, ontologically, human sin forestalls complete historical fulfilment.

(i) He asserts first the given limits of human rational understanding of the temporal process. Natural science does not, it seems, have such limits; although his awareness of the depths of human self-deception leads him to be cautious about being indiscriminate in his ascriptions of objectivity to the conclusions of scientific research, he has no doubts about the basic rationality of science. Human understanding of history, however, has very definite limits. The main reason for this is that history is the realm of freedom, of the self's transcendence over the coherences of nature. Such freedom, although adequate to ensure the non-predictability of human behaviour, is not so absolute as to break the organic relation of mind and body or the combination of 'freedom and necessity' in all human action. But it is sufficient to show that the sequences of natural causation cannot form an adequate basis for understanding the ultimate coherence of history.[47] He also has other reasons for thinking that the meaning of history is not amenable to reason. History, like other human sciences, is not assimilable to the methods of natural science, because of the inscrutability of human motivation; because every human action takes place in several dimensions, which multiplies enormously the problems of underdetermination of theory; and because of the ideological effects of the involvement of the whole self in the observation of historical events.[48] There are difficulties, therefore, even for the conventional historian, let alone the speculative philosopher of history. This does not imply that nothing can be known from history: Niebuhr willingly (though somewhat anomalously) asserts that 'history is actually the story of man's developing freedom'.[49] But it does imply that a complete understanding of the overall movement of history is impossible. For such an undertaking must be from a viewpoint, but those viewpoints accessible to finite human beings do not transcend history. In particular, reason bears no intrinsic relation to the eternal, and efforts to use it to gain a transcendent perspective will necessarily be interested and inadequate.

This belief in the limits of the rational intelligibility of history has a theological as well as a 'public' foundation. It lies in those

[47] See *NDM* i. *passim*, for Niebuhr's theory of the self.

[48] See Stone, *Reinhold Niebuhr*, 102; *FH* 11–13; *DST* 12–13; *BT* 36; and in general 'Ideology and the Scientific Method', in R. M. Brown (ed.), *Essential Niebuhr*, 205–17. Thus his criticisms of Dewey's search for a 'disinterested intelligence', *NDM* i. 118–19.

[49] *FH* 232. It is anomalous in that talk of the 'actual' story of history presupposes (at least within Niebuhr's terms) precisely the transcendent perspective he denies to finite creatures. The line of thought that gives rise to this assertion is indicated at the end of this section.

doctrines that stress the otherness of God and the distinction between derived and underived, such as the doctrines of creation and of the sovereignty and grace of God. Thus, time, as the 'stage' of history,[50] while it receives its significance from its divine creation, by the same token has limits to its rational intelligibility. The concept of creation 'agrees with classical, as against modern, thought that the temporal process is not self-derived, self-explanatory or self-fulfilling'.[51] It should be noted that Niebuhr does not base this ignorance of the meaning of history on the Fall. The Fall is used by him to describe the human response to finitude; it is a misuse of freedom, rather than the loss of any kind of eternity or transcendent perspective.[52]

There is therefore a theologically grounded factual impossibility of obtaining any immanently derived comprehensive account of history. This has several consequences. It explains how, while some appear to discern hints of a framework of meaning in parts of history, the whole appears to be on a scale inconceivable to the human mind. Again, it becomes possible to see how the correlations employed by historians and speculative philosophers of history to show its unity fail to do history justice. In particular, it follows that it cannot be shown that, even if there is progress in some areas, the whole of history is moving towards perfection. And so the bourgeois liberal account of progress, according to which 'an unconditioned fulfilment in terms of infinite duration'[53] is projected, cannot be justified in principle.

(ii) Second, ontologically, Niebuhr argues that self-derived human fulfilment in history is impossible, since the inevitability of sin prevents the resolution of all historical contradictions. His understanding of sin is derived from his analysis of the self. Human beings are situated in ambiguity because of their 'amphibious' position in the universe, as finite but free, part of nature but partly freed from it. This does not directly cause sin—living at the junction of nature and spirit, human beings sin 'inevitably though not necessarily'.[54] But it is the occasion of sin, for it leads to anxiety, which is 'the internal description of the state of temptation',[55] the basis of creativity as well as the pre-condition of sin. While the ideal response to temptation, and one possible at every

[50] *FH* 33–54.   [51] *FH* 46–7.
[52] *BT* 10–13; *FH* 121–2.   [53] *BT* 23.
[54] Cf. *NDM* i. 161.   [55] *NDM* i. 195.

moment, is freedom from anxiety through faith in the security of God's love, the universal response is that of unbelief, which is thus rightly held in the Christian tradition to be the root of sin. Unbelief compensates for the insecurity of the human condition in two ways: either through sinful self-assertion, a will-to-power trying to overreach the limits of creatureliness, or through sensuality, the self's attempt to escape self-love through deification of another, and then to immerse itself in unconsciousness.[56] In practice, at least in connection with his theology of history, he rarely mentions sensuality: the central human sin is hubris, or pride.[57]

Liberalism, it follows, has a mistaken anthropology. It shares in the error of optimism: namely, 'a too-simple confidence in man, particularly in rational man, and . . . a too-simple hope in the progressive achievement of virtue in history, by reason of the progressive extension of intelligence'.[58] Thus, on the one hand, it treats humankind as 'essentially a harmless animal',[59] rejecting the idea of original sin. It sometimes attributes evil to social institutions,[60] more commonly to ignorance[61] or else to nature; sharing essentially classical views of human nature, liberalism is thus a form of Pelagianism.[62] On the other hand, it disregards the message of the doctrine of the Antichrist, that because of the pervasiveness of sin, historical advance leads to new perils as well as new promises; new power and freedom will not emancipate from historical ambiguity.[63]

Liberalism also fails to see that it is itself an example of the hubristic attempt in search of security and redemption to turn the finite into the infinite. While denying the fact of sin, it yet commits

---

[56] Sensuality 'is always: (1) an extension of self-love to the point where it defeats its own ends; (2) an effort to escape the prison house of self by finding a god in a process or person outside the self; and (3) finally an effort to escape from the confusion which sin has created into some form of sub-conscious existence' (*NDM* i. 255).

[57] Thus 'pride is more basic than sensuality' (*NDM* i. 198). For this he has been widely criticized by feminist writers: see Judith Plaskow, *Sex, Sin and Grace: Women's Experience and the Theologies of Reinhold Niebuhr and Paul Tillich* (Lanham, Md.: University Press of America, 1980), esp. 51–94; and Daphne Hampson, 'Reinhold Niebuhr on Sin: A Critique', in Richard Harries (ed.), *Reinhold Niebuhr and the Issues of Our Time* (London and Oxford: Mowbrays, 1986), 46–60.

[58] 'A Faith for History's Greatest Crisis', 126.

[59] 'Ten Years', 543; *CLCD* 20.

[60] 'Sickness of American Culture', 268.

[61] *FH* 11–13; *BT* 141; *NDM* ii. 91.

[62] *NDM* i. 261.

[63] *NDM* ii. 327–30; 'A Faith for History's Greatest Crisis', 122; *FH* 15–16.

the greatest sin. Evil is not, as liberalism often supposes, due to
finiteness. Rather, the Incarnation demonstrates that 'what seems
to be an inherent defect in life itself is really a contingent defect in
the soul of each man, the defect of the sin which he commits in his
freedom';[64] and the doctrine of Christ as Judge shows that sin
rather than finiteness will be judged.[65] Evil flows from sin,
particularly from pride. Such pride is manifested in the denial of
historical relativism in an effort to uncondition the inevitably
conditioned, and in the attempts of tribes or nations to assert an
ultimate validity for their values.[66] But it is also found in the
elevation of bourgeois ideals to the status of timeless universals,
and in the optimist's construction of little worlds of meaning, the
illusions of which are eventually revealed by circumstances.[67]

This understanding of sin as pride shapes Niebuhr's theology of
history, as well as his theological anthropology. It is ascribed to the
liberal view of progress: 'The belief that man could solve his
problem . . . by the historical process itself is a mistake which is
partly prompted by the most universal of all "ideological" taints:
the pride, not of particular men and cultures, but of man as
man.'[68] Such hubris inevitably leads to destructiveness: the experience of the twentieth century is a nemesis. From such immanent
schemes of redemption come the grossest evils. Liberal universalism, for example, led to nationalistic fanaticism, since the unwillingness of some to accept universal liberal values constituted
evidence that they must be subhuman.[69] But these terms of
Greek tragedy are also interpreted theologically: God's power,
revealed in the structures of existence, executes his judgement on
human sin.[70] The tower of Babel is thus symbolic of human
history.[71] 'The most obvious meaning of history is that every
nation, culture and civilization brings destruction upon itself by
exceeding the bounds of creatureliness which God has set upon all
human enterprises.'[72]

[64] *BT* 168. The logic of the passage from which this is taken is inperspicuous.
[65] *NDM* ii. 302.   [66] *FH* 116–19, 218.
[67] *BT* 34–6, 115–16.   [68] *NDM* ii. 331.
[69] *BT* 237. This passage is expounded with reference to the Nazi treatment of the
Jews by Stanley Hauerwas in (*Against the Nations: War and Survival in a Liberal
Society* (Minneapolis: Winston Press, 1985), 84–5.
[70] *FH* 8, 27–8.
[71] *BT* 25–46; cf. also his treatment of the Temple, built through David's
recognition of his creatureliness (ibid. 47–68).
[72] *NDM* i. 150; cf. *FH* 104.

It is clear from this why Niebuhr criticizes the liberal conception of history. On the one hand, it pretends to an understanding of history that is unattainable by finite beings. As the realm of free action, unlike the object of study of natural science, history cannot be known as a unity by finite beings; as finite, its meaning is not self-derived but transcendent. The belief that history is the story of progress towards perfection cannot therefore be justified even in principle. On the other hand, the view of human nature entertained by liberalism, in which evil is ascribed to nature, ignorance, finitude, or other sources outside the self, prevents it from comprehending that the sinful use of human freedom implies that the capacity for creativity also becomes the basis of destructiveness. Progress towards improved technology or 'more inclusive harmonies' has led also to the possibility of greater evil. Thus immanently derived fulfilment or salvation is impossible. Like its professed universalism, the liberal belief in progress is fundamentally an expression of human pride, an attempt at self-redemption.

(b) In defence of the meaningfulness of history

Although Niebuhr is better known for his negative attack on progressivist theories of history, he also presents a positive theory. The meaning of history is not self-derived, but this does not imply that history has no meaning. Finite human beings cannot of themselves grasp the story of history but this does not imply that history has no story. History may not be the source of human fulfilment, but this does not imply that it is not the locus of that fulfilment. It may be tragic that human beings constantly transgress the laws of their creaturely being, but this does not imply meaninglessness. For beyond tragedy the grace of the God who transcends history and redeems as well as judges is revealed in Christ. 'Our most reliable understanding [of human destiny] is the fruit of "grace" in which faith completes our ignorance without pretending to possess its certainties as knowledge; and in which contrition mitigates our pride without destroying our hope.'[73] Against cynics and nihilists on the one hand and dualists on the other, then, he defends the meaningfulness of historical existence in a theology of history which undergirds his own revised liberalism.

[73] *NDM* ii. 332.

According to Niebuhr, as we have seen, the narrative of history is not immanently discernible; nor is salvation in history self-derived. Yet, he holds, there is a transcendent source of meaning. As always, this is argued from two directions. First, in the public realm, he claims—with regard to the interpretation of history—that there is judgement (which points to the existence of a meaning), although it is imperfect (which points to the need for a final judgement). With regard to meaning understood as human fulfilment, he mentions the 'provisional meanings in history, capable of being recognized and fulfilled by individuals and cultures'.[74] Second, theologically, the transcendent nature of historical meaning is illustrated for Niebuhr in the relation of eternity to time. This again has two dimensions, reflecting the two meanings of 'meaning in history'. On the one hand, eternity stands at the end of time in that, unlike time, it cannot be conceived as having a finis: this is connected with the claim that any historical action or event can be understood only in the light of the whole temporal process, which is possible only at the 'end' of history in a 'last judgment'.[75] On the other hand, eternity stands over time, not as a separate order of being, but as the source of temporal existence and the basis of the indeterminate possibilities open at each moment. This dimension shows 'those qualities and meanings of history which seem to have absolute significance without reference to their relation to the continuum of history', such as martyrdom and sacrifice.[76] Both claims are necessary for the transcendent nature of historical meaning. If merely the vertical were held, the historical and social meaning of life would be denied, Niebuhr argues. Thus he alleges that Barthian eschatology 'pays little attention to a possible meaning of history as a continuum and speaks of eschatology in terms of the eternity which impinges upon every moment of time'.[77] But opposition to such 'other-worldliness', though it might stress the temporally extended nature of history, runs the opposite danger of trying to fulfil meaning within history.

The meaning of history must be derived from beyond history, therefore. But if so, how is the content of history's meaning discovered? And how are the contradictions of history resolved? To answer these questions, Niebuhr turns to the claims at the centre of the Christian faith. 'The Christian faith begins with, and

---

[74] *FH* 214.
[75] *NDM* ii. 310–12.
[76] *NDM* ii. 310.
[77] *NDM* ii. 319–20.

is founded upon, the affirmation that the life, death, and resurrection of Christ represent an event in history, in and through which a disclosure of the whole meaning of history occurs.'[78] The Incarnation is essentially a revelation of the reconciliation between God and the world. The content of this revelation is that God has taken into himself the sins of the world, in that he has laid upon himself the suffering which is the consequence of his wrath against sin, as that wrath is expressed in the structures of the world which react against creaturely attempts to transcend them. Christ, as the suffering servant guiltlessly suffering for the sins of the guilty, reveals the character of the divine as one who is involved in the world and 'vicariously suffers' for human iniquity. Thus, in the death of Christ it becomes clear that judgement is not God's final word. Rather, Christ's death reveals that God 'overcomes in His own heart what cannot be overcome in human life', since human life always remains prone to hubris. In this way Christianity provides what Greek tragedy never could: namely, escape from nemesis.[79] On the Cross God shows that beyond judgement there is love: that is, that God is power beyond the structures of history in which judgement necessarily follows transgression, and that his merciful involvement in history is an expression of his transcendence over its forms and necessities.[80]

This revelation serves as the principle of interpretation for the whole meaning of history. It achieves this in three ways. First, it completes the incomplete knowledge drawn from the tangents of meaning in history that point beyond history, by showing the content of the transcendent source of meaning. Second, it clarifies obscurities and contradictions in history by showing that the execution of judgement is not the final word on history. Third, it corrects the false interpretations of history which human egoism has adopted, but which result only in the comprehension of history from a finite viewpoint.[81] From this ultimate perspective it becomes clear that history is the story, not of continual progress, but of judgement upon sin and of the possibility through grace of renewal and rebirth. At the level of civilizations, history from this standpoint is meaningful 'because eternal principles are vindicated

[78] *FH* 26.
[79] *NDM* i. 153.
[80] *FH* 26, 47; *NDM* ii. 74.
[81] *NDM* ii. 69–70, 85.

in both the life which overcomes death in rising civilizations, and in the death which overtakes proud life in dying ones'. [82]

But revelation in Christ is not only the source of principles for the interpretation of history. The Gospel also offers power to redeem sinners from their continual propensity to aggravate the human predicament by immanent and partial efforts to escape it.[83] Such power is available only to the faith that responds to the revelation of God. For this revelation necessarily involves for biblical religion the 'scandal of particularity', and cannot be apprehended except by faith. But faith cannot be reduced to the intellectual acceptance of metaphysical truths, such as those of traditional Christologies.

The relation between 'power' and 'wisdom' is thereby destroyed because the final truth about life is not apprehended in such a way that the 'existing individual' (Kierkegaard) is shattered in his self-esteem at the very centre of his being; his insecurity as a finite individual in the flux of time is not robbed of all false securities of power or pride; his anxiety is not heightened until it reaches despair. Out of such despair contrition is born; and of contrition faith is conceived; and in that faith there is 'newness of life', which is to say 'power'.[84]

In Christ a new beginning—power—is available for those who repent, whether they be individuals, nations, or civilizations. And in the 'longsuffering' of the divine mercy there are many such opportunities for repentance.

According to the degree with which civilizations and cultures accept these possibilities of renewal, they may extend their life indeterminately. But at some point or other they make the fatal mistake, or a whole series of fatal mistakes. Then they perish; and the divine majesty is vindicated in that destruction.[85]

In the revelation of Christ, centrally, then, the meaningfulness of history—in respect of both interpretation and the possibility of human fulfilment—is affirmed. Taken with the earlier negative movement, this implies a dialectical approach to history. Grace both contradicts and completes nature, in that it shows by its possibility the fulfilment of the structure of meaning and by its

---

[82] *NDM* ii. 318.
[83] *FH* 34.
[84] *NDM* ii. 63.
[85] *NDM* ii. 316–17.

necessity the judgement on all human attempts at such fulfilment. Immanently derived accounts of the course of history fail, yet the revelation of Christ shows history to be the story of judgement and the possibility of rebirth. Human attempts to find fulfilment in history merely aggravate the human condition, yet the power in the Cross provides the possibility of a new beginning to those who repent.

It is at this stage that the two senses of 'meaning in history', which have so far been distinguished in this account, may be seen to be two dimensions of one 'meaning in history', when that meaning is understood in a third sense to refer to the mean-ingfulness of historical existence: that is, to the point or value of acting in history. Such meaningfulness of historical action was denied by cynics for whom no historical goal is more valuable than any other, and by other-worldly dualists for whom this world is of no significance. But if we know how history is to be interpreted properly, and if we have access to the power not to misdirect it, action in history becomes intelligible. Thus, for Niebuhr historical good and evil do matter: the resurrection of the *body* shows that history is fulfilled and not annulled by eternity.[86] Moreover, although no life can fully justify itself in the sight of God and there is need for the ultimate mercy, the distinction between good and evil is not erased by the Atonement.[87] Social and political involvement is therefore intelligible and justified.

If historical existence is meaningful, it follows for Niebuhr that there is always reason for hope, since the intelligibility of action presumes a hopefulness about the outcome. Hope is not to be understood as preferential treatment for the believer, but as an awareness that the Kingdom is relevant at each moment. 'The participation of individuals of all ages in the age of fulfilment is implausible when taken literally; but it is symbolically profound. It relates the eternity which stands over each moment of time to the eternity in which the time process is fulfilled.'[88] Eternity—the Kingdom, perfection—serves at every point of history as a principle of judgement, but, by the same token, as an indicator of higher possibilities. There are indeterminately greater potentialities

---

[86] *BT* 302.
[87] *BT* 249–69; *NDM* ii. 302–3.
[88] *NDM* ii. 322 n. 1.

for any decision or action than are actually achieved: hence there is room for a duly contrite hopefulness.

But the narrative of history also sustains hope. For it turns out that for Niebuhr history is not just the story of cycles of death and renewal. There is increasing freedom in history: in so far as the narrative of history can be discerned, it is that of the development of freedom (through technology) and of the tendency towards more geographically inclusive harmonies.[89] The recognition of this progress in technology and geographical unification was the virtue of the modern sense of history, but modernity wrongly deduced from this that time was the stage of inevitable progress. The burden of Niebuhr's attack on the liberal understanding of history centred on its belief that increasing freedom guaranteed the simple achievement of these wider goals. But liberal self-deception in that regard does not invalidate the residual truth in progressivism.

Niebuhr's dialectical approach to history, according to which meaning in history is transcendently but not immanently derived, leads, therefore, to a justification of the meaningfulness of historical action. By combining this with an account of hope as the potential fulfilment of ever higher possibilities, supported by a narrative of history which bespeaks a chastened progressivism, Niebuhr aims to provide a justification of, and motivation for, social and political action which avoids the difficulties he finds in liberalism.

5 CRITICISM

Niebuhr restores the broadly Augustinian perspective on history, and therefore on politics, which had been largely lost by American Protestant modernism and the social gospel. In so doing, he provides a profound analysis of some of the deepest pretensions of secular liberalism, in which he discerns the ultimately religious ground-motive for the belief in progress—namely, a hubristic attempt at human self-justification.[90] Nevertheless, two general criticisms of his position must be raised. The first concerns the

[89] This is rightly recognized by Langdon Gilkey, 'Reinhold Niebuhr's Theology of History', *Journal of Religion*, 54 (1974), 360–86; see esp. p. 369 n. 22 for references.

[90] The criticisms of progressivism presented here do not nullify the possibility of other kinds of progress between Pentecost and the Parousia: notably, progress in the spread of the Gospel, development (perhaps) in the understanding of doctrine, and the growth of demonic world empires.

plausibility of his understanding of liberalism. The second questions whether the ultimately dualist basis of his theology finally prevents him from treating history seriously, despite his own protestations.

(a) Is Niebuhr's progressivist interpretation of the liberal philosophy of history plausible?

The object of Niebuhr's polemic, as Ronald Stone rightly claims, was not ultimately liberalism, but optimism.[91] Nevertheless, even if he sometimes talked of liberalism when properly he meant optimism, he clearly regarded the former as a species of the latter. But it is this assumption which is open to question. Not all liberals have been naïve progressivists.

Clearly there are examples of the massively optimistic view of history and human nature that Niebuhr pillories. Condorcet, for example, wrote (while hiding from the Jacobins) that 'nature has set no term to the perfection of human faculties; that the perfectibility of man is truly indefinite; and that the progress of this perfectibility . . . has no other limit than the duration of the globe upon which nature has cast us';[92] and again that 'the moral goodness of man, the necessary consequence of his constitution, is capable of indefinite perfection like all his other faculties, and that nature has linked together in an unbreakable chain truth, happiness and virtue'.[93] This extended to the hope that, even if immortality was beyond human power, the span between birth and death might be of indefinite length.[94] This widespread contemporary belief in progress was also expressed by his contemporary, Turgot.[95] Again, for the liberally inspired Godwin, 'every perfection or excellence that human beings are competent to conceive, human beings, unless in cases that are palpably and unequivocally excluded by the structure of their frame, are competent to attain.'[96]

---

[91] Stone, *Reinhold Niebuhr*, 38–9, 105.

[92] Antoine Nicolas de Condorcet, *Sketch for a Historical Picture of the Progress of the Human Mind* (1795), trans. J. Barraclough (London: Weidenfeld and Nicolson, 1955), 4.

[93] Ibid. 193.

[94] Ibid. 208.

[95] See A. R. J. Turgot, 'A Philosophical Review of the Successive Advances of the Human Mind' (1750), in *Turgot on Progress, Sociology and Economics*, trans. and ed. Ronald L. Meek (Cambridge: Cambridge University Press, 1973), 41–59.

[96] William Godwin, *Enquiry Concerning Political Justice* (1793), abridged and ed. K. Codell Carter (Oxford: Clarendon Press, 1971), 59; cf. Godwin's comment on

However, the five liberal writers discussed in Chapter 2, even though all but Locke were seen to hold some doctrine of progress, represent a problem for Niebuhr's characterization. This can be seen by separating out some of the constituent elements in the various progressivisms. Amongst these are the beliefs in (i) technological progress, (ii) the possibility of universal history and the eventual unity of humankind, (iii) human perfectibility, and (iv) moral progress.[97] Now, as mentioned above, Niebuhr believes in technological progress as a statement of historical fact: part of his criticism of modern views of history is that they wrongly deduce the other three strands from this. But of the four liberal writers discussed earlier who did believe in progress, none believed in all of (ii)–(iv). Kant looked forward to perpetual peace and the unity of humankind, but was relatively pessimistic about human perfectibility. Mill, although he thought that 'the general tendency is, and will continue to be, saving occasional and temporary exceptions, one of improvement . . . a tendency towards a better and happier state',[98] and while being dispositionally a perfectibi-list,[99] still feared the coming of democracy, and hardly owned to a massive historical idealism. Hobhouse also undergirded his liberalism with a belief in the ideal of social progress; yet he recognized that moral progress was not guaranteed and depended on continued vigilance, and was of sufficiently empirical temperament not to indulge fantasies about universal history. Finally, Hayek's conception of progress turns out to be merely in terms of the growth of scientific knowledge and the standard of living. None of them, that is, holds to the combination of highly implausible

the book: '[the] great doctrine of the treatise is . . . the perfectibility . . . the progressive nature of man, in knowledge, in virtuous propensities, and in social institutions' (ibid. 326). Carter's counter-example (pp. xxi–xxii) hardly qualifies very seriously the degree to which Godwin believed in progress.

[97] Morris Ginsberg, 'Progress in the Modern Era', in P. P. Wiener (ed.), *Dictionary of the History of Ideas* (5 vols., New York: Scribner's, 1973), iii. 633–50, also mentions belief in laws of development and evolution and differing opinions about the determinism and non-determinism of progress. Niebuhr criticized all of these.

[98] *System of Logic*, VI x. 3.

[99] John Passmore points out the passage in Mill's *Autobiography* where he describes 'the depths of melancholy to which he was reduced when it suddenly occurred to him that since musical combinations are limited in number, music would sooner or later come to a standstill' (*The Perfectibility of Man* (London: Duckworth, 1970), 174 n.).

conceptions of human nature and the possibilities of human history that Niebuhr's account of liberalism suggests.

The same conclusion may be drawn even from those who Niebuhr regarded as paradigmatic liberals. Many preachers of the social gospel were caricatured by his account of the movement. Walter Rauschenbusch, for example, although capable of saying silly things, could confess that 'in actual life there is no case of complete Christian transformation'[100] and that '[by] our very nature we are involved in tragedy',[101] so that 'there is no perfection for man in this life . . . there is only growth towards perfection'.[102] Admittedly, for Niebuhr, he was the 'most brilliant and generally satisfying exponent to the present day' of social Christianity,[103] but many others were similar. Willard Sperry and Harry Emerson Fosdick, for example, still believed in progress after the Great War, yet recognized that it was not simply attainable and that loyalties to groups had to be sacrificially transcended.[104] Indeed, later Niebuhr felt embarrassment when asked to 'name names' of those who fitted his account of the Social Gospel.[105]

The same held for Niebuhr's former colleague on the executive of the League for Independent Political Action, John Dewey. Dewey clearly was optimistic, valued education, and tended to attribute evil to ignorance or 'cultural lag'. His epistemology, stressing experimentation rather than reflection, demands public and self-corrective enquiry for knowledge to flourish. This in turn requires a free and courageous democratic community, employing intelligence and scientific method to reconstruct its self-understanding, and so to adjust 'that body of traditions which constitute the actual mind of man to scientific tendencies and political aspirations which are novel and incompatible with received authorities'.[106] This is connected with a theory of the self as social in nature, so that social

---

[100] Walter Rauschenbusch, *A Theology for the Social Gospel* (1917) (Nashville: Abingdon, 1945), 98.

[101] Ibid. 32.

[102] Rauschenbusch, *Christianity and the Social Crisis* (1907); excerpts in Benson Y. Landis (ed.), *A Rauschenbusch Reader: The Kingdom of God and the Social Gospel* (New York: Harper, 1957), 27–8.

[103] *ICE* 7.

[104] Hutchison, *Modernist Impulse*, 251–6.

[105] 'Reply', 441, to D. D. Williams, 'Niebuhr and Liberalism', 196–7. Cf. Hutchison, *Modernist Impulse*, 301–2, for other complaints of misrepresentation.

[106] John Dewey, 'Philosophy and Civilization', in *Philosophy and Civilization* (New York: Putnam's, 1931), 3–4.

modifications are 'the only means of the creation of changed personalities';[107] and in particular as malleable by education, which was 'the fundamental method of social progress and reform' and 'the deepest and best guaranty of a larger society which is worthy, lovely and harmonious'.[108] But Dewey was also aware of human limitations, that there is disappointment and loss: although hopeful and reformist, he was never utopian.[109] Thus in 1944 he could grant that the events of the previous fifty years had destroyed the general faith in the abolition of war, in the growth of rationality and enlightenment through increased scientific knowledge,[110] and that democracy was in the present circumstances difficult to realize. 'Democracy is not an easy road to take and follow. On the contrary, it is as far as its realization is concerned in the complex conditions of the contemporary world, a supremely difficult one.'[111]

In treating liberalism as a perfectibilist utopianism committed to moral progress and the immanent development of history, then, Niebuhr seems seriously to caricature it, failing to see its more plausible and pragmatic elements. This misrepresentation might appear purely accidental, the consequence of a tendency to schematize which, as we saw earlier, is not without value.

But there is surely a more cogent explanation, insufficiently emphasized by Niebuhr's commentators. From the mid-1930s Niebuhr's positive theory and political practice suggest a pragmatism and meliorism whose distinctiveness was self-conscious, and so had to be marked out from other approaches. In the case of naïve and sentimental optimisms this was easy enough. But to admit the existence of attempted justifications of a more cautious liberalism other than his dialectical 'neo-orthodoxy' presented special difficulties: for it was essential to his apologetic approach that only a Christian understanding of history and politics could avoid both this-worldly utopianism and pessimistic dualism. Liberalism for Niebuhr had to be seen to be characterized by this salvific progressivism. If it could not, the distinctiveness of his dialectical approach would be lost, and the basis—indeed, one is tempted to say, the *raison d'être*—of his apologetic would collapse. In short,

---

[107] Dewey, *Reconstruction in Philosophy* (1920) (Boston: Beacon Press, 1948), 196.
[108] From 'My Pedagogic Creed', quoted in Richard J. Bernstein, *John Dewey* (New York: Washington Square Press, 1966), 42.
[109] Bernstein, *John Dewey*, 167–85.
[110] Dewey, 'The Democratic Faith and Education', in *Problems of Men* (New York: Philosophical Library, 1946), 23–33.   [111] Ibid. 33.

Niebuhr's understanding of liberalism was essential to his defence of the Christian faith, and his caricature of the one was in part generated by the nature of his prior commitment to the other.

Although he was undoubtedly amongst its most influential critics, Niebuhr was not the only one to see the problems of liberalism, and liberals across the board learned to shun heavy-handed historicism. Just as forward-looking thinkers in the eighteenth century had been brought to recognize the values of conservatism by the French Revolution, so in this century the Hegelian-inspired conception of history as the progressive self-unfolding of reason was shown by the First World War to be wrong, and by the rise of Communist and Nazi totalitarianisms to be dangerously wrong.[112]

Perhaps the clearest of the mid-century rejections of historicism is found in Karl Popper.[113] For him, historicism is the belief that a truly scientific or philosophical understanding of politics must be founded on an interpretation of history which can make predictions, thus showing which actions will be successful.[114] On this view, Plato counts as a historicist, since his political theory turned on a belief that change was decay.[115] The problem Popper finds with historicism is that instead of looking for illumination for present action to history, it looks to history to discover the secret of human destiny. But history has no meaning except that given to it by the historian. For there cannot be an account of universal history, since all historical interpretation is selective and perspectival (though not thereby non-objective), and so-called histories of the world are merely histories of political power. There is therefore no destiny to be submitted to. Historicism, with all its baleful consequences, shrinks from the dualism of facts and decisions, and is born of the fear that human beings might genuinely be in control of their destiny. Yet history can be given a meaning, by using it to support the fight for the open society, for piecemeal social engineering, for freedom.[116]

---

[112] In fact, liberals were not wholly put out by the First World War. Hobhouse's response is typical: 'in the long run and at a greater depth there is harmony' (*Social Evolution*, 154); cf. ibid. 162: 'the halting, broken, and uneven nature of progress'.

[113] Although many others share it: Hayek, as was seen earlier, and Berlin, 'Historical Inevitability', in *Four Essays on Liberty*, 41–117.

[114] Popper, *The Open Society and its Enemies*, 6th edn. (2 vols., London: Routledge and Kegan Paul, 1966), i. 7–8.   [115] Ibid. 19.

[116] Ibid. ii. 259–80. Compare Charles Frankel's claims, in Dewey-like terms, that

Liberalism, then, is not committed to the strong progressivism that Niebuhr rightly castigates. Meliorism, however, does seem to be constitutive, as the evidence of Popper corroborates. The same conclusion may be drawn from contemporary English-speaking liberal political philosophy in the manner of Rawls, Nozick, and Dworkin. The question of the philosophy of history lies for this school somewhere on the scale between irrelevance and impertinence: if these thinkers are at all utopian, it is in a rather different mode from the earlier kinds of liberalism. Nevertheless, they might still be termed meliorist, at least in the minimalist sense that they believe that, even though individuals should not be forced to conform to a substantive, externally defined conception of the good, society can be better organized—namely, if it is organized in accordance with the reflectively derived principles which constitute the theory of justice and ensure a just distribution of goods and services, of benefits and burdens, for individuals who must pursue their goals within a social setting.

Niebuhr granted in later life that he 'define[d] liberalism too consistently in terms of its American versions'.[117] Yet, while this afforded him the posture of the liberal anti-liberal, it was (as intimated above) as much a response to the demands of the apologetic structure of his work as intellectual oversight. But this should not cloud appreciation of Niebuhr's acute sensitivity to the slightest indications of human pride, folly, self-deception, or self-justification: that is, to those characteristics which were, to employ a term he used perhaps too sparingly, idolatrous.

(b) Does Niebuhr have a sufficient theological basis for his notion of meaningfulness in history?

Niebuhr's understanding of human ignorance and sin produced a theory of far greater explanatory power than that of the liberals, religious and secular, whom he attacked. And many of his

the idea of progress, considered as a moral standard requiring open enquiry, 'would appear to be an indispensable belief for a fully liberal civilization' ('Progress, The Idea of', in Paul Edwards (ed.), *The Encyclopaedia of Philosophy* (8 vols., New York: Macmillan and Free Press, 1967), vi. 487).

[117] 'Reply', 441. Louis Hartz, *The Liberal Tradition in America* (New York: Harcourt, Brace and World, 1955), seems to reserve belief in this kind of progressivism not for liberals, but for various massively marginalized groups of European-style socialists. He may, however, have been polemically defending liberalism from just the kinds of criticisms Niebuhr brought.

conclusions would command the assent of much of the catholic mainstream of the Christian tradition. An Augustinian under-standing of the relation of time and eternity would accept that history is inscrutable to the human mind; its meaning is written in the scroll which can only be opened by the victorious Lamb (Rev. 5: 1–7). It would also agree that there will be no perfection in history: human sinfulness implies that whatever historical progress there is will not have the finality which is attributed to it by progressivist philosophies of history, and that politics will never achieve more than a relative justice or harmonization of interests. Again, Niebuhr's assertion of the necessity of grace is important: the eschatological transformation is shown thereby to come from beyond the natural, being neither demanded by anything immanent in creation, nor a reaction to the course that history has taken. In rebutting human misunderstandings and judging pretensions, grace destroys not nature, but creaturely transgressions of the created limits. Likewise, the fulfilment of history in eternity does not render history meaningless: its completion beyond its intrinsic possibilities does not nullify the significance of relative good and evil. Finally, an Augustinian would accept that since wisdom comes from revelation, the story of the Incarnation is determinative for the Christian understanding of history: as the eschatological event has taken place in God's self-disclosure in Christ, there can be no further turning-point in history which is decisive for salvation history.[118]

However, it is questionable whether Niebuhr's understanding of theological doctrines can provide a sufficiently firm basis for the conclusions he reaches. For behind his biblical and theological language there remains a set of beliefs which are finally dualist in orientation, despite his attempts to overcome the divide between time and eternity, the conditioned and the unconditioned, by his use of the language of paradox. If this claim can be substantiated, it would suggest that his theology may not be able to sustain the

---

[118] For this interpretation of Augustine, see R. A. Markus, *Saeculum: History and Society in the Theology of St Augustine*, rev. edn. (Cambridge: Cambridge University Press, 1988), esp. 1–71. It is arguable that Niebuhr's tendency to emphasize human inability to understand history, rather than human knowledge of history through revelation, can resemble Averroist scepticism (based on epistemological finitude) more than Augustinian humility (based on original sin). Certainly the Fall and finitude sometimes come nearer in his thought than perhaps they ought, but he does in the end keep them separate.

significance he wishes to claim for history. To establish the claim, we will consider two sets of theological themes: first, his doctrine of the Trinity together with his account of the Atonement; and second, his eschatology.

(i) First, in respect of his doctrine of God, it could be argued that, despite his use of Trinitarian language, his thought remains operatively unitarian. In his Christology, for example, he asserts that 'Father and Son are equally God'.[119] But he is unwilling to give this statement its full prima-facie ontological weight. One reason for this is the irrationality he finds in the ontologically expressed account. 'It is possible for a character, event or fact of history to point symbolically beyond history and to become a source of disclosure of an eternal meaning, purpose and power which bears history. But it is not possible for any person to be historical and unconditioned at the same time.'[120] Rather, the convictions that the Church Fathers tried to express in the doctrine of the two natures were 'Jesus' historical and human character on the one hand, and his significance as the revelation of the divine on the other'.[121] Yet he believes that it is important to maintain the central truth obscured by the Greek metaphysical terminology, for it contains the basic affirmations of Christianity concerning the relations of time and eternity[122] and the bridged gap between the passible and the impassible.[123] It also shows that God's word is important for human life, and that an event in history can reveal the character of history.[124]

Again, in his pneumatology, he is orthodox in pronouncing that the Holy Spirit is 'the Spirit of God indwelling in man',[125] but he appears to remove the substance of that assertion through his later talk of Christ as 'the criterion of the holiness of spirit'[126] in the context of a discussion of the Holy Spirit, which suggests that he is referring to the holiness of the *human* spirit. Indeed, it turns out that for Niebuhr the doctrine of the Spirit is important as a sign that all indications of holiness or redemption in history are not the immanent product of human abilities, but the result of the divine breaking through human self-sufficiency, presumably as the power engendered in the contrite acceptance of revelation.[127]

It seems from these examples that for Niebuhr eternity cannot

---

[119] *NDM* ii. 58.   [120] *NDM* ii. 63.   [121] Ibid.
[122] *NDM* i. 156.   [123] *NDM* ii. 62.   [124] *BT* 14.
[125] *NDM* ii. 103.   [126] *NDM* ii. 116.   [127] *FH* 168.

enter or become part of history: there is a 'barrier of creation'[128] which perfection can never cross. Niebuhr's Christ is not identical with, but the finite counterpart or representative of, the infinite. This 'counterpart' approach to the relation of the infinite to the finite is reflected elsewhere: mutual love and justice are the finite representatives of an agape that can itself never be justified in historical terms; and in history the divine goodness can be portrayed only through powerlessness, since all power held by finite beings is partial.

But it is also found in Niebuhr's doctrine of the Atonement, discussed earlier in the chapter. For Niebuhr, the contradictions of history are resolved outside history: it is at the level of the eternal and divine that God takes sin into himself, and the Cross, as the centre and point of the Incarnation, is the revelation to humankind of that divine mercy. In this conception, history is given significance in two ways: God is revealed on the one hand as 'involved in' history, rather than detached, and on the other as a personal being rather than an undifferentiated unity which destroys history in the process of destroying evil. Thus the Cross here represents an ethical isomorphism of the person of Christ. For just as Christ could not be both eternal and human, so the Cross shows that perfect love is not possible in history. Christ is 'the historic incarnation of a perfect love which actually transcends history, and can appear in it only to be crucified'.[129]

However, in none of these three cases is it clear that Niebuhr can affirm the significance of history, and therefore of historical action, which he claims. Christ reveals God, but is not himself God; the Spirit indwells human beings, but is not himself (itself) fully and ontically divine; the Cross reveals that God has taken sin upon himself, but does not itself constitute any part of the substance of God's saving work. Each of these positions engenders its own distinct theological problems (if Christ is not divine, for example, we may yet be confronted with an unknown God behind him; again, if the Spirit is not fully God, our knowledge and experience of God are not certain to avoid dissolution into personal subjectivity), but they all converge in this one respect: none of them can ground the importance of history which Niebuhr requires.

---

[128] The term is from Rachel Hadley King, *The Omission of the Holy Spirit from Reinhold Niebuhr's Theology* (New York: Philosophical Library, 1964).

[129] *NDM* i. 158.

None of them can admit the strongest reason for ascribing significance to temporality: namely, that the eternal has deigned to enter time and take it upon himself.

The point may be put to Niebuhr in his own terms. He attributes the supreme revelation of God to Christ. Yet, if God has himself done nothing in history, Niebuhr might be asked, it is not clear why the life, death, and resurrection of Christ should be assigned special significance. The question is even sharper in that in respect of the resurrection he considers that it is 'the revelatory depth of the fact which is the primary concern of faith', and that the supposed empty tomb is a kind of miracle 'in opposition to true faith'.[130] Niebuhr would have two kinds of response to this. Apologetically, the general structure of his argument is that a belief in these events as determinative for history provides a better interpretation of the whole of history, explains better human transcendence over—yet engagement in—time and nature, defends more convincingly belief in individuality, and so on, than any rival creed. But it is his second response that is important for the present argument: theologically, he argues, it is in those events that God's self-disclosure takes place. However, if that is so, and if the content of revelation is certain information about God—that he suffers because of human sin, for example—it must be asked why the particular person Jesus Christ should be regarded as necessary or irreplaceable for that revelation: Christ becomes just a token, perhaps the supreme token, of the type 'Suffering Servant', but with no deeper intrinsic significance.

How might Niebuhr obtain grounds for giving Christ the special significance his theology requires? Niebuhr's dualist presuppositions create the basic problem, which he tries to resolve in terms of the paradoxical relations between time and eternity. But paradox is no proper substitute for the full ontological engagement of history and eternity: it can allow only an external relationship between the two, never a meeting-place in which the two are substantially linked. One way in which Niebuhr could have come to this conclusion, though there are many others, would have been by placing a greater stress on revelation's nature as the revelation of a free God than on a priori constraints on the content of that revelation. If his theological epistemology had allowed knowledge

---

[130] *FH* 148.

to be a reflexive rather than an absolute operation, so that theological possibilities were derived a posteriori from the revelation given in Christ, rather than vice versa, he might have argued from an analysis not of the concept of revelation, but of the content of what has been revealed, to the conclusion that in *this* person *this* God with whom we have to deal has revealed himself, and thus that in *these* events the meaning of history has been decisively determined and the importance of historical action affirmed. Such an approach would not be entirely without public corroboration or confirmation, but it would ground the insistence that God in Christ is the clue to history. Whether this general approach or another is preferred, it is ultimately this ontological claim which is critical: at any rate, without such an affirmation, Niebuhr's Christ has in the end no better purchase on eternity than the liberal Jesus whom he rightly derides as being worthy of devotion only because of the number of superlatives that can be attached to descriptions of his goodness.[131]

(ii) Second, it must be asked whether his eschatology will carry the weight he gives it. Niebuhr stresses regularly that the eschatological symbols should be taken seriously but not literally. It has been the recurrent error of Christian orthodoxy to interpret them literally as events in time. But '[the] end of history is not a point in history'.[132] This does not prevent Niebuhr from employing traditional formulas: history after Christ is 'an interim between the disclosure of its true meaning and the fulfilment of that meaning, between the revelation of divine sovereignty and the full establishment of that sovereignty'.[133] Yet it is difficult to know what he can mean by this if, for example, he believes that '[the] end of an individual life is, for him, the end of history; and every individual is a Moses who perishes outside the promised land'.[134] Or if he can assert of the doctrine of the general resurrection of the dead that '[t]he participation of individuals of all ages in the age of fulfillment is implausible when taken literally; but it is symbolically profound. It relates the eternity which stands over each moment of time to the eternity in which the time process is fulfilled.'[135] These statements appear to suggest an account of the Christian hope that differs from traditional formulations: that for Niebuhr, human

---

[131] Cf. *NDM* i. 157. [132] *BT* 22.
[133] *NDM* ii. 51. [134] *NDM* ii. 319.
[135] *NDM* ii. 322 n. 1.

transcendence over the flux of time does not necessarily translate into a continuation of life after physical death.

The problem here for a theology of history is not simply that a realist belief in the resurrection of the dead is a central article of Christian doctrine: Christianity is not primarily concerned with buttressing the yearning of the human ego for indefinite temporal extension, an effort which is potentially corrupting. Rather, it is that the doctrine of the general resurrection is one way of making intelligible the creation of the world as an episode in the life of God. To assert that human beings will participate in the age of fulfilment gives point to God's initial act of creation as the work of one whose overflowing love expresses itself in the desire for eternal communion with his creatures.

Niebuhr's account, lacking a substantial doctrine of the general resurrection, seems to allow little room for such a line of thought. Of course, he might respond that such questions are beyond the realm of human understanding. But another reading of his theology might lend weight to the notion that it is ultimately focused not on God, but on the project of giving significance to human finitude, and in particular of prompting people 'to accept their historical responsibilities gladly', as he concludes *Human Destiny*.[136] Such an interpretation is supported by his account of the importance of eschatological symbols, according to which they convey '[the] sense that the final fulfilment impinges on the present moment, the feeling of urgency in regard to anticipating this fulfilment', which is wrongly turned into 'the feeling that the fulfilment of history is chronologically imminent'.[137] In other words, the eschatological realities that give a point to history are in danger of being absorbed by Niebuhr into the ethical demands of the present moment.

From this discussion of his doctrine of the Trinity, the Atonement, and eschatology, it appears that Niebuhr's language promises more than his theological system can deliver. He promises an account which will show Christ as the meaning of history; but what he delivers is neither a Christology which gives the Incarnation its full significance of God himself taking human flesh and investing this historical world with divine significance, nor an eschatology which fulfils the Incarnation by bringing the created order into

---

[136] *NDM* ii. 332.
[137] *NDM* ii. 51–2.

communion with the divine life. A theological critique of liberal progressivism should reject the idealist theological orientation which gives rise to these: only then will it be able to give substantial grounding to his proper assertions that in Christ the meaning of history is disclosed, that salvation cannot be a conclusion of the historical process, and therefore that the perfect order of society will not be established before the eschaton.

Niebuhr's work points the way to the constraints which Christian political thought must place on an acceptable philosophy of history. Although twentieth-century liberalism has generally been more cautious, and although contemporary liberal political philosophy limits itself to the theory of just distribution, liberals in the past have often espoused a progressivism which, in their ignorance of the limits of human knowledge and the pervasiveness of human sinfulness, is prone to underwrite, and itself to become, a form of salvation without grace. It is ultimately, as he put it, 'faith in man'.[138] All this Niebuhr rightly explodes.

To achieve this required profound adjustments to the liberal theological anthropology and theology of history that he inherited. That the changes he instituted were ultimately insufficient has been argued above. But their inadequacy stemmed not merely from a failure to affirm some fore-ordained set of orthodox theological doctrines; rather, it is symptomatic of a more deeply seated nexus of commitments.

Niebuhr's first book was entitled *Does Civilization need Religion?* (1927). The converse question, that religion might point to a God whose demands could not simply be identified with the requirements of civilization, was never considered seriously enough; both in the direction of his life's interests and in the structure of his thought he posited politics and deduced theology. In the end, Niebuhr could allow that religion might be construed as projection, its doctrines as 'believed poetry', its God more a principle of transcendence than the living God of Abraham, Isaac, and Jacob. Not that for him religion was ever merely projection, or theology purely a deduction from anthropology: on the contrary, his mythical approach to language about God should be seen in part as an attempt to preserve a theological realism, and his

---

[138] 'Ten Years', 543.

believed-poetry account of religious doctrines as a means of asserting their truth. But his search for a theology which would justify his politics, when set within the context of his failure to break with the dominant idealist theology, prevented him from securing a firm theological basis for his position. The fact that the crucial issue for him was the motivation to sustain political action and maintain a meaningful historical existence ultimately opens the door to the possibility of religion being harnessed to the less than ethical requirements of civilization. And in the end, it mistakes the proper direction of the symbolism: it is not so much that Christian theological language is a disguised form of talking about earthly politics, as that Christian participation in earthly politics is a symbolic means of pointing to Kingdom realities.

4

George Grant and the Basis of Liberal Values

I INTRODUCTION

If progessivism has rightly been regarded as a central feature of the liberal understanding of history, the idea of individual moral autonomy should be seen as no less central to its understanding of moral value. It was observed in Chapter 2 that this emphasis on individual moral autonomy has been susceptible to a variety of interpretations within the liberal tradition, from the idea that it is no part of the good life that one be forced to live it, at the one end, to a moral scepticism and a championing of the subjectivity of values, at the other. This has clear affinities with the account given in Chapter 2 of the self as sovereign chooser of its ends, whether this be construed simply as the right of individuals to exercise their conscience in matters of morals or religion without reference to superior authority or, in a decidedly more voluntarist vein, as the freedom of individuals to create for themselves the values by which they shall live. But it also consorts well with a contractarian basis for political value, in which individuals bargain with each other about the terms of co-operation in their common life, and construct political obligation and governmental legitimacy on the basis of a founding agreement.

The power of George Grant's searching analysis of the liberal conception of value derives from his ability to connect these characteristically liberal understandings of the self and of moral and political value to a wider account of modernity as an interconnected whole. That he criticizes liberalism and modernity from the perspective of metaphysical and axiological commitments that are close to the heart of the Christian tradition makes his work an especially suitable basis for a theological critique of these aspects of liberalism. Drawing on the thought of Nietzsche, Heidegger, Leo Strauss, and Jacques Ellul, amongst others, he constructs with considerable lucidity and intensity a picture of the modern age as fate, and contrasts it with an alternative understanding, hesitantly and apophatically expressed, that is illuminated by Plato, the Gospels, and Simone Weil. The multi-faceted nature of his thought is such that an exposition of his account of modernity could with equal propriety take any of several themes as primary—history, technology, justice, human self-interpretation, philosophy, nature, freedom, and science, amongst others. In this chapter I will give priority to his account of the modern notion of value: in particular, to his attack in his 1974 lectures, published as *English-Speaking Justice*, on John Rawls's liberalism.

Rawls's work provides what is still the most rigorous and sophisticated account of contractual liberalism yet presented. As Robert Nozick, an early critic, wrote: 'Political philosophers must now either work within Rawls' theory or explain why not.'[1] His account of method in political philosophy, and, connnected with this, of the nature of moral and political value, has been widely influential within the dominant school of political philosophy in the contemporary English-speaking world, even amongst those who reject his substantive conclusions. Present-day liberalism is by no means confined to Rawls's method or conclusions (and indeed, he has developed his views considerably in the last two decades), but the widespread influence of his theory fully justifies considering his work more closely.

Grant claims that Rawls fails to provide the foundational affirmations necessary to defend human beings against the predations of technology, and indeed encourages a conception of the self that serves to legitimate the hegemony of technology. There is, he says, a contradiction within contemporary Western civilization: liberal values are being overturned by technology, but liberalism can appeal to no justification of its values which does not also validate the technological mind-set which is overturning them. In this chapter we will explore the idea that Rawls's account of political liberalism and justice as fairness does nothing to avert this technological fate. I will argue that Grant importantly mis-interprets Rawls's device of the 'original position', and that Rawls's more recent work escapes many of Grant's strictures. Nevertheless, I shall also try to develop Grant's arguments to show that Rawls's account of the basis of value, and his distinction of

---

[1] Robert Nozick, *Anarchy, State and Utopia* (Oxford: Blackwell, 1974), 183.

'political' and 'comprehensive' doctrines, may in practice still result in the subversion of liberal values.

2 THE CIVILIZATIONAL CONTRADICTION

Grant opens *English-Speaking Justice* by considering the relations of technology and liberalism. The 'dominant form of self-definition' found in the English-speaking West is, he claims, 'a sustaining faith in a necessary interdependence between the developments in technological science and political liberalism'.[2] Liberalism is widely accepted as the most plausible modern political rhetoric: thus lip-service is paid to freedom, its central value, by all sides in public debate, providing strong evidence that it expresses what Western cultural élites regard as the best available articulation of moral truth.[3] Likewise, technological science is generally seen as the most powerful engine of progress in modern society and the primary means to the freedom necessary to lead the good life. Whether it is believed that science is necessary to realize the goals of liberalism, or that liberalism is most likely to ensure scientific progress, their close relationship is such that liberalism is often thought to be verified through the same account of rationality and objectivity as science.

How does Grant understand liberalism and technology? He argues that they were born of the same cultural moment, and that the historical roots of both reflect the typically modern understanding of humanity and 'the whole'. 'Modernity', a term used by Grant to refer to 'the civilization of the age of progress',[4] is conceived as a unified historical totality, whose essence may be 'enucleated'[5] in several ways, such as history, technology, or liberalism. Its origins Grant finds most closely articulated in terms of the will, 'that primal western affirmation which stands shaping our whole civilization, before modern science and technology, before liberalism and capitalism, before our philosophies and theologies'.[6] This in turn, despite the clear influence of Heidegger, he finds to be due not to some ancient Greek forgetfulness of

---

[2] *ESJ* 3.   [3] *ESJ* 5–8.   [4] *LN* 53 n. 15.
[5] 'Enucleation' is a term of art coined by Grant, to refer to the extraction of the animating source of an entity, beyond its purely phenomenal or behavioural aspects (*TH* 8).
[6] *ESJ* 63–4.

Being, but to the exclusivity and manner of reliance on revelation that has been associated with the Western use of Scripture.

It is within this account of modernity as the rise to ascendancy of voluntarism that his understanding of liberalism and technology should be placed. In the case of technology, it led him to reject Ellul's definition of *la technique* as 'the totality of methods rationally arrived at and having absolute efficiency (for a given stage of development) in every field of human activity'.[7] He felt that Ellul's theological framework was too strongly indebted to voluntarism, scorning philosophy in the classical sense of the contemplative desiring love of wisdom, and failing to recognize that the technological civilization first arose in Western Europe because of the Hebraic elements introduced by Christianity. Thus, although much of his sociological spadework is useful, Ellul fails to uncover the essence of technology in its relation to the will. Instead, Grant observes that 'technology' is a neologism which captures in its conjunction of *technē* and *logos* the co-penetration of the arts and the sciences, of knowing and making, such that they are united in the will to mastery of the earth.[8] Correspondingly, he describes it in broadly Heideggerian terms as 'the endeavour which summons forth everything (both human and non-human) to give its reasons, and through the summoning forth of those reasons turns the world into potential raw material, at the disposal of our "creative" wills'.[9] The Nietzschean overtones of this are accented when he talks of technique as 'our vision of ourselves as creative freedom, making ourselves, and conquering the chances of an indifferent world'.[10] More than a way of thinking, it is a way of being, 'the basic way western men experience their own existence in the world'.[11]

Grant's understanding of liberalism is more complicated. He appears to use the term 'liberalism' in two ways. The first is adopted on polemical grounds, and is too broad to be illuminating.

[7] Jacques Ellul, *The Technological Society* (New York: Vintage Books, 1964), p. xxv; quoted in *TE* 11, 113.

[8] *T&J* 11–14. It is this purported etymology which attracts Grant to the word 'technology' for the modern reality, despite the multiplicity of inappropriate connotations it invokes; like many Heideggerians, he sometimes attaches particular significance to what is unveiled through such etymologies. The word *technologia* is in fact found in Philodemus, and the cognate verb *technologeō* in Aristotle.

[9] *ESJ* 82.

[10] *TE* 137.

[11] Grant, 'A Conversation on Technology' (with Gad Horowitz), *Journal of Canadian Studies*, 4/3 (1969), 3.

It refers to 'the broad tradition of sane discourse in the western world', in that '[in] so far as the word "liberalism" is used to describe the belief that political liberty is a central human good, it is difficult for me to consider as sane those who would deny that they are liberals'.[12] On this definition, Plato, Hegel, and Rousseau are counted unproblematically as liberals. While it is valuable as a reminder to English-speaking liberals that Russell, Popper, and the like represent not 'liberalism itself, but a particular species of it',[13] the definition will not be further discussed here. It is peculiar to Grant, and too broad to be of value for present purposes.

His second and more common account of liberalism, by contrast, in which liberalism is the whole of modernity from one aspect, promises (no doubt partly through its neglect of detail) a theory of wide explanatory power. Occasionally distinguished as 'modern' liberalism, this kind of liberalism refers to 'a set of beliefs which proceed from the central assumption that man's essence is his freedom and therefore that what chiefly concerns man in this life is to shape the world as we want it'.[14] In the Straussian contest between the ancients and the moderns, it comfortably sits on the side of the latter, and amongst its number Grant includes Machiavelli, Hobbes, Spinoza, Vico, Rousseau, Hegel, Marx, and Darwin.[15] The alternatives to this liberalism he lists as, on the one hand, Plato and Aristotle and their Jewish and Christian interpreters, and on the other, those indebted to Marx and Nietzsche.[16] Contractual liberalism is one form of it, with 'right prior to good; a foundational contract protecting individual rights; the neutrality of the state concerning moral "values"; social pluralism supported by and supporting this neutrality'.[17] A characteristic feature of this liberalism has been its general hostility to Christianity: at its centre lies the belief that the idea of the supernatural must be eliminated. Among other things, liberalism and Christianity disagree about the role of self-restraint. For liberalism, 'the emancipation of the passions and optimism about the result' has been a central tenet; but for Christianity, fulfilment of desire is found through obedience to Christ. Again, for liberalism, freedom is the ability of human beings to make themselves and the world as

[12] *ESJ* 4.   [13] *ESJ* 5.   [14] *TE* 114 n. 3.
[15] *LN* 95. Grant submits to Strauss in his interpretation of past political philosophers.
[16] *ESJ* 95.   [17] *ESJ* 70.

they want them to be; but for the Gospels, it is the ability of human beings to give themselves to God. In general, as he puts it: 'To liberalism, man is the measure; to Christianity, God is the measure. To liberalism man creates himself, and measures and defines the order which he makes. To Christianity, man is measured and defined by an order which he does not make.'[18]

There are certain difficulties in Grant's account of liberalism, even given its alarming brevity and typification. Marx, for example, is described variously as a liberal, a modern post-liberal, and (elsewhere[19]) a pre-modern. Again, although liberalism is for Grant the whole of modernity in its political aspect, Nietzsche, who is the modern *par excellence* for Grant, is here a post-liberal. Furthermore, Grant names as representatives of liberalism figures none of whom would occupy more than a marginal position in the standard canon of liberals, and some of whom are not even political thinkers. This certainly need not be taken as confusion: it is precisely Grant's point that because modernity is a totality, the similarities between different traditions of political thought, and indeed between different discourses, are more important than the dissimilarities. It is a revisionary account, whose rationale is derived from Grant's preferred method of interpreting liberalism in terms of the metaphysics that grounds modernity. How much of this can be recruited for the purposes of the present book will be discussed at the end of this chapter.

The historical outworking of liberalism and technology is exemplified by North America. In particular, the evolution of modernity and the working out of this Western affirmation of the will is emblematized in the history of the United States, which he regards as 'the most progressive society on earth', and which as an imperial centre is becoming a universal destiny through its technological expansion.[20]

Grant explains American identity in terms of its rejection of one

[18] Grant, 'How Deception Lurks in The Secular City' (review of Harvey Cox, *The Secular City*), *United Church Observer* (1 July 1966), 17, 26.

[19] *LN* 56. The three interpretations are probably compatible once some distinctions are made clear.

[20] *LN* 54–66. The relation of Canada to the American project was one of Grant's abiding concerns. Cf. e.g. *The Empire: Yes or No?* (Toronto: Ryerson Press, 1945); 'Have We a Canadian Nation?', *Public Affairs* (Institute of Public Affairs, Dalhousie University), 8 (1945), 161–6; *LN*; and 'Canadian Fate and Imperialism', *TE* 63–78.

of the two 'primals' of Western civilization.[21] These 'primals', or originating presences determinative of thought and action, are ancient Greece and Christianity. The former, at its height in Plato and Aristotle, was oriented to eternity and thus to contemplation of the good as the highest end; justice was conceived as a given order for which human beings were fitted, and morality as a desiring attention to a timeless perfection. The latter, although in its truest form in the Gospels compatible with the truth given in Plato, differed through its identification of charity as the highest good.[22] Moreover, exalting the will through its doctrine of creation, oriented to time through its doctrines of providence and redemption in history, and directed to the future in its eschatology, Christianity was responsible when secularized for the modern idea of progress.[23] While for Europeans the more contemplative primal of ancient Greece was still present to inform their lives and their polities, North Americans had for their primal the meeting of the New World with a Calvinism which represented a rejection of the classical world in the name of the Bible.

This fateful conjunction occurred in the context of the joint seventeenth-century attack on medieval Aristotelianism by Protestantism and the new natural sciences. These two movements agreed negatively in their opposition to Aristotelianism, the one demanding total dependence on divine revelation, the other seeking explanation through efficient rather than final causality. But they were also joined together positively: the naked Calvinist soul before its transcendent, sovereign God, seeking the divine will and securing divine approval through its activity rather than its contemplation, came to regard the self as radically free and the external world (including the body) as matter of no intrinsic value, to be subdued in accordance with the demands of the soul's 'unappeasable responsibility'.[24] Likewise, the traditional contemplative understanding of science gave way to the utilitarian

[21] See in general 'In Defence of North America', *TE* 15–40.

[22] See Joan E. O'Donovan, *George Grant and the Twilight of Justice* (Toronto: University of Toronto Press, 1984), 100–1, for the relationship between charity and contemplation.

[23] See e.g. *TE* 18–19; *TH* 21–2; J. E. O'Donovan, *George Grant*, 129–30, for the resolution of Grant's apparent contradictions. In later writings he suggests that Pope Gregory VII's victory in the Investiture contest contributed to the technological society by turning the Church 'from its traditional role of holding forth the mystery of perfection, to the role of control in worldly affairs' (*T&J* 58).

[24] *TE* 23.

and empirical interrogation of nature, the ceaseless efforts of a detached Archimedean self striving to move the world to prove its own designs. The human will in this way became no longer one of many natural agents oriented to the good, but alone able through its activity to impose good on an indifferent material world. The historicist understanding of the self as creative freedom and the technological account of the natural world as ruled by necessity and chance formed (through its English-speaking founders) the 'spiritual primal'[25] of North America, and led to the portrayal of the unspoiled continent as a *tabula rasa*, ready to yield to the impressions of the overriding conqueror. In combination with the 'practical primal', shared by all North Americans, of crossing the seas and settling the land, there came to be that primal which still shapes North America: 'the omnipresence of that practicality which trusts in technology to create the rationalized kingdom of man'.[26] In this is expressed a will to mastery and an orientation to the future which seeks an emancipation both practical (in freedom from disease, poverty, and overwork) and theoretical (in freedom from traditional and irrational prejudice), but which serves to veil the eternal order of the good.

The results of this Grant finds in every area of contemporary life. Because the political good is widely accepted to be the overcoming of chance in the building of the technological society, politics as negotiation between differing conceptions of the good is being replaced by the administrative search for means to secure the technical good.[27] Likewise, political conservatives 'in the sense of being the custodians of something that is not subject to change' no longer present a viable political option,[28] while local cultures and traditions are particulars in the process of becoming little more than charming residual customs because of the universalizing effects of technology.[29] Again, education is conceived as the teaching of the sciences of mastery over human and non-human nature,[30] while the sciences are treated as value-free, quantifica-

[25] J. E. O'Donovan, *George Grant*, 94.
[26] *TE* 25.
[27] Grant, 'Ideology in Modern Empires', in J. E. Flint and G. Williams (eds.), *Perspectives of Empire* (London: Longmans Group, 1973), 190–1; *idem*, 'Nationalism and Rationality', *Canadian Forum*, 50 (1971), 336–7.
[28] *LN* 67; cf. the introduction to 'Religion and the State', *TE* 43–5.
[29] *LN* 54; *TE* 67.
[30] *TE* 115; 'Faith and the Multiversity', *Compass*, 4 (1978), 3–14.

tional, and behaviourist,[31] and the humanities as a museum culture for intellectual tourists.[32] Further, computers, like 'those crisp rationalized managers, who are the first necessity of the kingdom of man',[33] contribute to homogeneity by their need to classify.[34] And public religion has become 'an unimportant litany of objectified self-righteousness necessary for the more anal of our managers',[35] while in 'personal relationships' ecstatic relations are sought that transcend the merely contractual,[36] but in which only the loss of the other results.[37] Underlying the superficial variety of a pluralist society is the dreary monism of the religion of progress. 'Some like pizza, some like steaks; some like girls, some like boys; some like synagogue, some like the mass. But we all do it in churches, motels, restaurants indistinguishable from the Atlantic to the Pacific.'[38]

The goal and destiny of modernity Grant describes, following Strauss's Hegel, as the 'universal and homogeneous state'.[39] This liberal ideal is a world society without class or national division, in which freedom and equality are realized on the back of technological growth. For Grant, this ideal would be the perfection of tyranny, rather than of freedom. In making the most important truths available to and practicable by all, the universal, homogeneous state represents the final identification of philosophy, religion, and politics. And in affirming that the most important truths are self-evident, and identifying these with the truths of the

---

[31] *TE* 115.

[32] 'Research in the Humanities', *T&J* 97–102.

[33] *TE* 25. Cf. Philip Rieff, *The Triumph of the Therapeutic: Uses of Faith after Freud* (1966) (Chicago: University of Chicago Press, ²1987), pp. ix–x: 'Now the bureaucrat sits behind his impersonality, an expert at redistributing jargon and managing case history files. Any good bureaucrat knows his true end: enlarging his own little piece of power. The bureaucrat is the master organizer of our passionate indifference to the real needs of given individuals, each different from every other in his identity, his incommunicability, his inwardness.'

[34] Grant, ' "The Computer does not Impose on us the Way it should be Used" ', in Abraham Rotstein (ed.), *Beyond Industrial Growth* (Toronto: University of Toronto Press, 1976), 122; cf. *T&J* 19–31. Grant further claims that because computers can only exist in societies with larger corporations, they limit the forms of community now practicable, whatever political or social ideals people may have (*T&J* 32).

[35] *TE* 24.

[36] *ESJ* 11.

[37] Grant, 'The Uses of Freedom—A Word and our World', *Queen's Quarterly*, 62 (1956), 524.

[38] *TE* 26.

[39] See in general, 'Tyranny and Wisdom', *TE*, 81–109.

religion of progress, it represents the improper replacement of religion by philosophy as the arbiter of public truth.[40]

However, even within its own terms, and even for those who reject Grant's belief that 'reverence rather than freedom is the matrix of human nobility',[41] this political ideal of modernity encounters a deep problem: its content is becoming more vacuous as it is replaced by the pursuit of technical expansion. For, by a powerful and tragic irony, technology is now turning against human freedom and in fact limiting the liberty that it was originally intended to enhance. In the name of control over nature, of efficiency, and of freedom of choice, technology is now effecting the rise of cybernetics and the managerial, of eugenics and behaviourism, with the result that the traditional and largely Christian notions of justice and human worth which form much of the content of liberal justice are being swept away. And, ironically, liberalism is contributing to its own demise.

When modern liberals, positivist or existentialist, have criticised the idea of human excellence, they may have thought that they were clearing the ground of religious and metaphysical superstitions which stood in the way of the liberty of the individual. Rather they were serving the social purpose of legitimizing the totally technological society by destroying anything from before the age of progress which might inhibit its victory.[42]

The problem that liberalism faces, Grant argues, is that the conceptions of self and the world, of rationality and history, which provide the background for its intelligibility and the basis of its justification, are precisely those which justify and further the progress of that technology which is undermining liberal values. Liberalism, even if it had the motive, can find no independent ground from which to criticize technology. Nor, moreover, can it prevent the erosion by technology of liberal values: it is being 'played out within a destiny more comprehensive than itself'.[43] For although liberalism and technological science have their joint origins in the flowering of the will in Reformed Protestantism and the new natural sciences, their continued mutual sustenance is not guaranteed by their common origin. This twofold problem Grant attributes to the 'civilizational contradiction'[44] of the modern

---

[40] See 'Religion and the State', *TE* 43–60; J. E. O'Donovan, *George Grant*, 62–8, 162–3.   [41] *TE* 43.

[42] *TE* 129.   [43] *ESJ* 82.   [44] *ESJ* 75.

world, the contradiction involved in attempting to hold together the scientific world of chance and necessity and the notions of justice inherited from the pre-modern world. For modern science revealed a world apparently indifferent to moral values, which thus had to be conceived of as imposed on nature by the will, and not derived from it through the reason. While this led the moderns to reject the ancient account of the justification of value, at the same time they wished to preserve the traditional values.

The potential danger this threatens to the traditional under-standings of justice that were taken over by liberalism has been avoided till now, but only for extraneous and historical reasons, not because of the adequacy of the intellectual defence of liberal values.[45] The increasing cultural dominance of the various Eng-lish-speaking middle classes has ensured that their moral and political beliefs required no deeply considered intellectual justifica-tion; thus, in this century, 'the expansion of the United States around the world, as the great capitalist empire, was so fast and successful that the constitutional principles of bourgeois hegemony became even more self-evident' than they were before.[46] Again, the religious traditions of the English-speaking countries, Calvinist and Anglican in Britain, small-town pietist in North America, were able to provide 'that necessary moral cement which could not be present for those who were consistently directed by contractualism or utilitarianism or a combination of both'.[47] The continued existence of the traditional understanding of justice was an accident of history: it did not require justification in thought, since it was sustained on other grounds.[48]

There were of course attempts to reconcile the old justice and the new science: Grant mentions Locke, Rousseau, Kant, and Marx, as examples.[49] But these represented the 'secularised Christianity' which Nietzsche ridiculed.[50] Thus Kant, who attempted to hold together science and human autonomy, was the 'great delayer', because of his self-anaesthetization from the modern through maintaining morality as the one fact of reason.

[45] *ESJ*, 48–68.   [46] *ESJ* 57.   [47] *ESJ* 62.
[48] Friedrich Nietzsche, *The Gay Science*, trans. Walter Kaufmann (New York: Vintage Books, 1974), has his own account (Prelude 32): 'Wie jeder, der einst Ketten trug, Hört überall er—Kettenklirren.' Cf. s. 108: 'God is dead: but given the way of men, there may still be caves for thousands of years in which his shadow will be shown.'
[49] *ESJ* 75.   [50] *TH* 22, 28; *TE* 129–30 n.

The full horror of the discontinuity between the impersonal universe and the moral values of Western civilization was incomparably expressed by Nietzsche, who recognized that if justice were merely the imposition by will of values on facts, then there is no reason beyond the contingencies of history why the values of liberty or equality or the worth of others should be respected. Such values become merely horizons, and once horizons are recognized as horizons, they no longer have power to sustain those who live within them. The death of the Christian God is the end of all horizons, the admission of chaos outside of the will to power.[51] But for Nietzsche such an admission properly owned is not trivial, 'something after which we can get on with the business of making life cosy'.[52] For with the recognition that human purposes are not guaranteed by the order of things, the whole burden of meaning falls on the will, and with that an immense darkness. It is neither possible to return to the enchanted world of the past, nor clear how to lift the curse of living without horizons.

But such a recognition also entails that it is unnecessary to accept the *décadence* values of the Platonism-for-the-people that modernity has adopted. Liberalism is unable to defend the content of the justice it upholds. There is no reason, on its account of the foundations of justice, why the conveniences technology affords should not be exploited by those with sufficiently strong wills, whatever the moral cost. Although it might be thought that we could decide to will the liberal values of equality, freedom, and rationality, the recognition of these values as willed, and not as 'cosmically sustained',[53] prevents them from acting as horizons, and forces the admission that their acceptance derives ultimately from the play of power. Grant hints at the danger to an age which believes in time as history but which has given up belief in progress because of the experiences of the twentieth century. The corporations will be free to replace justice with convenience values, and while liberal justice will still be dispensed, those who are too weak to enforce contracts—'the imprisoned, the mentally unstable, the unborn, the aged, the defeated, and sometimes even the morally unconforming'[54]—will be excluded. Fascism, he declared in what

---

[51] *TH* 29–30.   [52] *TH* 30.   [53] *TH* 32.
[54] *ESJ* 83–4. For Nietzsche's version of justice, see Grant, 'Nietzsche and the Ancients', *T&J* 79–93.

was to be his last publication before his death, 'is a growing possibility in advanced industrial countries'.[55]

3 GRANT AND RAWLS

If liberalism is to be sustained as the principal expression of Western self-understanding, then it faces, according to Grant, the task of showing how its central values of liberty and equality may be justified in the face of the technological forces which threaten to undermine them. John Rawls's liberal contractarianism is the most prominent contemporary justification of the values of what is fated to be a world-historical class, and if Grant is correct, it is clearly incumbent on Rawls's theory to address the problems of this civilizational contradiction.

(a) Grant's questions to Rawls

The questions Grant directs specifically to Rawls are found in Part II of *English-Speaking Justice*. They may be conveniently summarized through a number of passages of questions in the text. In this section I will argue, by way of interpretive clarification, that Grant poses questions of three basic kinds.

The first passage of questions turns on the justification of equality.

Why is it good that all human beings should live in a society to which they can give consent and in which they are guaranteed an equality of political liberties? Why is it good that human beings should have political rights of a quite different order from members of the other species? Why should equality in legal rights stand above and not be influenced by the obvious inequalities in contribution to progress whether in production, in the arts or in the sciences? . . . [Why] does Rawls's account of the 'person' make equality our due? Why are beings who can calculate and cannot avoid choices worthy of equal inalienable rights? After all, some humans can calculate better than others. Why then should they not have fuller legal rights than the poor calculators? Why do either of these human abilities justify the primacy of equality, or the different level of our rights compared with those of other species?[56]

---

[55] 'The Triumph of the Will', in Denyse O'Leary (ed.), *The Issue is Life: A Christian Response to Abortion in Canada* (Burlington, Ont.: Welch Publications, 1988), 157.

[56] *ESJ* 32–3.

These boil down to two questions:

> (i) In virtue of what are *only* human beings (and not, say, animals) worthy of this level of respect?
> (ii) In virtue of what are *all* human beings equally worthy of this level of respect?

There is perhaps the hint of a third:

> (iii) In virtue of what are *any* human beings worthy of this level of respect?

The second passage of questions centres on the practicability of Rawls's combination of individualism and egalitarianism, given the power of the public and private corporations in late state capitalism.

Can his calculating individualism bring forth a doctrine of the common good strong enough to control the ambitions of these mammoths? Can the calculating individual be a citizen in such a world, or does this account of human beings only lead to individuals concerned with consumption— above all entertainment and the orgasm as consumption?[57]

This passage raises at least two more questions:

> (iv) Is Rawls's ideal practicable in this society? Is the liberty and equality he would like to have for all in abstract theory nevertheless impossible in practice?
> (v) Is Rawls's ideal, in so far as it is practicable, incompatible in practice with other independently specified ideals, specifically life as a citizen and the individual as more than a consumer?

The third passage contains 'the fundamental question' about Rawls's theory, which does not require glossing:

> (vi) 'Can the content of justice he advocates be derived from his contractual theory?'[58]

The last passage of questions addressed specifically to Rawls concerns his attempt to justify contractarianism within what Grant sees as the assumptions of analytical philosophy.

---

[57] *ESJ* 41.
[58] *ESJ* 42; cf. 43–4.

Is justice pursued because of convenience, even when the calculation is in terms of an account of self-interest reached in abstraction from any knowledge of the way things are as a whole? Is such justification of justice able to support the pursuit of liberty and equality at a time when the inconveniences of technology do not seem to favour them?[59]

At least one question arises from this passage:

> (vii) Can the pursuit of justice, liberty and equality be defended if it is inconvenient?

But also implicit is another:

> (viii) Can a knowledge of justice be abstracted from the way things are as a whole?

Questions (i)–(viii) reduce to questions of three basic kinds. (1) The first concerns whether justice can be derived from a contract by calculating self-interested individuals. This might include questions (vi), and (vii), and the last part of (v). There are several overlapping questions under this heading. First, will Rawls's contract ensure justice in the sense of preserving the pre-modern values of equality, dignity, and freedom? Second, what sort of conception of the self does Rawls's version of the contract imply? Specifically, does it not lead to treating human beings as consumers, searching to satisfy their wants without regard to externally given ends? Third, can justice interpreted as giving others their due be derived from prudential calculation in the moderns' sense of prudence, in which it is contrasted with morality? That is, can a contract show me why I should be altruistic rather than self-interested? If another's good is construed simply as a function of the agent's self-interest, it will have no independently founded claim against the demands of technology, should they conflict.

(2) The second basic kind of question concerns whether justice, and value in general, can be understood except on the basis of what Grant calls 'ontological affirmations'.[60] This would include questions (i), (ii), (iii), and (viii). Grant compares Rawls with Kant, his supposed mentor. Kant makes axiological claims for the good will, grounded ontologically in the idea that moral willing is participation in the very form of reason; whereas Rawls, by contrast, accepts the naturalistic fallacy as a fallacy.[61] Grant

---

[59] *ESJ* 46–7.   [60] *ESJ* 29.   [61] *ESJ* 25, 32.

interprets this to mean that 'propositions concerning how human beings ought to act cannot be derived solely from factual propositions about nature', and that 'the principles of justice cannot be derived from such metaphysical propositions as the state of nature'.[62] This he connects with the distinction between 'nature' and 'freedom' and between 'is' and 'ought', with Max Weber's formulation of the distinction between judgements of fact and judgements of value, with the denial of a teleological knowledge of nature, and with the removal of political philosophy from dependence on metaphysical assumptions.[63] Thus the fact–value distinction grounds values outside 'the whole'. 'Facts are now identified with objects and are abstracted from things in their wholeness. The rest is labelled "values" and is tucked away as part of one's own subjectivity. Values are detached from "objective" being.'[64]

There are a number of reasons for distinguishing between questions of types (1) and (2). First, this highlights the similarities and differences between Rawls and earlier contractarians. Although the questions under (1) are here addressed specifically to Rawls, they (or at least similar questions) can well be asked of the contractarian tradition as a whole. Questions under (2), by contrast, turn on Rawls's alleged metaphysical denials, which were not shared by previous contractarians. Further, the questions relate to different issues subsumed under the question of personal identity. The first type are related to the question of the nature of human agency and the self; the second, as will be seen, are concerned in part with what distinguishes persons from non-persons and makes them worthy of respect.

(3) The third fundamental type of question considers the practicability of Rawls's ideal. This includes questions (iv) and the first part of (v). Grant's sociological understanding of contemporary society sees the dynamics of corporations as the threat to the feasibility of Rawls's ideals of equality and liberty. But he wonders also whether Rawls's theory allows room in practice for the good of citizenship, understood perhaps in the classical republican sense of the development and exercise by citizens of their political virtues through responsible and effectual participation in public life.

[62] *ESJ* 22.
[63] *ESJ* 22, 23–4, 30, 37.
[64] 'Faith and the Multiversity', 9.

There are, then, three basic kinds of question that Grant puts to Rawls: (1) whether justice can be derived from contracts by self-interested individuals; (2) whether justice can be understood except on the basis of ontological affirmations; (3) whether Rawls's ideal is practicable. In what follows, less attention will be paid to the last kind of question than to the first two; although I will make initial responses to some of Rawls's general claims about the stability of a 'well-ordered society', serious treatment of the issues raised by questions of the third type would require a social and psychological theory that is much more empirically informed than it is possible to give here.

(b) A response to Grant on behalf of Rawls

Rawls's theory has developed from his elaboration of 'justice as fairness' in *A Theory of Justice* (1971) to his account of a 'political conception of justice' in *Political Liberalism* (1993).[65] Although the political conception of justice was developed in order to address perceived inadequacies in the original account of justice as fairness, analytically justice as fairness is now best understood as one element within the overall framework of the political conception. Hence in this chapter we will start from his more recent account, and refer back to his earlier work only when appropriate. The direction of this development in his thought was of course not available to Grant; however, since the issue for us is not primarily the antiquarian question of whether Grant was justified in his criticisms, but the practical question of whether those criticisms still have force, it is reasonable to start from the version Rawls himself now considers most adequate.

Rawls starts from a central feature of modern Western democracies: namely, the plurality of comprehensive religious, moral, and

---

[65] *PL* was foreshadowed in a succession of articles, including 'Kantian Constructivism in Moral Theory', *Journal of Philosophy*, 77 (1980), 515–72; 'Justice as Fairness: Political not Metaphysical', *Philosophy and Public Affairs*, 14 (1985), 223–51; 'The Idea of an Overlapping Consensus', *Oxford Journal of Legal Studies*, 7 (1987), 1–25; and 'The Priority of the Right and Ideas of the Good', *Philosophy and Public Affairs*, 17 (1988), 251–74.

Amongst the vast secondary literature on Rawls, see e.g. Barry, *Liberal Theory of Justice*; Norman Daniels (ed.), *Reading Rawls: Critical Studies on Rawls' 'A Theory of Justice'* (Oxford: Blackwell, 1975); and Robert Paul Wolff, *Understanding Rawls: A Reconstruction and Critique of* A Theory of Justice (Princeton: Princeton University Press, 1977). A recent introduction is Stephen Mulhall and Adam Swift, *Liberals and Communitarians* (Oxford: Blackwell, 1992), esp. 1–33, 167–205.

philosophical doctrines which they display. Not only is there disagreement between different understandings of the world and of conceptions of the good; there is also disagreement about the terms under which people with such different comprehensive doctrines should live together. Since the Reformation, it has been impossible for any single comprehensive doctrine to provide publicly recognized principles of justice for the basic structure of society. Even within democratic theory there has been a conflict, in Benjamin Constant's terms,[66] between the more Rousseauan and egalitarian 'liberties of the ancients' and the more Lockean and libertarian 'liberties of the moderns'. Given this conflict, and given further that it is a conflict of reasonable doctrines which is not likely to be resolved in the foreseeable future, political liberalism asks how people with deeply opposed but still reasonable comprehensive doctrines can live together and affirm a single constitutional order. In other words, it enquires what might be fair terms of co-operation for a society characterized by reasonable pluralism, on the assumption that its citizens are to be regarded as free and equal.

To answer this question, Rawls argues that we need to look for a shared basis for co-operation which all citizens could affirm and which would be, as far as possible, independent of their comprehensive doctrines. Such a shared basis would form a 'political conception of justice': it would neither presume nor deny the truth of any particular comprehensive doctrine, and would provide canons of shared, public reason that could be applied to questions concerning the basic structure of society. His hope is that this basis can be found in the traditions embedded in the public culture of democracies. From these traditions an intuitive notion will be discerned which accords with our considered convictions, but which is more fundamental than disputed questions about (for example) the best interpretation of values such as liberty and equality. This will lay the basis for an agreement on the fundamental questions of political justice by providing a framework for relating those other values. This fundamental ideal, he claims, is that of 'society as a fair system of social co-operation between free and equal persons'.[67]

The notion of the person involved here is not descriptive, drawn

---

[66] Benjamin Constant, 'The Liberty of the Ancients Compared with that of the Moderns', in *Political Writings*, ed. Biancamaria Fontana (Cambridge: Cambridge University Press, 1988), 307–28.   [67] *PL* 9.

from the natural or human sciences; nor is it dependent on any particular comprehensive doctrine. Rather, in keeping with the idea that no controverted religious, moral, or philosophical doctrines should be used in the development of a public basis for justice, it is a normative, 'political' conception which is implicit in the shared public culture of modern democracies. Specifically, it is the idea of 'someone who can be a citizen, that is, a normal and fully co-operating member of society over a complete life'.[68] Persons in this political conception are regarded as free and equal by virtue of their possessing the two moral powers which are associated with participation in a system of fair social co-operation: namely, a capacity for a sense of justice and for a conception of the good, as well as the powers of reason connected with those moral powers.[69]

From this fundamental shared understanding of a society and of persons are to be drawn the principles of justice which define the terms of fair social co-operation. For Rawls's theory of justice as fairness, the means for deriving these is the original position. This device is a way of providing constraints on what will count as appropriate terms of bargaining in order to ensure fair agreement. These constraints are again derived from our considered convictions: most notably, they include the veil of ignorance, which contributes to fairness by abstracting from the contingencies of history, social background, natural talent, and so on. The parties in the original position, who are the representatives of citizens, and accept the constraints on their reasoning specified by the terms of the original position, then choose principles of justice which will form the terms of social co-operation. The basis for fair co-operation cannot be one that can reasonably be disputed, such as an appeal to the deliverances of (Rawls's instances) rational intuition or natural law. Rather, it must be grounded solely in what the parties in the original position can agree to, bargaining as free and equal citizens under conditions that ensure fairness. Thus the aim of each party is to agree to those principles which they think will be of most advantage to those whom they represent; this is to be understood in terms not of any egoistic maximal desire-satisfaction of each, but of the greatest possible development of moral personality, suitably defined.[70]

---

[68] *PL* 18.   [69] *PL* 19.   [70] *PL* 73–5, 105–6.

How could the principles of justice derived from such a procedure possess any binding power on us in the actual world? After all, it is not clear how a hypothetical contract can bind. Rawls's answer is in two stages. The first is the elaboration of a political conception of justice, as outlined above. This is rooted in the notion that no comprehensive doctrine can act as the basis of a constitutional order in a modern democracy without an oppressive use of state power; in deciding questions of the basic structure of society, citizens should rather appeal to a public conception of reason and public principles of justice which avoid controversy over disputed moral, religious, or philosophical issues. This political conception is intended as a free-standing doctrine, justified on its own terms out of resources available in the public traditions of democracies, and dependent on no comprehensive doctrine.

However—and this is the second stage in Rawls's answer—he hopes that it will gain the support of an 'overlapping consensus' of those with opposing religious and philosophical beliefs, in which all citizens justify justice as fairness to themselves within the terms of their own doctrines. People are motivated to co-operate under its terms, because they can recognize that its values are 'derived from, or congruent with, or at least not in conflict with, their other values'.[71] This is not to say that the kernel of the overlapping consensus is simply the 'centre of gravity' of the comprehensive doctrines which form the background culture, such that the public terms of co-operation are merely a *modus vivendi*, specified by whatever citizens will agree to for the sake of getting on together. Rather, citizens will affirm the public principles of justice as publicly justified in themselves, and as a fully reasonable political conception for a democratic society characterized by a plurality of reasonable but conflicting comprehensive doctrines.

This account of Rawls's political liberalism is brief, and elides many important features of his overall theory, as well as a number of interpretive difficulties; but it provides the setting for the questions Grant puts to Rawls. Grant's first set of questions centred, it will be recalled, on the question of whether justice can be derived from a contract between calculating individuals. This general question had three aspects: about the possibility of deriving

[71] *PL* 11.

the pre-modern content of justice from contract, about the nature of the self implicit in Rawls's theory, and about the possibility of deriving other-regard from self-regard.

Before we look at any of these three sub-questions, we should briefly recall what the basis for Grant's suspicions might be. Rawls explicitly places justice as fairness within the social contract tradition.[72] According to this tradition, individuals situated in a state of nature or some other suitably defined pre-governmental (and perhaps pre-social) condition draw up a contract with one another from which they may derive a basis for governmental legitimacy and political obligation (and perhaps for social existence itself). In many versions of social contract theory, the motivation of individual contractors is taken to be rational self-interest, and the contract is entered upon in order to further their individual good. Now Rawls appears to belong straightforwardly to this tradition: he wrote in *A Theory of Justice*, for example, that the theory of justice 'is a part, perhaps the most significant part, of the theory of rational choice',[73] and the device of the original position models a situation in which 'free and rational persons concerned to further their own interests' are to choose the principles of justice that will regulate their life together.[74]

The impression is somewhat misleading, however. Rawls's later political liberalism makes clear the difference between the conceptions of the person, of society, and of reason that will characterize the political conception of justice and those of the various comprehensive doctrines endorsed by citizens. The different features of the political conception are taken as givens embedded in the public culture, and the original position is an attempt to model them; it is only in the original position that the parties behave in a way that could remotely be described as rational self-interested calculation. But even here their aims 'are not egoistic but entirely fitting and proper',[75] inasmuch as they are concerned with securing the higher-order interests of those they represent: namely, the development of their moral powers and the furthering of their determinate conceptions of the good. There is no egoistic assumption that interests *of* the self are necessarily interests *in* the self, or any idea that either public justice or morality in general can be derived solely from rational choice procedures. When justice as

---

[72] See e.g. *TJ* 3.   [73] *TJ* 16.
[74] *TJ* 11.   [75] *PL* 106.

fairness is construed as a political conception of justice, the continuities between it and traditional contractarian theories are significantly qualified.

In relation to the first aspect of Grant's question, therefore, concerning whether Rawls's contract allows for the derivation of the pre-modern content of justice, it should be made clear that if the values of equality, justice, and freedom are to be interpreted roughly as those which Rawls finds embedded in the public culture, then they are built in to the political conception of justice. Moreover the principles of justice constructed from the original position can themselves be modified if we are unable to accept them on due reflection. Whether or not what Grant regards as the pre-modern contents of justice (including liberty and equality, neither very precisely defined) are present in Rawls's principles of justice turns on whether they are present in the public culture, therefore, and not on whether such values can be derived from Rawls's contract.[76]

The other two aspects of this general question turn on the relation of the political conception of persons to people in real life. This is the fundamental issue in determining Rawls's conception of the self, which has also been much misunderstood. Thus the communitarian Michael Sandel claims that '[looking] from one direction through the lens of the original position we see the two principles of justice; looking from the other direction we see a reflection of ourselves'.[77] For Rawls it is not ourselves that we see, but the parties in the original position. These are related to us in that, for the purposes of political agreement, we are willing to see ourselves as such: they portray our political or public identities, but not our individual self-understandings. Rawls is willing to make affirmations about our public identities—for example, that they involve freedom in the three respects that citizens are regarded as having the moral power to have a conception of the good, as self-authenticating sources of valid claims, and as capable of taking responsibility for their ends. But none of these imply that this is how citizens do or should view themselves from the point of view of their comprehensive doctrines. 'It is essential to stress that

---

[76] Whether they are guaranteed by Rawls's contractarianism is an issue to which I return below.

[77] Michael J. Sandel, *Liberalism and the Limits of Justice* (Cambridge: Cambridge University Press, 1982), 47–8.

citizens in their personal affairs, or in the internal life of associations to which they belong, may regard their final ends and attachments in a way very different from the way the political conception involves.'[78]

Thus Rawls is not committed, as Sandel claims, to seeing us as selves prior to our ends, choosing our conceptions of the good, rather than as in part constituted by them. When the heuristic device of the original position is employed, 'our reasoning no more commits us to a particular metaphysical doctrine about the nature of the self than our acting a part in a play, say of Macbeth or Lady Macbeth, commits us to thinking that we are really a king or a queen engaged in a desperate struggle for political power'.[79] Nevertheless, Rawls is bound in his political conception of the person to the distinction between the public and non-public identities of citizens, and it is the reasonableness of this distinction, not the question of the thickness of Rawls's conception of the self, on which a communitarian critique should concentrate.

A parallel defence to that against Sandel can be made on Rawls's behalf concerning Grant's specific claim that justice as fairness treats human beings as self-interested calculators. It is not as private individuals that Rawls invites us to see ourselves as rational choosers, but only as public citizens seeking fair terms of social co-operation. It is not merely that, as we have seen, interests of the self are not necessarily self-interests, but also that these interests of the self which are the ends of calculation apply to public identities only, and these are logically separate from private identities. Moreover, in the original position there is at work the ideal of aiming at citizens' higher-order interests; while this may not be beyond criticism, it does not lead to a conception of human beings as consumers as readily as might the account of the self in standard rational choice theory.[80]

This understanding of the relation of the parties to people in ordinary life also implies an answer to the third aspect, concerning the derivation of other-regard from self-regard. For Rawls this is a matter of moral theory, not of political philosophy. The justice he is concerned with is that applicable to the basic structure of

[78] 'Justice as Fairness', 241.
[79] *PL* 27.
[80] Norman Daniels criticizes Grant for not distinguishing the self-interest of the contracting parties from the self-identities of citizens (review of *ESJ*, *Canadian Journal of Philosophy*, 9 (1979), 563–7).

society, and has no logical connection with justice as a virtue of individuals. While he has claimed that in a well-ordered society a just distribution would, for example, make people more just and more likely to pursue other aims, because the acquisition of wealth was less important,[81] this is tentative psychology, not a claim about the nature of justice. To Grant's possible rejoinder that this is to divide up justice in a way not given in the order of things, he would appeal to the practical nature of his enterprise, the securing of fair terms of co-operation in situations of reasonable pluralism.

In general terms, therefore, Rawls's political liberalism, separating a public conception of justice from citizens' comprehensive doctrines, distances him from the contractarian tradition, and rescues him from some of its problems in a manner that Grant does not allow for. Rawls does not assume that justice is to be derived from a contract between calculating individuals in the way that Grant supposes. This is not to say, however, that there are not problems with Rawls's account. But to see some of these, we should turn to Grant's second question to Rawls.

Grant's second question was concerned with Rawls's alleged separation of facts and values, and thus his failure to see justice as part of 'the whole'. Justice, he asserted, is not for Rawls in some sense grounded in reality, but conceived independently of knowledge of 'the nature of things'. Now this would certainly appear to hold for Rawls's notion of pure procedural justice from within the original position. For 'the idea of approximating to moral truth has no place in a constructivist doctrine: the parties in the original position do not recognize any principles of justice as true or correct and so as antecedently given: their aim is simply to select the conception most rational for them, given their circumstances'.[82] The principles chosen in the original position are defined as just; there is no question of correspondence to an independent order. However, the question regarding pure procedural justice is not really to the point; since the original position is a special device within a more general understanding of the justification of justice, it is more important to examine whether Grant's question is well asked of the theory as a whole.

In an important sense, Rawls's political conception makes no metaphysical assumptions. He refuses to ground his theory in

---

[81] 'Fairness to Goodness', *Philosophical Review*, 84 (1975), 545–6.
[82] 'Kantian Constructivism', 564.

some 'moral reality', because he hopes by a method of avoidance to evade controversies about the status and justification of moral and political values. 'Philosophy as the search for truth about an independent metaphysical and moral order cannot, I believe, provide a workable and shared basis for a political conception of justice in a democratic society.'[83] Political liberalism is concerned not with finding the truth about the issues it covers, but with discovering public terms of fair co-operation between people with differing and incompatible comprehensive doctrines. Its primary aim is practical and political, not epistemological or metaphysical.

But it does not follow that political liberalism is committed to a 'fact–value distinction' or to denying moral realism. Even if Rawls himself may think moral realism mistaken, political liberalism is not committed to this. Nor does it require constructivism in political philosophy in any sense that denies that the nature of justice or the political good is somehow discernible in the order of things. The questions of whether the principles of justice are susceptible to truth assessment, and if so, whether they are true are bracketed; for political purposes they are to be regarded as reasonable, not as true. On the other hand, although political liberalism does not deny a realist moral ontology, it does not require it: it simply prescinds from such controverted questions in order that a shared basis for public justice can be assured.

That Rawls's political liberalism does not simply deny moral realism does not, however, imply that the bottom of Grant's question has been plumbed. To see this, let us start by considering the question of whether Rawls does not just provide a rationalization of a form of liberal democracy. When he formulates the fundamental question of political liberalism as 'How is it possible for there to exist over time a just and stable society of free and equal citizens, who remain profoundly divided by reasonable religious, philosophical and moral doctrines?',[84] the characterization of citizens as free and equal is assumed, rather than argued for. Yet, Grant might quite reasonably enquire, it is unclear what the basis of this assumption is. Human history has scarcely been monopolized by the political values of the freedom and equality of persons: why should they be assumed here?

[83] 'Justice as Fairness', 230.
[84] *PL* 4.

Political liberalism, it will be recalled, attempts first to justify the political conception of justice as fairness as a free-standing doctrine. To whom is it justified, and by what criterion? It is not justified to people from the point of view of their comprehensive doctrines; that is the task involved in securing an overlapping consensus, and is a matter of the stability of a well-ordered society, not of the justification of its fundamental principles. Rather, political liberalism is justified from the point of view of public reason to those who are reasonable. Rawls describes public reason as follows. First, it is 'characteristic of a democratic people: it is the reason of its citizens, of those sharing the status of equal citizenship'.[85] Second, public reason is public in three ways: 'as the reason of citizens as such, it is the reason of the public; its subject is the good of the public and matters of fundamental justice; and its nature and content is public, being given by the ideals and principles expressed by society's conception of political justice, and conducted open to view on that basis.'[86] For our purposes the most important of these three features is the first: namely, that public reason is to be understood as the reason of the public—that is, presumably, of citizens conceived as free and equal. In other words, the argument goes: the principles of justice which elaborate the idea of the freedom and equality of citizens are justified by appeal to public reason; but that is, in turn, to be understood as public because it is the reason of citizens conceived as free and equal.

The charge that this procedure is circular seems unavoidable. Granted that the steps in the overall argument are not otiose, appealing from public reason to the public culture, and thence moving via the original position to the principles of justice as fairness; and granted (for the sake of argument) that the original position specifies principles that could not be directly derived from a divided public culture; nevertheless, the freedom and equality of citizens are everywhere assumed, and nowhere defended. Either the principle of appealing to the public culture must be taken as of universal application, such that it is true for any society that whatever can be justified in that society by 'public reason', using its own internally derived canons, is *eo facto* just—even if that society be Nazi Germany or slave-owning Athens. Or Rawls must

---

[85] *PL* 213.   [86] Ibid.

affirm that appeal to the public culture is justified only when it recognizes people as free and equal. But the latter alternative requires either acceptance of the parochiality of his understanding of public reason—that in effect it just does rationalize liberal democratic values—or a furnishing of the grounds for assuming that people are free and equal. And such grounds can presumably be provided only within the terms of a comprehensive doctrine: whether this be a simple comprehensive doctrine, which would probably be open to dispute from other simple comprehensive doctrines on the matter of whether people are to be conceived as free and equal, and so could not form the basis for a political conception of justice, or a 'reasonable comprehensive doctrine', as Rawls terms it,[87] which would not be disputed by other reasonable comprehensive doctrines on this matter, but only at the price of having begged the question.[88]

Rawls's appeal to the political conception as a free-standing doctrine does not justify the liberal democratic values of liberty and equality, except within public cultures already committed to them, therefore. Why does this matter? After all, he claims only to be providing a theory for societies committed to such democratic values; so long as justice as fairness is stable, one might imagine, there is no obvious problem.

Aside from the questionable intellectual adequacy of such a determinedly culture-relative political theory, with its evident lack of concern for any universal claims about justice, the issue of stability is surely more serious than Rawls admits. Certainly, he gives some reasons for thinking that justice as fairness could be identified by the kernel of an overlapping consensus of comprehensive doctrines, and that this could remain stable over time. For example, he details (i) a moral psychology which reasonable and rational citizens of a well-ordered society would have, which would

---

[87] A reasonable comprehensive doctrine accepts, *inter alia*, that citizens should be treated as free and equal (see *PL* 58–66). A 'simple' comprehensive doctrine (my coinage) is a comprehensive doctrine without any constraints of reasonableness.

[88] For this argument, cf. Mulhall and Swift, *Liberals and Communitarians*, 220–6. A similar set of considerations could be raised concerning Rawls's distinction between three points of view: that of the contracting parties in the original position, that of citizens in a well-ordered society, and that of 'ourselves—of you and me who are elaborating justice as fairness and examining it as a political conception of justice' (*PL* 28). Who are 'ourselves' here? Why should 'we' accept Rawls's account of what is to be found in the public culture?

make citizens more likely to develop the virtues of co-operation;[89] (ii) an account of how a mere *modus vivendi* could develop first into a constitutional consensus (that is, an agreement over basic political institutions), and then into a fully-fledged overlapping consensus;[90] and (iii) the educative value of a publicly acknowledged political conception of justice such as justice as fairness, in which people recognize and come to desire for themselves the ideals of citizenship within a well-ordered society.[91]

These are telling considerations, and should not be underestimated. Nevertheless, Rawls does not take into account any factors on the opposite side. Most importantly, the stability of a political conception is finally a matter for a detailed empirical sociology, and this is hardly satisfied by the limited number of a priori suggestions he offers. For example, his account displays no awareness of the claim that political stability in late capitalist societies is in fact secured not by allegiance to a common set of values (liberal or otherwise), but rather by a variety of other mechanisms. Among them, in the view of one sociologist, should be included

the apparatus of modern administration itself, the neutralizing of genuine political dissent, the system of palliative welfare benefits, the reduction of the franchise to an almost passive formality, and the social dependency induced by the nature of economic and employment relations in a technologically advanced multinational economy.[92]

Others might produce different lists and point out that the issue of the stability of a political conception should not be confused with that of political stability as such, whilst still agreeing that shared public values would play a relatively minor role in achieving or maintaining an overlapping consensus.

Nor does Rawls consider how comprehensive doctrines might come to be viewed in practice, as a political conception gained an increasing grip on a society. It is quite plausible to imagine that they would increasingly lose their role as views of the world proposed by people to each other as claims to truth, and come

---

[89] *PL* 81–6.
[90] *PL* 158–68.
[91] e.g. *PL* 71, 85–6.
[92] Bryan Turner, as described by Rowan Williams, 'Postmodern Theology and the Judgment of the World', in Fredric B. Burnham (ed.), *Christian Faith in a Pluralist World* (New York: HarperCollins, 1989), 99.

instead to be regarded as intellectually irresolvable but subjectively engaging forms of personal fulfilment, slight in importance when compared with the ostensibly objective truth of the dominant public culture. In practice, of course, many comprehensive doctrines are now seen in this way—with deleterious consequences on their capacity to sustain any kind of public culture, sense of shared values, or, for that matter, overlapping consensus.

Finally, it is not hard to imagine how, in an increasingly individualized and deracinated culture, justice as fairness might come to seem a relatively weak attraction for some, compared with those comprehensive doctrines which look to, say, public implementation of the sharia law or to nationalist fascist doctrines for their inspiration. The values of the domain of the political will not in practice always outweigh other values, and conceivably may not do so for significant numbers of people who may just refuse to remain politically invisible.

None of these points implies that a political conception of justice would have no causal role at all in establishing its own stability, but only that it would probably not have a decisive role, and would certainly be relatively weak without other supporting factors. What they clearly do indicate, however, is the danger of not caring about the content or deeper motions of the background culture, provided that it supports the political conception of justice. To be sure, the political conception is not analytically dependent on the principles picked out by the kernel of an overlapping consensus. But it may be practically unsustainable over any extended period of time, should the focus of the overlapping consensus shift decisively or disintegrate altogether. In general, we may say, the stability of the overlapping consensus concerning the principles of justice is more open to doubt than Rawls allows for: in the long term the content of the public conception of justice will be determined by the content of the various elements of the background culture.

It is possible to bring out some specific applications of this conclusion. For it is precisely these shifts in people's comprehensive doctrines and the sociological consequences thereof which it is one part of Grant's account of technology to analyse. If the mindset of technology is changing our views in the background culture of modern Western societies in such a way that, as described earlier, those who are 'too weak to enforce contracts' may be excluded from liberal justice, the question must arise whether publicly instituting justice as fairness would be able to prevent this from occurring. While the issue in principle relates to many people, for Grant it focuses on unborn children. If justice is not anchored in foundational ontological statements about human beings, he claims, it will slide in accordance with convenience.

What is it about our species that makes it appropriate that we have rights at all? If the fetuses are accidental blobs of matter, aren't we also? It is this that is frightening about those who argue that the fetus in the womb has no rights. In that affirmation is implied a view of human beings that destroys any reason why any of us should have rights.[93]

The point needs a certain amount of elaboration to be wholly cogent; but the plausibility of the idea that justice as convenience is a threat not only to the unborn but to others as well—people with severe disabilities, or who are elderly and ill, or very young and ill, or are marginalized or surplus to society's needs for any number of other reasons—seems evident.

Now, as was discussed earlier, Rawls does explain in virtue of what somebody is to be counted as a person from the point of view of the political conception: a person is 'somebody who can be a citizen, that is, a normal and fully co-operating member of society over a complete life'.[94] It would be premature to assume that this immediately excludes those mentioned in the last paragraph, since this is a normative, political conception of the person and not an empirical description of those who are to count as citizens in real life. However, it is central to the political conception that disputed features of reasonable comprehensive doctrines are not introduced into the domain of the political, and questions of personhood presumably often count amongst these—think of the status of the unborn or those in the persistent vegetative state, for example. The political conception tries to take no position on these. Thus, concerning abortion, Rawls's theory neither defends the rights of the unborn; nor (one ill-argued footnote aside[95]) does it attack them. It is presumably regarded as a matter of ordinary political, and perhaps judicial, process.[96]

[93] 'The Case against Abortion', *Today Magazine* (3 Oct. 1981), 13. 'Abortion and Rights' (written with Sheila Grant; *T&J* 117–30) is the nearest approach to an extended treatment of abortion that Grant provides; but cf. also 'Triumph of the Will'.
[94] *PL* 18. [95] *PL* 243–4 n. 32.
[96] Concerning those who are clearly not 'normal and fully-cooperating' members of society but whose status in the sight of reasonable comprehensive doctrines might be thought less ambiguous (such as those with significant but not severe mental

But this is sufficient to expose Rawls to Grant's main charge; that justice as fairness as such will do nothing to prevent the dynamics of technology from controlling and fashioning human beings, and indeed powerfully influencing decisions about who are to count as human beings in the fullest sense. Of course, Rawls could reply that this criticism could be made of many versions of democratic theory that emphasize the process of democracy and downplay its content. On the other hand, his is a theory of justice which claims to provide an account of the distribution of benefits and burdens in a society, and any failure in such a theory to identify who should be the subjects of such benefits and burdens must be considered a serious deficiency in it. The ramifications of such an inadequacy are highlighted in sociological theories such as Grant's, which suggest that it would be a matter of historical accident if the beneficiaries of justice in a well-ordered society were to turn out to match those defended in the tradition of Jewish and Christian moral thinking.

How might the defects in Rawls's approach be addressed? One possible alternative, which pays heed to the problem of stability, would be to detail a public conception of justice which was prepared to address the content of the background culture. This would face squarely Grant's fears about the influence of technology on people's comprehensive doctrines. It would also highlight the problem of dividing justice into personal morality on the one hand and the distributive justice of the basic structure on the other, a division which Grant disputes.

In the western tradition it was believed that acting out of justice in human relationships was the essential way in which human beings are opened to eternity. Inward and outward justice were considered to be mutually interdependent, in the sense that the inward openness to eternity depended on just practice, and just practice depended on that inward openness to eternity. When public justice is conceived as conventional and contractual, the division between inward and outward is so widened as to prevent any such mutual interdependence. Both openness to eternity and practical justice are weakened in that separation.[97]

disability?), political liberalism is less clear; at any rate, it seems that any ascription of dignity to them would be by extension from the normative understanding of personhood, based more on a concession to the Western moral tradition than on recognition of any anterior or independent foundation for their equal humanity.

[97] *ESJ* 85; cf. *T&J* 54, where justice is understood as 'rendering due', to oneself, to others, to the non-human world, and to God, thereby including and integrating

There are also severe practical consequences of a sharp distinction between private and public identities. Grant notes: '[The] widespread concentration of most North Americans on private life, and their acceptance that the public realm is something external to them, takes us far away from the original liberal picture of autonomous and equal human beings participating in the government and production of their society.'[98] It leads to 'either the necessity of finding one's role in the public engineering or the necessity of retreating into the privacy of pleasure'.[99]

Of course, talk of bridging the gap between public and private quite rightly raises deep anxieties for anybody of remotely liberal sensibility. Grant himself is well aware of the issues. For him they are interpreted through an acceptance of the classical understanding of the relation of philosophy and religion, such that all human beings are inevitably religious, but not all will become philosophers. One consequence of this is that 'religion has a more direct relation to the public sphere than has philosophy'.[100] To assimilate the two, as has happened under the religion of progress, so that philosophy with its claims about the self-evidence of progress takes the place of religious and public truth, is the totalitarianism of modernity, the absorption of the private (that is, philosophy) into the public. The problem for conservatism, as Grant sees it, is that it recognizes the need for a public religion which is not a philosophy (that is, a public religion which is not the present *de facto* public religion) at a time when only the religion of progress seems to have the 'right of tradition'.[101] Rawls, by contrast, depends precisely on this right of tradition, the values embedded in the public institutions of democratic societies, to give content to his theory.

Whether or not one is impressed by this account of philosophy and religion, the dilemma remains. Either a sharp distinction is maintained between public and private (or, in Rawls's terms, between citizens' comprehensive doctrines and the political con-

both personal and political justice. Contrast, e.g., R. M. Hare, *Moral Thinking: Its Levels, Method, and Point* (Oxford: Clarendon Press, 1981), 54: 'For cases where the interests of others are not affected, I make no claim to provide canons of moral reasoning.' Rawls, 'The Basic Structure as Subject', *American Philosophical Quarterly*, 14 (1977), 159–65, discusses Nozick's attack on end-state distribution, not the present issue.

[98] *ESJ* 11.   [99] *LN* 57.   [100] *TE* 59.
[101] J. E. O'Donovan, *George Grant*, 65.

ception of justice), with the possible consequence that the background culture may finally subvert the public liberal values. Or those who elaborate public principles of justice will have to grasp the nettle and address themselves also to the content of citizens' beliefs. This latter approach need not deny fundamental liberties, and indeed may be the only sociologically shrewd way of ensuring them.

We will consider some preliminary points regarding this in the next chapter. Suffice it to say for the present that Grant's talk of 'ontological affirmations', with all the attendant difficulties of the notion, may turn out to be part of the solution; after all, saying what we think people in fact are, and not just asserting what we choose them to be or side-stepping the whole question by a method of avoidance, may be the first stage in ensuring them justice.

(c) Conclusion

Rawls's political liberalism, I have argued in this section, is significantly different from standard contractarian theories, and avoids many of the objections Grant makes to them. His distinction between public and non-public identities means that he is not committed to treating human beings as self-interested rational calculators. Grant is wrong,[102] therefore, to identify people in the real world straightforwardly with the contracting parties. And the derivation of the public conception of justice from the values embedded in the public culture, such that the bargaining of parties in the original position is a secondary rather than foundational feature in the structure of justification, implies that the role of contract in establishing principles of justice is not as central in Rawls's thought as in many contractarian theories.

However, the attempt to explicate justice as fairness as a freestanding doctrine, justified on the basis of public reason to those who are reasonable, is circular. While this might not matter in liberal democracies if the stability of justice as fairness were not at stake, the sociology of a putatively well-ordered society might make it difficult in practice to maintain over time an overlapping consensus centring on the principles of justice. Moreover, justice as fairness as such would do little to hinder the convenience values fostered by the technological society expounded by Grant—unless

---

[102] Though not unreasonably. Rawls admits the unclarity of *TJ* on many of these points ('Justice as Fairness', 223–4).

there were to be some public attention to acceptable comprehensive doctrines, an effort deeply alien to the instincts of political liberalism.

Behind the discussion between these two writers we should also note two different understandings of political philosophy. For Grant, political philosophy seeks the truth about political things.[103] For Rawls, 'the task of political philosophy for our time', which political liberalism undertakes, is to find 'a reasonably systematic and practicable conception of justice for a constitutional democracy, a conception that offers an alternative to the dominant utilitarianism of our tradition of political thought'.[104] The task is practical and political, not epistemological or metaphysical. Nothing in his position is incompatible with Grant's substantive claims about justice being right; it is simply that not everybody in present society agrees with Grant, and some practical resolution of the differences must be found.

This practical task cannot be pretended away by Christian political theology. Indeed, as we shall explore in later chapters, it is one of the consequences of the Fall that the need for people to get on together despite their differences is a fundamental feature of political society, prior even to its possession of justice. However, the parochial nature of Rawls's theory, with its procedural refusal to look further than the givens of democratic public culture for the content of public justice, must cast some doubt on the final adequacy of his approach to the exercise. The practical task calls for a somewhat different theorization. Furthermore, it needs to be complemented by the endeavour to think through with Grant what has been lost in the technological drive to mastery. Whatever the practical demands, as supremely relevant is the task of recollection, of loving, and of gathering from the tradition 'intimations of essential deprivals'.[105] While the idea of time as history cannot be abandoned 'as if it had never been',[106] for through it there have been given elements of the good,[107] yet there remains a need to think in unity what in this civilization has been contradiction:

---

[103] It is not a pleasant game for the culturally impotent: *LN* 94 n. 36.

[104] 'Justice as Fairness', 223, 226.

[105] *TE* 141.

[106] *TH* 52: for interpretation, see J. E. O'Donovan, *George Grant*, 131: 'Our present darkness must have meaning even as darkness.'

[107] *TH* 51. It has involved 'a great achievement of the intellect' ('Faith and the Multiversity', 13; cf. *T&J* 59–60), and has in part realized the hope of relieving famine, toil, disease, and war (*T&J* 15).

to those of us who for varying reasons cannot but trust the lineaments of liberal justice, and who somehow have been told that some such justice is due to all human beings and that its living out is, above all, what we are fitted for,—to those of such trust comes the call from that darkness to understand how justice can be thought together with what has been discovered of truth in the coming to be of technology.[108]

4 CRITICAL ASSESSMENT

Up to this point, I have accepted for the sake of the argument Grant's account of modernity, technology, and liberalism. However, in order to incorporate this debate between Grant and Rawls into the wider project of a theological critique of political liberalism, we need to analyse critically some of his assumptions. We will look at two areas: (a) the theological basis of Grant's criticism and (b) the role of Grant's understanding of technological modernity.

(a) A theological perspective on Grant[109]

Grant rarely wrote explicitly on theological matters, and indeed displayed only occasional interest in the traditional concerns of theology. While this paucity of material makes criticism of his theological position difficult, it may also allow a greater latitude for incorporating his thought as a whole into other theological frameworks.

While his theology is broadly Christian, it is not bound to the formulations of traditional orthodoxy. Led to the Gospel by way of Greek philosophy rather than the Old Testament, Grant places himself on the side of Christianity that is 'farthest away from Judaism, and nearest to the account of Christianity that is close to Hinduism in its philosophic expression'.[110] Thus he identifies belief in God with the affirmation that there is order beyond space and time,[111] and opposes the project of the biblical theology movement to the extent that it bases Christianity on the history of

---

[108] *ESJ* 86. John Badertscher, 'The Prophecy of George Grant', *Canadian Journal of Social and Political Theory*, 4 (1980), 183–9, helpfully indicates the tensions in Grant's account here.

[109] For theological criticism, see esp. J. E. O'Donovan, *George Grant*, 166–80.

[110] Grant, Conversation, in Larry Schmidt (ed.), *George Grant in Process: Essays and Conversations* (Toronto: House of Anansi Press, 1978), 102.

[111] Grant, Tape 1 (Canadian Broadcasting Association): 'that's what one means by God.'

Israel and stresses the historical to the exclusion of the universal teaching of perfection and affliction.[112] Christ is a universal truth, and should not be connected with an account of God's dynamic action in the world; the latter seems 'unthinkable and to lead directly to atheism',[113] for it believes in a scrutable providence and justifies the culture-destroying aggression of triumphalist missionary expansionism.

He counts Simone Weil as his ultimate theological authority.[114] She has known Christ, he believes; those who have not experienced such a vision cannot speak with authority, but can only speculate about theological matters. For her, he holds, God is perfection and can have no purposes, and so cannot be thought to intervene in history; there is an infinite distance between the order of necessity and the order of the good, so that human beings can never improve themselves by their own efforts, but only by participation in God's being, the corresponding attitude to the realm of necessity is one of submission rather than mastery, a love of fate which will lead to the discovery of beauty.[115] Again from her, he accepts that 'faith is the experience that the intelligence is illuminated by love',[116] and the belief that justice should not have been separated from love in the Western tradition, that something can be known truly only by the one who loves it.[117]

Now Weil's Platonism can be regarded as valuable when it leads Grant to conceive of justice as 'what we are fitted for', and thus to recognize the existence of a moral order not grounded in history. Again, its attitude to the course of history as one of acceptance rather than control helpfully illuminates the nature of technological hubris.

Nevertheless, it has theological drawbacks. First, it leads Grant to deny, or at least not positively to affirm, the doctrine of creation.[118] He appears to associate belief in creation with a belief in the radical contingency of nature and an arbitrary divine

---

[112] Grant, Conversation, 102.   [113] Ibid. 102–3.
[114] See esp. J. E. O'Donovan, *George Grant*, 176–7; Edwin B. Heaven and David R. Heaven, 'Some Influences of Simone Weil on George Grant's Silence', in Schmidt (ed.), *George Grant in Process*, 68–78.
[115] Grant, Tape 3.
[116] Expounded in 'Faith and the Multiversity', 3–5, and *T&J* 35–77. On Weil, see *T&J* 54–6.
[117] Grant, Conversation, 105; Tape 3.
[118] Grant, Tape 2.

sovereignty.[119] However, neither of these follow from the doctrine of creation. It is possible to assert both God's ultimate freedom and the non-arbitrariness of nature and the moral order through a doctrine of creation in which God has in freedom committed himself to acting in certain ways towards the creation. An emphasis on the Aristotelian notion of the good as embodied in the structures of existence and on the Augustinian teaching about the necessary connection between created existence and ordering to the good would admit both the doctrine of creation, which is necessary to preserve God's ultimate sovereignty, and the objectivity of the moral order, which is necessary to render intelligible creaturely existence.

Second, such a Platonism runs the risk of exaggerating its response to historicism by rendering history insignificant. In attacking the assertions implicated in the notion of time as history, such as 'the finality of becoming, the assertion that potentiality is higher than actuality, that motion is nobler than rest, that dynamism rather than peace is the height',[120] and recalling us to recollection and to 'wondering or marvelling at what is',[121] salvation may begin to resemble a gnostic redemption from the world. Thus one critic complains that Grant refuses to allow his belief in an ahistorical standard of morality to be tested in historical struggle: his vision is a too easy historical fatalism that cannot be translated into politics, a 'panic remembrance' which falters at the edge of Nietzsche's abyss, and reaches back for 'the sinecure of natural law'.[122] And Grant's self-appointed task in his later career of not reflecting on the modern but thinking the truth of what is absent in the modern might suggest an unwillingness to engage with the practicalities of justice.

It should be said, however, that Grant's practice belies any impression that historical action lacks significance. His political engagement from the beginning of his career supports his approval of More's advice, 'When you can't expect the good to happen, try and prevent the very worst',[123] and his claim never to have despaired of politics. In theory also, he agrees with Nietzsche

[119] Grant's Augustine is the author of 'Quid sumus nisi voluntates?' (*TH* 34).
[120] *TH* 44. [121] *TE* 35.
[122] Arthur Kroker, *Technology and the Canadian Mind: Innis/McLuhan/Grant* (Montreal: New World Perspectives, 1984), 48–51.
[123] Grant, 'Conversation on Technology', 5.

that love of fate is not a passive acceptance of 'destiny', while any
search of the past that insulated one from the present would be
'cowardly, trivializing, and at worst despairing'.[124] 'Getting on with
the job' is a necessary moral maxim for all: '[What] the world tends
toward without it is seen in quietist societies, and against this we
may thank God for our activist tradition.'[125] Compassion comes
before thought: Heidegger is indicted for speaking of Being but
condoning tyranny.[126] And to love is 'to pay attention to other
people and this means to communicate with them'.[127] But philosophy also has a public role: not (in the present circumstances)
effecting goods, but subversively unmasking 'the assurances that
move us to pursue less than the highest ends'.[128]

But if Grant, as a theologically oriented thinker, is to attribute
significance to historical action, he must provide (whether explicitly or not) a theological context for this. Not only does he need,
as was argued above, a doctrine of creation: he also needs a
Christology which affirms the Incarnation without a Platonic
lapse into docetism, and which, through pointing to the Christ-
event as the climax of history, can confer uniqueness on the
particular events of history and thus enable a narrative of those
events to be given. Moreover, he needs an eschatology in which
history is gathered up through the divine purpose to its fulfilment.

Grant does not speak to any of these issues. Nevertheless, the
last is connected with the doctrine of providence, and this he does
address. Here we may contrast his theology with another Christian
tradition. For the Augustinian tradition, divine providence must be
distinguished from the decree of election, the former being
purposive but inscrutable, the latter simply arbitrary. Grant,
however, while his thought is crudely compatible with the latter
when he talks of faith as a matter of 'luck'—it just is given to some
to know that experience—even if he identifies the call of election
with the phenomenal experience of faith,[129] explicitly denies the

[124] *TH* 45, 48.
[125] 'Conceptions of Health', in Helmut Schoek and James W. Wiggins (eds.),
Psychiatry and Responsibility (Princeton: Van Nostrand, 1962), 122.
[126] *TE* 102–3.
[127] 'How Deception Lurks', 16.
[128] Laurence Lampert, 'The Uses of Philosophy in George Grant', *Queen's
Quarterly*, 81 (1974), 509–10.
[129] 'Faith and the Multiversity', 5.

existence of the former, appearing to think that to deny the scrutability of providence is tantamount to denying providence itself. Such a denial of providence prevents the possibility of faithful historical action whose meaningfulness is neither dismissed nor imagined to be absolute or independent of the divine initiative. Providence cannot be conflated with creation, for creation has to be complete to render intelligible the notion of the fulfilment of history; nor can it be eliminated, for the divine government of history and the theological founding of politics would be lost. While Grant may rightly regret aspects of Christian missionary expansion, the solution lies elsewhere than in denying the doctrine of providence.

Aspects of Grant's few excursions into theology are problematic, therefore, but this is not tantamount to an assertion of heterodoxy. As we have argued, he does not allow his Platonism to cause him to neglect the value of action in history; moreover his sense of immanent teleologies displayed in his attacks on abortion and euthanasia[130] is consistent with a Christian conception of the created moral order. But more importantly, his Christianity is never swallowed up by his Platonism. Thus, while he perceives the infinite gap between necessity and the good, he also finds the gap bridged in the act of love which is Christ crucified. And while Christianity shares the classical account of justice, it extends what is due to others (by emphasizing forgiveness), and adds an account of how that due should be fulfilled: participation in the divine goodness involves attention to 'the immediate requirements of the world',[131] since the second great commandment is like unto the first. Indeed, it is his conviction that the Gospels as well as Plato are the primal revelations for the two dominant Western traditions that leads him in his later work to find tragic and unresolved tensions between the claims of contemplation and of charity.[132] In general, therefore, although we may have reservations about some

[130] See *T&J* 103–30; 'Triumph of the Will'.
[131] *T&J* 55.
[132] See J. E. O'Donovan, *George Grant*, 100–1; the tension was explicit from his earliest work (cf. ibid. 15–17), though during his Hegelian phase in *Philosophy in the Mass Age* (Toronto: Copp Clark, ²1966) he thought it rationally resolvable within history. It is to the Christian emphasis on charity that Grant attributes (and defends against Strauss's élitism) the Western belief in the equality of all human beings.

of his theological claims, Grant is properly to be included amongst Christian critics of liberalism.

(b) Grant's understanding of modernity, technology, and liberalism

We must now return to Grant's account of modernity. A full explication of modernity along the lines which Grant suggests is not possible here, even if it were desirable. But our particular concern, a theological interpretation of liberalism, can be considerably enriched by engaging with his account. Although his general understanding of liberalism is broader than the one I gave in Chapter 2 (in including non-political thinkers, for example), his account of it as the political aspect of modernity, rooted in the will, accounts for most of the features of liberalism described there, from the conception of the self as sovereign chooser, through the progressivist philosophy of history, to the supreme liberal values of liberty and equality. But it also indicates the importance of making a distinction which Grant, like Niebuhr, is insufficiently clear about, that one can be a liberal in some respects but not in others: in particular, the liberal conception of the self, of the basis of value, of history, and of rationality, can be rejected by a theory that nevertheless accepts central aspects of constitutional, economic, and welfare liberalism as being either true or at any rate most appropriate for some contemporary societies. Grant's tendency to emphasize liberalism's shortcomings and self-deceptions leads him to neglect, or at least not to show forth, his basic agreement with many of the central affirmations of liberalism.

A similar consideration arises when we turn to his account of the dependence of liberalism on technology. It would be possible to come away from a reading of Grant with the impression that he regards liberalism as peculiarly vulnerable to ensnarement by some form of technological tyranny. Certainly it is the civilizational contradiction caused by the joint origins of technology and liberalism which concerns him and to which he devotes his energy. But there is no doubt that liberalism is the centre of his attention, because it is the dominant tradition of the modern world, and one which ironically regards itself as least liable to fall for tyranny precisely because it is liberal. Technology, as was discussed at the beginning of the chapter, stands for Grant as the dominant shaping force of the whole of Western civilization, and he would surely have agreed with Heidegger about technology being the subject of which both capitalism and communism are predicates. When he criticizes liberalism, it is out of love for the central Western values which are still present in it, not because he wishes to advocate another set of political values that might lend themselves to illiberality even more quickly.

We will return to some of these issues in the last chapter. For the present we shall consider just one final question. Grant's talk of technological fate may engender a sense of helplessness. Are we simply fated to enter technological tyranny?

For Grant, as for Ellul and Heidegger, technology is a 'destining'. A product of the Western tradition, technology has paradoxically broken with that tradition, being at once the necessary historical outcome of the Christian revelation and the rejection of the truth given in that revelation.[133] But Grant differs from Ellul and Heidegger concerning the nature of the destining. For Ellul, technology is primarily a sociological, not an intellectual or spiritual phenomenon; only restraints of a sociological kind could change technology, but none such exist, he holds: it is an irreducible social reality, 'essentially independent of the human being'.[134] For Heidegger, technology is a destining of Being: it is not merely humanly derived instrumentality, but the demand upon human beings, which follows from the way that they find the world to be, to focus on themselves rather than the world as the source of certainty, and thus to objectify reality and to understand it by representing it as system.[135] Although for Heidegger technology is a destining, he is not a determinist:

[133] Joan E. O'Donovan, 'The Battleground of Liberalism: Politics of Eternity and Politics of Time', *Chesterton Review*, 11 (1985), 134–5.

[134] Ellul, *Technological Society*, 306. This is compatible with technological fate working through, rather than despite, human decisions: if a field of choice is weighted such that for a particular agent only one course of action is acceptable, the outcome will be inevitable, on the assumption of that agent's rationality; 'technological fate' is what weights the alternatives. Compare, in a Marxist context, G. A. Cohen, *Karl Marx's Theory of History: A Defence* (Oxford: Clarendon Press, 1978), 147 n. 1.

[135] In Heidegger's terms, the call in the unconcealment of Being is a challenging claim, a *Ge-stell*, to order the self-revealed as standing-reserve, to turn *Gegenstand* into *Bestand*. See the essays collected in *The Question Concerning Technology and Other Essays* (1952–62), trans. William Lovitt (New York: Harper and Row, 1977). Grant's title *Time as History* could be read as an ironic quotation of Heidegger: thus, under the sway of technology, 'time has ceased to be anything other than velocity, instantaneousness, and simultaneity, and time as history has vanished from the lives of all peoples' (Heidegger, *An Introduction to Metaphysics*, trans. Ralph Manheim (New Haven: Yale University Press, 1959), 38).

human beings are free at least in the sense that they can open themselves to the essence of technology, and recognize their destining as destining without being constrained simply to obey it uncomprehendingly. For Grant, however, technology is a fate of thinking: 'I mean by "civilizational destiny" above all the fundamental presuppositions that the majority of human beings inherit in a civilization, and which are so taken for granted as the way things are that they are given an almost absolute status.'[136] Likewise, political philosophy becomes the unfolding of fate because of its concern with judgements about the good which are then acted upon by those engaged in practical affairs.[137] This moderately idealist account of the nature of historical change—'theories are at work in the decisions of the world, and we had better understand them'[138]—explains why he places such stress on the intellectual task for the present era of thinking together ancient justice and modern science: a supposedly untheorized praxis alone is no solution, nor is waiting with Heidegger for a 'turning'.

Yet that suggests the possibility of hope. If there is at least an intellectual task to be done, which might bear fruit in the decisions of the world, then perhaps some small gap opens up against brute determination of the future. At the level of politics, liberal political orders can allow for counter-movements that join thought and practice in rejection of the totalizing proclivities of technology. And, in theological terms, necessity in history can only be the necessity that arises from human sinning—the primary human response to technology must be that of repentance. Moreover, if technology is a perversion of the good, and not a sham entity with no ultimate ontological status (such as sin or death)—that is, if a more positive normative account of the will can be given, in which it is in harmony with reason—it could be handled within the scriptural categories of the principalities and powers.[139] It could

---

[136] *T&J* 22.

[137] *LN* 94 n. 36.

[138] *ESJ* 47.

[139] See, at different levels of theological and exegetical depth, Karl Barth, *The Christian Life*, trans. Geoffrey W. Bromiley (Grand Rapids, Mich.: Eerdmans, 1981), 213–33; Hendrik Berkhof, *Christ and the Powers*, trans. John H. Yoder (Scottdale, Pa.: Mennonite Publishing House, 1962); G. B. Caird, *Principalities and Powers: A Study in Pauline Theology* (Oxford: Clarendon Press, 1956); Walter Wink, *Naming the Powers: The Language of Power in the New Testament* (Philadelphia: Fortress Press, 1984); idem., *Unmasking the Powers: The Invisible Forces that*

be taken as a corrupted good which has forsaken its subordinate role and sought absolute authority. And to that the Christian response starts from the prayer, 'Thy Kingdom come!'[140]

Determine Human Existence (Philadephia: Fortress Press, 1986); *idem.*, *Engaging the Powers: Discernment and Resistance in a World of Domination* (Minneapolis: Fortress Press, 1992); James W. McClendon, jun., *Systematic Theology: Ethics* (Nashville: Abingdon Press, 1986).

[140] For further theological discussion of technology see e.g. Oliver O'Donovan, *Begotten or Made?* (Oxford: Clarendon Press, 1984), esp. ch. 1; Egbert Schuurman, *Technology and the Future: A Philosophical Challenge*, trans. Herbert Donald Morton (Toronto: Wedge Publishing Foundation, 1981); Stephen V. Monsma (ed.), *Responsible Technology* (Grand Rapids, Mich.: Eerdmans, 1986); Carl Mitcham and Jim Grote, *Theology and Technology: Essays in Christian Analysis and Exegesis* (Lanham, Md.: University Press of America, 1984).

5

Jacques Maritain and the Liberal Defence of Pluralism

I INTRODUCTION

The focus of interest within English-speaking political theory has shifted decisively in the last two decades. Liberals, more self-assured against their external enemies as a result of the moral unattractiveness and now wholly evident economic incompetence of revolutionary socialism in practice, have turned their attention instead towards domestic issues concerning the definition and distribution of goods and rights. Arguments within the broad liberal consensus of Western democracies have come to centre-stage, and the rehabilitations of the quasi-Kantian theory of contract by John Rawls, which we looked at in the last chapter, and of a quasi-Lockean theory of property by Robert Nozick have become the most prominent philosophical emblems of the wider political argument between welfare left-liberals and conservative libertarians. Nevertheless, while the imaginative plausibility of collectivist societies of any kind remains apparently expunged, the submerged quest for 'community' which emerged in the humanistic Marxism of the New Left re-emerged during the 1980s as a response to the alleged 'individualism' of much analytical political philosophy. It is this new family of criticisms of liberalism, drawing on the tradition of Aristotle, Hegel, and the German Romantics, as well as on Heideggerian analyses of mass society, which have attracted much attention in the last decade.

Representative of these 'communitarian' critics of liberalism is Charles Taylor.[1] The understanding of human beings and society

---

[1] See esp. the essays in *Philosophy and the Human Sciences: Philosophical Papers 2* (Cambridge: Cambridge University Press, 1985), 1–12, 187–337. The most celebrated example of this trend in political theory is Sandel, *Liberalism and the Limits of Justice*. Alasdair MacIntyre has (in discussion) rejected the label 'communitarian' as a description of his own position, dismissing communitarian politics as 'the children of the bourgeoisie playing with themselves'. It is, he says, politics in the head—an imagined engagement with reality—which, like most political pronouncements of

typical of modernity is, he argues, one of 'atomism'. According to this doctrine, individuals are conceived as metaphysically distinct from society; society is an aggregate of individuals, who enter into it with the instrumental purpose of fulfilling their anteriorly defined ends: hence rights are granted primacy, and obligations are justified by consent. Against Aristotle, for whom the characteristically human excellences were made possible only by living in society, atomists believe that human beings are self-sufficient as individuals: they deny that the individual is constituted by the self-interpretations communicated by the language, culture, and historical traditions of a community. This belief has been sustained, Taylor claims, by a notion of the agent as disengaged from the world of scientifically neutral facts and as thereby able to experience the heady freedom of a self-defining subjectivity.[2] This view of the agent as detached from nature has produced the modern understanding of natural science (with its stress on objectification and primary qualities), the attempted modelling of the human on the natural sciences, and an account of linguistic meaning as basically designative. But it has also made plausible the idea that no background understanding of human capacities is required to make intelligible the specification of rights, and thus also the idea that rights can be ascribed without a consideration of the social and cultural circumstances which are constitutively necessary for human agency. However, if the social thesis is true—namely, that the distinctively human capacities (such as language-use, freedom of choice, capacity to worship, etc.) can only be developed (or at least properly or fully developed) in society—and if it is only such capacities that make intelligible what rights should be attributed to human beings, it follows that obligations to the society

professors, is ultimately fruitless; genuine community is not achieved by being chosen as an end in itself, but is supervenient on whole-hearted commitment to some other activity. Some notion of the kind of community he is looking for is given in 'The Idea of an Educated Public', in Graham Haydon (ed.), *Education and Values* (London: Institute of Education, University of London, 1987), 15–36. For some cogent criticism of Sandel and earlier MacIntyre, cf. Amy Gutmann, 'Communitarian Critics of Liberalism', *Philosophy and Public Affairs*, 14 (1985), 308–22; and for a good introduction to the issues in debate, see Mulhall and Swift, *Liberals and Communitarians*.

[2] Thus, by contrast with Grant, he argues that the seventeenth-century revolution should be read as being motivated by the desire for freedom from an external given order, rather than by the desire to manipulate the material world (*Hegel* (Cambridge: Cambridge University Press, 1975), 3–9).

which gives identity to an agent are as fundamental as the rights which that agent claims. That is, the considerations which justify rights should be recognized as simultaneously justifying obligations: duties are not derivative from rights. The individuals who populate modernity, with their armour of rights, are the products of a certain kind of civilization, and have duties to the institutional and communal bearers of the culture which have given them their identity.

Taylor's account, the details and difficulties of which do not concern us here, focuses the central issue in the debate between communitarians and liberals. An ideal frequently espoused by liberals is that of neutrality between conflicting and perhaps incommensurable conceptions of the good. But the communitarian notion of the agent implies that the fostering of the capacities that constitute the agent is of public concern, and perhaps, therefore, that the political and legal framework of a society should not be neutral. This suggests that if a neutral state is morally undesirable, the degree of pluralism possible within a society must be limited, and with it the range of conceptions of the good that may legitimately be pursued within that society. Are liberals correct to remain attached to their ideal of neutrality, or does the necessity of socialization for individual development imply that the public realm should embody substantive moral commitments?

The debate between liberals and communitarians, with its focus on the nature of agency, is the most recent guise of a complex of wider and more familiar disputes concerning the possibility of state neutrality, the justification of pluralism, and the legal enforcement of morality. On these issues, some of which we touched on in the previous chapter, the ideas of Jacques Maritain have been as important as those of perhaps any Catholic thinker of the twentieth century. Although their influence was chiefly during the middle decades of the century, they potentially have a renewed significance in the light of the communitarian critique of liberalism. Maritain's vision of a 'new Christendom' provides, I believe, theological foundations for a distinctive solution, a *tertium quid*, to these problems. Accepting the Aristotelian understanding of human beings as naturally social and of the common good as intrinsically moral as well as material, he nevertheless argues for a quasi-neutral state in which each religious group would justify the same foundational charter of rights within its own terms. Although the neutrality of the democratic charter is informed and qualified by his requirement that legislation should not approve conduct contrary to natural law and by his belief that his 'integral humanism' will produce a 'vitally Christian lay state', his insistence on religious freedom provides in effect the grounding for many other liberties.[3]

There is much that is attractive about Maritain's new Christendom and the Thomist understanding of the person and society which grounds it. However, I shall argue in this chapter that his reading of Aquinas serves to justify a version of political liberalism only through a tacit historical relativism and historicism. Moreover, although his defence of a pluralism which admits the importance of human socialization and cultural traditions has much to commend it over against secular liberalism, his notion that natural legislation is an essential feature of any political society has its own problems. These could be resolved, I shall suggest in the final section, by placing his theory within an Augustinian framework.

2 RELIGIOUS FREEDOM, HISTORICAL RELATIVISM

Maritain's distinctive contribution to the Thomist tradition of social and political thought lies in his defence of the ideal of a new Christendom. He has, he claims, 'sought inspiration in the general principles of St. Thomas Aquinas . . . and tried to feel . . . what would be his personal reaction to the conflicts of human

[3] Maritain's principal works that address issues in political theory are, in order of publication (English translation published in London by Geoffrey Bles, unless otherwise indicated): *The Things That Are Not Caesar's* (1927), trans. J. F. Scanlan (London: Sheed and Ward, 1930); *Religion and Culture* (1930), trans. J. F. Scanlan (London: Sheed and Ward, 1931); *FMW*; *IH*; *Scholasticism and Politics* (1940), trans. Mortimer J. Adler; 'The Conquest of Freedom', in Ruth Nanda Anshen (ed.), *Freedom: Its Meaning* (1940), repr. in Joseph W. Evans and Leo R. Ward, *The Social and Political Philosophy of Jacques Maritain: Selected Readings* (1956), 28–46; *Redeeming the Time* (1941), trans. Harry Loren Binsse (1943); *RMNL*; *Christianity and Democracy* (1948), trans. Doris C. Anson (1945); *PCG*; *The Range of Reason* (1947; trans. 1953); *MS*; *PH*. But see also 'Introduction' and 'On the Philosophy of Human Rights,' in UNESCO, *Human Rights: Comments and Interpretations* (London and New York: Allen Wingate, 1948), 9–17, 72–7; and *The Peasant of the Garonne: An Old Layman Questions Himself about the Present Time* (1966), trans. Michael Cuddihy and Elizabeth Hughes (London: Geoffrey Chapman, 1968).

Of the secondary literature on Maritain, see especially Joseph W. Evans, 'Jacques Maritain's Personalism', *Review of Politics* 14 (1952), 166–77; the essays in *Recherches*

history'.[4] To this end he has laid special stress on Aquinas's doctrine of analogy, a method of argument which he finds to be 'the truly living and universal instrument of research and of the truth'.[5] But, as we shall see, his manner of using the principle of analogy raises the question of whether he adopts an improper historical relativism, and indeed historicism, which is at variance with Aquinas. In this section, after an introductory outline of his new Christendom, I shall investigate the suspicion that his understanding of historical development leads to a relativism; in the course of this, I shall pay particular attention to the case of his defence of religious freedom, an issue which also foreshadows the later discussion.

(a) The new Christendom

There are three different but overlapping contexts of action which make intelligible Maritain's development of the ideal of the new Christendom. The first, reflected notably in *True Humanism* (1936), was that of Catholic Europe, and especially France, in the mid-1930s.[6] Here was founded his vision of a new Christian order, informed by a Christian social theory and intended as an alternative especially to atheistic communism but also to the rising fascist totalitarianism;[7] this would replace outmoded and dying capitalism,[8] would recognize the value of the historical gains made by (for example) the labour movements, and would uphold the Catholic Church, against internal medievalist conservatives and external modernist detractors, as the defender and invigorator of

et Débats (Centre Catholique des Intellectuels Français), 19 (July 1957), esp. Joseph de Finance, 'La Philosophie de la liberté chez Maritain' (95–116), and Louis Gardet, 'La Culture chrétienne et le dialogue des cultures' (148–65); Hwa Yol Jung, *The Foundations of Jacques Maritain's Political Philosophy* (Gainsville, Fla.: University of Florida Press, 1960); Henry Bars, *La Politique selon Jacques Maritain* (Paris: Les Éditions Ouvrières, 1961); Joseph W. Evans (ed.), *Jacques Maritain: The Man and His Achievement* (New York: Sheed and Ward, 1963); Deal W. Hudson and Matthew J. Mancini (eds.), *Understanding Maritain: Philosopher and Friend* (Macon, Ga.: Mercer University Press, 1987).

   [4] *IH* 202.
   [5] Ibid.
   [6] For the intellectual and historical context of *True Humanism*, see Jean-Marie Mayeur, 'Les Années 30 et *Humanisme intégral*', in J.-L. Allard, C. Blanchet, G. Cottier, and J.-M. Mayeur, *L'Humanisme intégral de Jacques Maritain* (Paris: Éditions Saint-Paul, 1988), 17–36.
   [7] *IH* 27–62, 71–87, for Marxism; 271–81 for fascism.
   [8] *IH* 184–6.

the temporal common good. The second context was that opened up by the prospect, in the latter years of the Second World War, of reconstructing European and world order: the task undertaken here, developed out of considerations such as had been outlined in *The Rights of Man and Natural Law* (1942), focused on constituting effective supranational institutions, and framing a universal declaration of human rights which could be acceptable at the level of moral agreement to people of any philosophical or religious creed.[9] The third context, into which *Man and the State* (lectures 1949, published 1951) partly fits, was that of the efforts of American Catholics to enter the mainstream of American public life. Maritain could be represented as contributing to a Catholic defence of the American experiment, a task which would involve defending Catholics against nativist fears of the Church's authoritarianism, and showing how Catholics would abide by the First Amendment's no establishment and free exercise clauses, provided that these were understood to be excluding preferential treatment for particular churches or denominations, rather than to be discriminating against religion as such and so establishing secularism by default.[10]

These three contexts were in no sense opposed to each other: indeed, Maritain's mature thought displays a remarkable continuity and basic unity. Thus he was to write in *Reflections on America* (1958) about *True Humanism* that, although it was originally written with reference to Europe, the congeniality of American civilization to him had led him to reflect that 'it appears now to be a book which had, so to speak, an affinity with the American climate by anticipation'.[11] It is not out of place, therefore, for us to begin with a discussion of the new Christendom, even though later we will be more concerned with the democratic charter, a notion he had not conceived at the time of *True Humanism*.

[9] Cf. Maritain's role in the UNESCO volume (1948). *MS* also engages with these questions.

[10] First Amendment issues were discussed explicitly by John Courtney Murray; see esp. 'Civil Unity and Religious Integrity: The Articles of Peace', in *We Hold These Truths: Catholic Reflections on the American Proposition* (London: Sheed and Ward, 1960), 45–78. For Maritain's influence on post-war American Catholicism, see, e.g. Jay P. Dolan, *The American Catholic Experience* (Garden City, NY: Doubleday, 1985), 352. Philip Gleason, 'American Catholics and Liberalism, 1789–1960', in Douglass and Hollenbach (eds.), *Catholicism and Liberalism*, 45–75, provides a recent historical overview.

[11] *Reflections on America* (New York: Scribner's, 1958), 174–5.

The ideal of a new Christendom signals for Maritain the goal of a vitally Christian lay polity appropriate for contemporary historical conditions. The historical ideal of medieval Christendom is no longer plausible, he argues: Catholics should work with all people of good will towards a Christian social order which will succeed capitalist social and economic structures and will avoid the errors of individualism, communism, and fascism. The temporal policy of medieval civilization was just one possible realization of the religious truth about the political order. In new circumstances an analogous realization of the same religious truth is necessary, avoiding, on the one hand, the dissolution of eternal principles through equivocation and, on the other, the false rigidity of univocal application in differing historical contexts.

There are certain abstract principles which apply to the temporal order invariably.[12] First, it is communal. The end of civil society is a common good which is more than an aggregation of individual goods and to which every individual as part of the social whole is subordinated. The common good is the proper temporal end of political society, and is both material and moral. But since the social whole is comprised of persons endowed with spiritual existence, the temporal common good is not its final end. Rather, it is ordained to the extra-temporal good of the person. Thus Maritain terms the temporal common good the 'infravalent' end of political society. Second, the social polity will be personalist. Unable of itself to lead to perfection of spirituality or the full autonomy of sanctity, it nevertheless should assist the final end of each person through providing the material, moral, intellectual, and social conditions necessary for achieving the goal of human existence, the vision of God. Third, because it is thus ordered to a supravalent end, the temporal order will be pilgrim in nature: the earthly city is a society of those travelling towards their eternal habitations. This does not entail a purely instrumental role for it, such that it has no value in itself: it should aim to procure 'a relative but very real earthly happiness for the assembled multitude'.[13]

Similarly, three immutable principles govern the relations of Church and State.[14] First, the transcendence of God above any earthly institution implies 'the freedom of the Church to teach and preach and worship, the freedom of the Gospel, the freedom of the

---

[12] *IH* 127–31.   [13] *IH* 131.   [14] *MS* 148–54.

Word of God'.[15] Second, the universality of the Church above every body politic, together with the essential secularity of the temporal order through the division of the things which are God's from those which are Caesar's, entails 'the superiority of the Church—that is, of the spiritual—over the body politic or the State'.[16] Nevertheless, third, since the Church and the body politic cannot live in separation from each other, and since persons may be members of both societies and cannot be divided, there follows the requirement of 'the necessary co-operation between the Church and the body politic or the State'.[17]

Although these principles are permanently valid, their realizations as concrete historical ideals will vary between contexts. These contexts differ in respect of the 'dominant dynamic idea' and the empirical conditions found in each. The historical ideal of medieval Christendom was that of the Holy Roman Empire. Its dominant dynamic idea was that of 'force in the service of God', and the attendant empirical fact was that the political order was 'a function of consecrated activity', and so needed religious unity.[18] This ideal of the *sacrum imperium* corresponded to a 'Christian consecrational conception of the temporal', which Maritain analyses into five elements.[19] First, there was a tendency towards an organic temporal unity in which political unification would be the expression of a more fundamental intellectual, spiritual, and cultural identification: 'national quarrels were quarrels within one family and did not break the unity of culture'.[20] Such unity was made possible through, second, the effective ministerial function of the temporal towards the spiritual: to the extent that this happened, the political order became merely instrumental to the end of eternal life.[21] Next, there was the willingness to use the institutional or coercive powers of the State to assist towards the spiritual good of persons or the spiritual unity of the body politic. Fourth, there was a 'diversity of social races': temporal authority was conceived in the manner of paternal authority, and social structure as a hierarchy of family relations. Finally, there was a distinctive conception of the city's common work: 'the faithful strove to build a figurative and symbolic image here on earth of the Kingdom of God.'[22]

---

[15] *MS* 151–2.   [16] *MS* 153.
[17] *MS* 154.   [18] *IH* 137.
[19] *IH* 140–7.   [20] *IH* 141.
[21] Maritain does not make clear how this relates to the non-instrumental nature of the temporal order mentioned above.   [22] *IH* 147.

For Maritain the dominant ideal of the new Christian society will be that not of the holy empire but of 'the holy freedom of the creature whom grace unites to God'.[23] The temporal order will be motivated by 'the conquest of freedom and the realization of human dignity':[24] it no longer requires religious unity to ensure its political stability. Maritain argues here also for five elements which correspond to, but replace those of, medieval civilization.[25] First, instead of a maximal organic unity there will be a pluralism of economic structures[26] and of juridical structures (which will recognize 'the differing juridical status of the diverse spiritual groups included in one commonweal'[27]). The unity will be of a shared aspiration to a common good that best subserves the person's supra-temporal goals, rather than a unity of fundamental doctrinal agreement. Joined in this way by a civic friendship rather than a common faith, it will aim at a unity which is, although minimal and at the level of the temporal, nevertheless 'organic' and 'much superior to that of the liberal–individualistic order'.[28] Second, the coming of age of the temporal order must be recognized: the authority of the State will be acknowledged as supreme in its own order, serving a genuinely infravalent end, and not just a minister to the spiritual order. Third, the manner of collaboration between Church and political authority will reflect the dominant dynamic idea of the autonomy of the person: the State's role in spiritual matters will be one not of legal coercion, but of moral influence through its cultivation of the common good. It will do less to promote the person's eternal interests on the 'objective' side, and more on the 'subjective' side. Similarly, the Church will pursue its mission through its 'vivifying inspiration' rather than its social power.[29] Fourth, instead of a hierarchy of social relations, authority will be founded on the fundamental equality of all persons: although government will still derive its authority from God, it will lose its sacral aura, and will be mediated through organs of popular consensus. Finally, the common task of the new Christendom will not aim at reflecting the Kingdom of God on earth, but at realizing a fraternal community: it will be this

---

[23] *IH* 156.   [24] *MS* 160; cf. *IH* 171.   [25] *IH* 156–201.
[26] What Reinhold Niebuhr was to call a 'type of guild socialism' (review of *FMW*, *Saturday Review* (8 Aug. 1936), repr. in John W. Cooper, *The Philosophy of Freedom: The Legacy of Jacques Maritain and Reinhold Niebuhr* (Macon, Ga.: Mercer University Press, 1985), 172).
[27] *IH* 160.   [28] *IH* 165 n. 1.   [29] *MS* 162–7.

practical common task, not a theoretical doctrinal unity, which will be the unifying force of Maritain's vitally Christian lay state.

(b) The defence of religious freedom

It is evident why this account of a new Christendom has been influential on many Christian politicians and thinkers of broadly Christian Democratic orientation. Not least, in distancing himself from medieval Christendom, Maritain lays the ground for a Christian understanding of political society which recognizes the facts of cultural, ideological, and religious plurality, is egalitarian rather than hierarchical in basic conception, and sees the Church's political engagement as fundamentally a matter of inspiration from below rather than control from above. Nevertheless, even in these general terms, Maritain's portraits of medieval and new Christendoms give rise to the question of whether his appeal to analogy is a legitimate justification or merely a sophisticated blind for a basic historical relativism. His belief that different concrete historical ideals obtain according to the different dominant dynamic ideas and empirical conditions of historical periods requires grounding if it is to avoid the charge of arbitrariness in its prescriptions.

To investigate this, I will first describe more closely an example which clearly demonstrates that Maritain prescribes different actions in different historical periods. The example we shall consider is his defence of religious freedom in the new Christendom, contrasted with his acceptance of the traditional double standard as appropriate for the Middle Ages. This brings out the issues clearly, though it is of course also germane to our background problematic of a theological analysis of political liberalism.

The traditional Catholic position concerning religious coercion, as it had come to be seen by Maritain's time, was particularly associated with Gregory XVI, Leo XIII, and Pius XII.[30] Its fundamental and determinative doctrine was that 'error has no rights': this was derived from an interpretation of the principle *extra ecclesiam nullum ius*, such that the Church had access to the temporal sword in order to ensure the religious unity of Christendom and the elimination of heresy. From the denial of rights to error came teaching on the rights of conscience and the constitutional incorporation of the Church. The *conscientia recta et vera*,

---

[30] This interpretation follows John Courtney Murray, SJ, *The Problem of Religious Freedom* (London: Geoffrey Chapman, 1965), 7–45.

guided by higher norms that are true, was the Catholic conscience, and had full claim to religious freedom. The *conscientia recta sed non vera* was granted inner freedom and the right not to be compelled to accept the true faith, but not the right to the outer freedoms of teaching, worship, and witness, though these might be granted for the sake of the common good. The *conscientia exlex*—that is, *non recta*—had no right to religious freedom. Constitutionally, the old position demanded intolerance where possible and tolerance where necessary. In 'thesis'—that is, in countries where Catholics were in a majority—error may and ought to be extinguished; in the situation of 'hypothesis', where Catholics were in a minority, the evil of error had to be tolerated as the lesser evil.

Maritain's own position concerning this doctrine of the double standard is somewhat ambivalent. It is clear that in general he regarded it, or at least an earlier version of the view just outlined, as appropriate for the Middle Ages. It is also clear that he advocated for the era of the new Christendom a doctrine of religious freedom. This is to be founded, as mentioned above, on a doctrine of the relations of Church and State which reflected the dominant dynamic ideal of the freedom of the person. The person's spiritual interests would be promoted more on the 'subjective' than the 'objective' side:[31] the political authority would not use legal coercion in religious matters, nor would the Church depend on its social power to fulfil its purpose.[32] This doctrine of religious freedom, while it would permit a civil tolerance that respected conscience, would not represent a dogmatic tolerance: there would be a freedom not to be coerced into the truth, but not a freedom to err.[33]

Now these ideas appear to imply that Maritain has overthrown the double standard altogether, rather than merely consigned the modern world to a period of indefinite hypothesis. They are supported by the statement that even if religious unity were to return, 'no return to the sacral regime in which the civil power was the instrument or secular arm of the spiritual power could be conceivable in a Christianly inspired modern democratic society'.[34] Moreover, he argues that nothing he says opposes the ideal that the Catholic Church alone should have the juridical privileges that rightfully belong to the true religion, but adds breezily that such a

---

[31] *FMW* 68.   [32] *MS* 162–7.
[33] *FMW* 68.   [34] *FMW* 181.

condition could only obtain if there was worldwide religious unity and therefore the Catholic Church alone enjoyed the privileges granted to every religious body.[35] Most explicitly of all, he quotes Cardinal Manning to the effect that if Catholics became the majority, they would not use political power to constrain faith: this statement of Manning's, he says, 'does not refer to the requirements of an hypothesis reluctantly accepted, but to the requirements of the very principles soundly applied in the existential framework of the modern historical climate'.[36]

Tolerance, it seems on this evidence, is justified not as a lesser evil, but as a positive good. But, disconcertingly for this interpretation, Maritain also argues that 'in order to avoid greater evils (that is, the ruin of the society's peace and either the petrification or the disintegration of consciences), the commonweal could and should tolerate (to tolerate is not to approve) ways of worship more or less distant from the true one'.[37] That is, toleration of non-Catholic rites is not a matter of right, but of the lesser evil. Again:

The Church does not lose any of the essential rights she has claimed or exercised in the past. Nevertheless, she can renounce the exercise of certain of them, not because she is forced to do so, but voluntarily and by virtue of the consideration of the common good, the historical context having changed.[38]

And he implies elsewhere that amongst these essential rights are legal constraint over religious profession.[39]

These other passages might suggest, then, that Maritain has not wholly excluded the double standard approach. Thus Sidney Hook argues that Maritain has no disagreement in principle with using force against heresy, and indeed that for him toleration of heresy is an evil, the Church merely acquiescing in the modern liberties until it can exercise again its own proper liberty.[40]

It is not evident how these two strands should be made compatible, the one suggesting that tolerance is now appropriate, and thus that the modern era is in a situation of hypothesis, the other that the thesis–hypothesis approach itself is no longer appropriate. The general flow of his thought, however, embracing

---

[35] *FMW* 173a-b n. 27.   [36] *FMW* 181.
[37] *MS* 169 n. 25 (a quotation from *IH* 160). Note further that this is a later work.
[38] *MS* 180 n. 30.   [39] *FMW* 69.
[40] Sidney Hook, *Reason, Social Myths and Democracy* (New York: Harper and Row, 1940), 80, 83.

the new Christendom and the analogical nature of the concrete historical ideals, surely indicates that the latter should be interpreted as the dominant theme. If this is right, Hook's understanding of Maritain is incorrect inasmuch as religious freedom in the present age is not a concession but fully appropriate for now, but correct in that for Maritain religious coercion is not straightforwardly wrong in timeless principle, but is justified according to historical context.

If the double standard was applicable during the Middle Ages but is not in the new Christendom, it appears to follow that Maritain is committed to a simple historical relativism. But before the charge can be pressed against him, we must first understand certain features of his philosophy of history.

Time, he argues, has an intrinsic reality. An absolute supratemporal ideal must be realized existentially and in time, and so must be relative to historical conditions. If the separation of thesis and hypothesis is understood in such a way that the normative ideal is insulated from contact with experience, the working principles of the practical order are liable to become the 'handmaid of opportunism'. The thesis–hypothesis distinction should rather contrast 'a *concrete historical ideal,* an image that incarnates eternal truth for a given historical firmament and under a form essentially adapted to it, and *the conditions of effective realization* of this practical ideal'.[41] Although no doubt difficult, such an ideal is not essentially impossible to realize: if it does not come to be, that is not because circumstances thwart our wills. Thus the ideal must be capable of being willed with integrity: it must be a possible end of rational action. Further, historical change is not continuous, but is divisible into discrete and discernible organic wholes; 'whereas in actual fact time has a meaning and a direction, human history is made up of periods each one of which is possessed of a particular intelligible structure and therefore of basic particular requirements, a fact that no political brain should ignore.'[42] Such periods are characterized by 'historical climates' or 'historical constellations'.[43] The Middle Ages was one such constellation; the new Christendom will incarnate the analogical principles appropriate to another.

An ideal must, then, be realizable and relative to its age. But it

41 *FMW* 112, emphasis original.
42 *MS* 155.
43 *MS* 156.

might be wondered why there is a difference in kind, rather than just a difference of degree, between realizing the new Christendom and returning to the ideals of medieval civilization: after all, however propitious the circumstances, incarnating ideals is no simple matter. Maritain offers three reasons for thinking that a revival of the medieval configuration is not just instrumentally difficult but also morally inappropriate.[44] First, he appeals to a law governing the relation of human beings to time, that 'a *too complete* experience cannot be recommenced'. Medieval Christendom has been lived once, has borne its fruit, and is now dead. Second, the modern age has aimed to rehabilitate the creature, and 'it is impossible to conceive that the sufferings and experiences of the modern age have been useless'.[45] Third, the Christian belief in the government of history by God means that to attempt to make the past immobile would be to deny his providence.[46]

These arguments are sketched so briefly and with so little reference to their assumed philosophical and theological background that it is difficult to evaluate them. At any rate, it is not clear whether the arguments do not each presuppose the periods whose very existence they are intended to establish. Further, the scrutability of history which each of them supposes is undefended; of course, historians can individualize discrete historical periods for their own purposes, but a theological argument must be given for according such periods theological significance, and Maritain provides none.

Even if such a periodization were shown to be justified, so that in different historical periods there properly obtained different moral and juridical prescriptions, the central question remains as to whether this acquits Maritain of the charge of relativism. He argues that the new Christendom, while incarnating the same analogical principles, should be regarded 'as belonging to an *essentially* (specifically) distinct type from that of the medieval world'.[47] But, as one critic enquires, although it is possible for

---

[44] *IH* 133–5.

[45] *IH* 134, emphasis original.

[46] These considerations might form part of the basis of a reply by Maritain to the possible criticism (connected to one made below) that he provides merely a rhetoric for the new Christendom, but no analysis of the social causality which would actualize his ideal. The criticism is nevertheless powerful, and his discussion of historical constellations and their underlying ontology would clearly require considerable development to allay doubts.

[47] *IH* 133, emphasis original.

there to be differences between the objects to which a concept applies, how is it possible for a concept to have *'essentially* different applications without undergoing *essential* alteration'?[48]

Maritain claims, in response, to avoid relativism through his analogical application of the immutable principles that govern the relations of Church and State. He does not say explicitly to what kind of analogy he is referring, beyond presenting it as a middle way between univocity and equivocation.[49] Of the two principal kinds of analogy traditional in philosophical theology, that of attribution and that of proper proportionality, the absence in Maritain's exposition of any prime analogate (such as medieval Christendom), to which other historical periods would be secondary, suggests that it is not the former. Presumably, therefore, it is the analogy of proper proportionality: that is, as certain principles applied under past historical conditions, so certain others obtain now. But such analogies require control: there must be specifiable features common to the relations within each pair of terms of the analogy in virtue of which the analogy holds. That is, each pair (empirical conditions: governing principles) must instantiate a universally specifiable relation, such that there is a universally applicable principle which may generate different prescriptions according to empirical circumstances.

Now such a requirement is satisfied by the double standard. For the prescriptions 'intolerance when Catholics are in a majority' and 'tolerance of Catholics when they are in a minority' are derivable from the universal principle that error has no rights together with secondary claims about the truth of Catholicism and the relevance of majorities. The question is whether Maritain can find a similar fundamental principle which will generate the two prescriptions (a) that the double standard should be adopted at times when political unity requires religious unity and it is generally accepted that force may be used in the service of God and (b) that there should be religious freedom at times when political unity is compatible with religious pluralism and the ideal of religious freedom is prevalent.

Maritain hints at two candidates (or perhaps a joint candidate)— namely, the common good and that which helps the Church's mission—when he refers to 'the ruin of the peace of the commun-

---

[48] Jules Meinvielle, *De Lammenais à Maritain* (Paris: La Cité Catholique, 1956), 79 (emphasis original; my translation).

[49] Cf. e.g. *IH* 132.

ity and the hardening or the weakening of consciences' as greater evils than religious pluralism.[50] But it is not clear that either of these is adequate. As they stand, neither is sufficiently specific. The latter is certainly a necessary condition, but can scarcely be criterial (that is, necessary and sufficient) without incurring the charge of 'Machiavellianism',[51] the ascription of rights for such periods as it conveniences the Church. The former requires filling out: while confronting new situations will require the political authority's judgement, the common good itself must be understood as a network of moral claims which are in principle universally specifiable, and it is amongst these that the principle must be found. Yet it is not at all clear what moral claim, if any, would generate the two prescriptions required.

If no principle can be found whereby to ground Maritain's acceptance of the double standard for the Middle Ages and of religious freedom for the new Christendom, it follows that Maritain is a historical relativist, despite his disclaimers. But he has two further lines of defence.

He appeals, first, to Albert the Great and Thomas Aquinas. They justified their contemporary practice against the patristic Church's refusal to use force through the notion of the diversity of states or ages of the Church. 'That in yet another age', Maritain claims, 'it will again be appropriate to make no use of [force for religious ends] is explicable in the same way'.[52] But neither of these authorities supports his claim. Aquinas, addressing the question 'whether it was the same church in the time of the apostles as it is now'[53] accepts Augustine's assertion against the Donatists of the different ages of the church', and says that 'there is a different *status* of the church between now and then, but not a different church'.[54] Again, Albert comments that Christ responded *Satis est* to the eager disciples offering the two swords on the grounds that 'although in the primitive church, when iniquity and unbelief were prevalent, there was no use for that sword, yet, as we have said, Christ wanted this help to be in the Church, knowing that the

---

[50] *FMW* 65. For the common good, cf. *MS* 184.
[51] Pietro Pavan, 'Declaration on Religious Freedom', in Herbert Vorgimler (ed.), *Commentary on the Documents of Vatican II* (5 vols., London: Burns and Oates; New York: Herder and Herder, 1967–9), iv. 51.
[52] *IH* 172.
[53] *Quaestiones Quodlibetales XII*, q. 13, ed. R. Spiazzi (Turin: Marietti, [9]1956).
[54] Ibid., ad 2.

Church once it had spread could not govern without the material sword'.[55] But both of these can be interpreted as versions of the double standard: Aquinas and Albert are earlier double-standard theorists, not believers in historical constellations.[56]

Maritain might wish to reply, second, that the approach just outlined is 'abstract' and insufficiently 'existentialist'. The brief answer to this is that it is one thing to take full account of particular historical circumstances before making a moral judgement, another to let those circumstances govern the content of that moral judgement. History is a morally relevant feature in certain respects: as Maritain himself grants, there is a historical change between the Age of the Old Law and that of the New Law.[57] But there are no morally relevant ages within the era of the Church. An existential grasp of circumstances is possible without succumbing to an historical relativism.

Here the Vatican II Declaration on Religious Freedom, *Dignitatis Humanae Personae*, may be compared.[58] In respect at least of its avoidance of historical relativism and its acceptance that the Church may need to repent over past complaisance in unevangelical behaviour, the Declaration is much more satisfactory. Explicitly intending 'to develop the doctrine of recent Popes' (Article 1), it declares right from the title its rejection of any form of the double standard, and accepts that in the past life of the people of God 'there have at times appeared ways of acting which were less in accord with the spirit of the gospel and even opposed to it' (Article 12). The Church fully disavows all use of coercion: religious freedom is not recommended as a concession to circumstances, but is argued for in its own right. Its central claim, that the right to religious freedom belongs to the inalienable dignity of the

---

[55] *In Evangelium Lucae*, 22. 35–8.

[56] A text of Aquinas which might be interpreted to suit Maritain's end reads: 'the just and the good . . . are formally and everywhere the same, because the principles of right in natural reason do not change . . . . Taken in the material sense, they are not the same everywhere and for all men, and this is so by reason of the mutability of man's nature and the diverse conditions in which men and things find themselves in different environments and times' (*De Malo*, q. 2, art. 4 ad 13, in *Quaestiones Disputatae*, ed. P. Bazzi *et al.* (2 vols., Turin: Marietti, [10]1965); quoted in John Mahoney, SJ, *The Making of Moral Theology: A Study of the Roman Catholic Tradition* (Oxford: Clarendon Press, 1987), 314).

[57] *PH* 65–7.

[58] Second Vatican Council, *Dignitatis Humanae Personae*, in Walter M. Abbott, SJ, (ed.), *The Documents of Vatican II* (London: Geoffrey Chapman, 1965), 675–96.

human person (Article 2), is regarded as applying without historical qualification. Not that the right is structurally unqualified:
there are regulatory norms which qualify this, as all other rights.
Morally, the norm is the 'principle of personal and social responsibility' (Article 7); juridically, limits are provided by the concept of
public order, which arises out of the need for justice and the
protection of rights, public peace, and the safeguarding of public
morality. Whether these limits were operative in the Middle Ages,
the Declaration does not venture to pronounce upon.[59] At all
events, although the Declaration is not without difficulties,[60] the
Council's route through development of doctrine (however that is
to be interpreted) is happier than Maritain's historical relativism.

Yet this raises the question: if the criticism of Maritain outlined
above is valid, why should he devote himself to such an elaborate
philosophy of history, with its stress on the *diversitas temporum*?
Why should he raise the suspicion of historicism, which he himself
condemns as 'epistemological time-worship' and 'chronolatry',[61] if
it is open to him to offer a non-relativist defence of religious
freedom in the manner of the Vatican Council's? Perhaps, the
thought runs, Maritain, writing before the Council, has worked up
the complex doctrine of analogy between historical periods just so
as to avoid the charge of developing doctrine: perhaps he was
seeking a means of rendering his temperamental liberalism compatible with his respect for the Magisterium.

In fact, whatever Maritain's motivations, the structure of his
thought shows greater complexity in his position than we have seen
so far. Two sections of the late work, *On the Philosophy of History*
(1959) throw some light, where he discusses the laws of 'the
passage from 'sacral' to 'secular' or 'lay' civilizations' and of 'the
political and social coming of age of the people'.[62] In the former
case, the distinction between sacral and secular civilizations is of
universal import, though the full autonomy of the temporal only
came to its proper historical significance through the Christian
distinction between the realm of Caesar and the realm of God. In
the latter case, which refers to the progressive movement from

---

[59] Enda McDonagh, 'Religious Freedom and the State', in *The Declaration of Religious Freedom of Vatican Council II* (London: Darton, Longman and Todd, 1967), 76–99, seems to think that they were.

[60] For which see e.g. *Sacramentum Mundi*, v. 295–8.

[61] *Peasant of the Garonne*, 12–14.

[62] *PH* 87–91.

subjection to democratic self-government, the Gospel leaven was again crucial; though such autonomy also responded to the call of natural law—'such a spontaneous universal spreading of the democratic process is an obvious sign of its basically natural character.'[63]

These two laws of historical change are 'typological formulas or vectorial laws'; that is, they 'manifest' particular yet typical historical developments.[64] But what sort of claim do they make? They are not merely historical generalizations about the secularizing tendency towards separation of Church and State and about the geographical spreading of democracy. They also appear to encapsulate the moral claims that a secular temporal order is normatively superior to a sacral order and that autonomy is in itself a good. Maritain's analogical treatment of the concrete historical ideals, it seems, masks an evolutionary periodization of history.

Further, the two laws suggest that it is no accident that the empirical and moral claims coincide: history and the improvement in the existential moral order run together because both are outworkings of a fundamentally natural law. This coalescence of historical and moral change may be compared with his reason for denying a conflict between the claims of ethics and of temporal success.[65] There is no need to fear such a conflict, he claims, because underlying natural forces ensure that the way of peace is more potent than the way of war: 'the Christian has a natural love of Being and a natural desire to co-operate with the push of creative forces at the heart of history.'[66]

The new Christendom turns out to be not just another analogical realization of the immutable principles: it is the order towards which history itself is tending, at least for the moment.[67] This is not to say that Maritain believes that human behaviour is improving: rather, history is moving towards a better moral framework within which human beings act.[68] Nor does it imply that history is determined in all its particulars: although history is

[63] *PH* 91. The Gospel leaven as the inspiration of democracy is a principal theme of *Christianity and Democracy*.

[64] *PH* xi.   [65] *FMW* 164–7.   [66] *FMW* 165.

[67] He allowed, at least earlier on (*IH* 204), for 'the hypothesis of an eventual cycle of culture in which it [sc., a consecrated Christian conception] will once again prevail, under conditions and with characteristics which we cannot foresee'.

[68] *PH* 83. His idea that Christianity can purify, in order to save, 'the truths towards which the modern age is striving in the cultural order' (*IH* 201) may refer to the same historical movement.

propelled by 'the immense dynamic mass of the past', it is wrong to deny with Marx that there is a 'sphere of indeterminateness' which allows for freedom.[69] Thus the new Christendom may also be a plausible end of Christian action.

Why should Maritain believe that history is tending towards a more natural order? In the end, he seems to have mapped intrinsically ahistorical natural law claims (for example, that self-determination is better than subjection) onto history, such that a law can be posited depicting the movement from darkness to light. Now there is no reason to deny that human knowledge of natural law grows (or better, is susceptible of growth), or that social organization has grown in complexity. But it is illegitimate to deduce—or at least, no persuasive argument has been produced to show—that the future can be bound in the manner that his vectorial laws suggest. That freedom is better than slavery tells us nothing about the future of the human race.

Maritain, it appears, is not only a historical relativist but also a historicist: such disclaimers of these positions as he makes should in view of this be rejected.[70] Does it follow that critics who reject these positions have nothing to learn from this aspect of Maritain's thought? Should they jettison without remainder all his talk of the intelligible structures of history and the historicism which informs it? Not necessarily, as may be seen from the fact that Maritain does not treat the defence of religious freedom as an abstract topos. The thrust of his thought is not towards a revision of Catholic teaching about heretics, or about Church and State, or indeed about any number of isolated issues, but towards the realization of a whole civilization. It is this ideal that animates and integrates his thought and action, and which leads him to conceptualize history in terms of discrete periods rather than a continuous flow. For Maritain, only if the building of a civilization forms the end of action, can there be an ideal sufficiently noble for a heroic humanism. Whatever the value of his specific proposals for this grander vision, it is this sense of the situatedness of human action and of

[69] *PH* 123–4.
[70] Maritain could escape by arguing for historical progress in moral conduct, or for a development ('organic growth') in natural law itself. The former he will not commit himself to (*PH* 83); the latter he never explicitly accepts. Whether or not his thought leads in this direction, considerable polemical difficulties would have arisen for him from consigning the ideals of medieval Catholic Christendom to the childhood of the human race.

the complexity of its practical outworking, of the civilizational context of moral issues, which finally abides.

In a memorable passage Maritain lamented:

Moralists are unhappy people. When they insist on the immutability of moral principles, they are reproached for imposing unlivable requirements on us. When they explain the way in which those immutable principles are to be put into force, taking into account the diversity of concrete situations, they are reproached for making morality relative. In both cases, however, they are only upholding the claims of reason to direct life.[71]

No doubt there was an element of irony here. Nevertheless, although he recognizes the falsity of the opposition, so that there can be immutable principles applied to particular situations without improper compromise, he does not succeed in avoiding returning to the dilemma and impaling himself on the latter (relativist) horn. Yet Maritain's better self would have agreed that with a correct doctrine of the Holy Spirit, an acceptance of the role of repentance in moral learning, and a proper understanding of the application of rules to cases, it is possible to construct a model in which reason can be seen to direct life without making impossible demands or making morality relative.

Such an approach would allow us to embrace the principle of religious freedom whole-heartedly, and not as a mere concession to circumstances. Of course, it may be that it is possible to justify placing some limits on the free exercise of religion, and it may be that the political conditions and cultural psychology of the Middle Ages constituted an occasion for this. But it is quite another to say that the principle of religious freedom simply did not apply then— which Maritain's historical periodization implies, and which rightly gives rise to charges of relativism against him.

Nevertheless, despite all his unsatisfactoriness on these issues, Maritain's evaluations of the model of medieval Christendom as appropriate for its time, and of the new Christendom as both appropriate for his time and an advance on medieval Christendom, are an effort to articulate two important and seemingly conflicting intuitions: on the one hand, that political ordering and legitimate political authority can take different forms in different societies, and on the other, that some legitimate forms of polity may be

[71] MS 74.

morally preferable to others. Maritain's use of historical constellations and vectorial laws attempted to do justice to both of these. If
his solution is unacceptable, we will need to provide an account
that is better. This I attempt to do in section 4.

3 A COMMITTED BUT PLURALIST POLITICAL SOCIETY

So far, we have looked at Maritain's vision of the new Christendom and, in the course of discussing his philosophy of history, at
his defence of religious freedom. The new Christendom was, it will
be recalled, the general background against which we proposed to
consider Maritain's reflections on liberalism and his possible
contribution to the issues between liberals and communitarians.
It is to these that we now turn.

His account of natural human sociality but political neutrality,
his proposals for state commitment but juridical pluralism, and his
attack on liberalism and instrumentalist accounts of politics,
together with his defence of rights in the name of democracy
draw us to the heart of Maritain's political thought. Eschewing the
term 'neutrality' because of the vitally Christian nature of his
projected lay state, he yet offers a pluralist society which also
admits the importance of human socialization and cultural traditions. There are difficulties with such a programme, I shall argue,
though in the next section I will discuss one possible resolution of
them.

(a) The rejection of liberalism

In an appendix, entitled 'On Liberalism', to *The Things That Are
Not Caesar's* (1927),[72] Maritain provided what were to be his
fullest explicit reflections on liberalism. While admittedly it is an
early work, indeed his earliest specifically political work, and
portrays some of his 'antimodernist' polemics and the conservatism that had originally educed his sympathies towards the Action
Française, much of the substance of his criticism of liberalism
made here was to endure throughout his life.

Liberalism he defined in accordance with Leo XIII's encyclical
Libertas, praestantissimum, as 'the application to morals and politics

---

[72] *Things*, 135–51.

of the claim to absolute independence which is the distinguishing characteristic in philosophy of rationalism and naturalism', and is therefore 'the refusal in practice to admit any control proceeding from anything other than ourselves'.[73] Though there are degrees of liberalism, every form of it tends to its perfect type in which all authority, natural or supernatural, is repudiated. It is centrally a teaching about freedom, and Maritain faults this doctrine of independence of the will from every external rule: 'Parity of truth and falsehood, of justice and injustice, of good and evil, is the metaphysical secret to which liberalism obscurely attunes the human soul.'[74] His understanding of freedom and the liberal misconception of it is expounded in the important essay 'A Philosophy of Freedom' (1935).[75] Here he distinguishes 'free will' from the 'freedom of autonomy'. The former a human being possesses as a person, which concept Maritain appears to understand with Boethius as the *individualis substantia rationalis naturae*: this 'initial freedom' is a metaphysical given that is inherited with a rational nature. But it requires development into the latter, 'terminal freedom',[76] and it is our duty to become in the psychological and moral orders what we are metaphysically: that is, 'by our own effort to make ourselves *persons* having dominion over our own acts and being to ourselves a rounded and a whole existence'.[77] Freedom of choice is teleologically ordered beyond itself to the freedom of autonomy.

This has implications in two significant areas. In 'the order of the spiritual life' two mistakes are to be avoided: the error, on the one hand, of assuming that the freedom of autonomy is a natural endowment, with a consequent self-divinization;[78] and, on the other, of making free will an end in itself, so that 'man, condemned to recurrent acts of choice without ever being able to bind himself, is launched into a dialectic of freedom which destroys freedom'.[79] Properly, the freedom of autonomy is realized perfectly only in the beatific vision, at which time freedom of choice will become redundant, since that object will have been gained to the choosing of which free will was itself ordered.[80]

In the order of social life, there are parallel errors. One is to base

---

[73] Ibid. 138.   [74] Ibid. 139.
[75] *FMW* 3–73. Cf. also 'Conquest of Freedom'. [76] *FMW* 42.
[77] *FMW* 30.   [78] *FMW* 33.
[79] *FMW* 31.   [80] *FMW* 34–6.

social life on the freedom of autonomy, which is reinterpreted 'as a type of transitive action, expressing itself in production and control . . . in material accomplishment, in the realization of power':[81] thus Hegelianism, Marxism, and fascism. The other is the liberal, individualist error. This takes freedom of choice as an end in itself: society functions to preserve this in such a way that all possible acts of free choice may be available and that people may appear 'like so many little gods', with no other restriction on their freedom save that they are not to hinder a similar freedom on the part of their neighbour.[82] But such an ideal in practice is hypocritical (since this freedom is available only to a few), and leads to an anarchy which both prevents effective realization of autonomy and requires compensation by a large, enslaving bureaucratic apparatus.

His identification of the liberal error which equates freedom with the initial freedom of choice and his sense that personhood is an object of moral striving as well as a given metaphysical status make clear Maritain's rejection of Enlightenment liberal conceptions of agency. But the constitutive role of society in the realization of human potential implies further for him the denial of three typically liberal notions: the ideals of an instrumental and material understanding of the common good, of uniting through common consent to a philosophical minimum, and of a neutral (that is, 'laicist') state. We shall look at each in turn.

People seek society, Maritain contends, because of the nature of human perfection and because of sheer physical need. As 'persons', they require communion since human beings naturally 'overflow into social communications in response to the law of superabundance inscribed in the depths of being, life, intelligence and love'.[83] As 'individuals' they need material sustenance. This distinction between individuality and personality is identified with that between matter and spirit. The ontological grounding of individuality is in matter, which of itself is lacking in the determination of form and tends internally to fragmentation and externally to the selfish exclusion of others. Personality is metaphysically rooted in the spirit, being 'the subsistence of the spiritual soul communicated to the human composite';[84] it is the form which endows the individual with independent existence and the possession of interiority, and

---

[81] *FMW* 41. [82] *FMW* 40. [83] *PCG* 34. [84] *PCG* 29.

which enables unification internally and relations with others through knowledge and love externally. This distinction between personality and individuality should not be mistaken for a Cartesian dualism of unextended mind and extended body, however: the two are co-principles of the one reality of the human being, just as chemical composition and aesthetic value are two aspects of the one reality of a painting.[85]

Because people desire society to achieve their ends in both these dimensions, the common good of society cannot be construed as the material goods or sum of material goods of the individuals that compose it. That idea 'would dissolve society as such to the advantage of its parts, and would amount to a frankly anarchistic conception, or to the old disguised anarchistic conception of individualistic materialism in which the whole function of the city is to safeguard the liberty of each'.[86] Nor, however, is the common good analogous to the public good of a hive in which individual bees are sustained merely for the sake of the whole. Since it is the common good of *persons*, it is redistributed back to each and is common to both whole and parts. Intrinsic to it, therefore, is respect for the rights of persons and families. Further, this correlation of the common good with the good of persons is the source of its principal value: namely, 'the highest access, compatible with the good of the whole, of the persons to their life of person and liberty of expansion, as well as to the communications of generosity consequent upon such expansion'.[87] But achievement of such a goal is inconsistent with an understanding of society in which a moral component is optional: the formation of society around justice rather than force is what distinguishes civil society from a gang of robbers. The common good is an ethical good, by which Maritain means both that it may be furthered only by ethical means and that it is a good in itself; it is not just a function of individual utilities, but is constituted by the achievement by each of 'real independence from the servitudes of nature'.[88]

---

[85] *PCG* 23–33.   [86] *PCG* 36.   [87] *PCG* 37.

[88] *PCG* 38–9. For John Finnis the common good is 'fundamentally the good of individuals' (*NLNR*, 168), and could in principle be wholly specified in terms of individual human rights, though such a specification would not be useful for other (partly linguistic) reasons. This position implies that there is no separable entity which is the subject of the common good beyond the individuals whose common good it is. Maritain would have rejected this on the grounds that '6 is not the same as

It follows that the common good is a moral as well as a material good, and it is one of the errors of liberalism to deny this.[89] Governments are obliged to secure the welfare of the soul, as well as external advantages and benefits:

the social polity is essentially directed, by reason of its own temporal end, towards such a development of social conditions as will lead the generality to a level of material, moral and intellectual life in accord with the good and peace of all, such as will positively assist each person in the progressive conquest of the fullness of personal life and spiritual liberty.[90]

Although political authorities may only apply external sanctions for external misdeeds and are not competent to ensure the eternal well-being of citizens, the law must yet be understood as the 'pedagogue' of liberty, educating citizens into freedom with a moral authority which has all but disappeared under liberalism.[91]

Human beings require society for the sake of their moral as well as their material needs, then, and this generates a richer notion of the common good than liberalism can provide. Yet, since Maritain's ideal is of a pluralist society, the issue arises of what the basis of social unity is and whether liberals are right to found this in a common subscription to a philosophical minimum. The source of medieval unity lay, he asserts, at the supra-temporal level, in a common Christian faith. In the modern period, however, philosophers (he mentions Descartes, Leibniz, Hegel, and Comte) attempted to usurp the function of religion by replacing faith by reason as the supra-temporal principle of unity. Such efforts have met with singular lack of success, which leads Maritain to the conclusion that 'nothing is more vain than to seek to unite men by a philosophic minimum'.

And, he continues, 'this quest of a common denominator in contrasting convictions can develop nothing but intellectual cowardice and mediocrity, a weakening of minds and a betrayal of the

3 + 3' (*PCG* 37). The difference between them lies in their philosophical grounding: Finnis establishes his legal theory on the basis of individual practical reason, whereas Maritain looks to Aristotelian metaphysics. Although the practical outworking of each of these positions (*ceteris paribus*) does not affect the logic of the relation of individual and common good for either, it may be that in practice the one view may lead to the subordination of the individual, and the other to the loss of public goods.

[89] *Things*, 139–42.
[90] *IH* 128. Cf. *IH* 131, *MS* 54–5.
[91] *IH* 176. The discussion in the preceding paragraphs might be profitably compared with L. T. Hobhouse's thought on similar matters; see Ch. 2 above.

rights of truth'.[92] Instead of an agreed doctrinal minimum, the practical common task of effecting the common good should be the basis for common action.[93] Instead of subscription to a common creed, whether of faith or reason, there must be a 'simple unity of friendship'.[94]

Maritain recognizes that this fraternal love will be insufficient, however. He notes the importance of 'a biological community of interests and passions, a social animality so to speak'.[95] More importantly, he indicates that this civic friendship itself presumes an ethical specification,[96] and that while force may be necessary for social order, it will be ineffective without religion.[97] For a secularly Christian political community, the ethic that will inform social unity will be Christian. This introduces the third liberal ideal which Maritain wishes to criticize.

The common good is directed towards obtaining for its citizens the greatest liberty of autonomy. Yet such autonomy, which in its purest form is perfect sanctity in the vision of God, is not achieved in earthly life. Because the highest goal of the person is a destiny beyond time, the temporal common good of the civil society must be indirectly subordinated to those ends which it is incompetent to achieve. Indeed, unless it is so subordinated, not as a pure means but 'infravalently', it fails to fulfil its own nature. The common good is destroyed once it claims to include within itself the higher ends of the human person.[98]

This is incompatible with the liberal ideal of neutrality or laicism, according to which no religion should have any public role. The temporal order is to be confessedly religious, and specifically Christian: every state, he proclaims, 'will be obliged to make a choice for or against the Gospel'.[99] The political order 'can and should also, while all the time remaining in its own order, bear in its proper political specification an impregnation of

---

[92] *IH* 167.
[93] *IH* 200. The criticisms given here, taken from *IH*, appear to confront not only those philosophers who sought common acceptance of 'substantial' truths of reason, but also those who have pursued social unity through the joint acceptance of 'formal' rules of co-operation. This does not conflict with the democratic charter presented below, which requires 'a fundamental agreement between minds and wills on the bases of life in common' (*MS* 109), since Maritain assumes there the background of an ethically and religiously rooted civic friendship.
[94] *IH* 168.   [95] *IH* 198.   [96] *IH* 168.
[97] *Things*, 140.   [98] *PCG* 43–6.   [99] *MS* 159.

Christianity. A Christian city or commonwealth is a temporal city intrinsically vivified and impregnated with Christianity.'[100]

(b) The democratic charter

It is questionable whether Maritain is right in thinking that the need of the commonwealth to be subordinated to the higher ends of the person implies that the temporal order must be specifically Christian; we return to this problem later. But there is much here that is important and worth defending. His distinction between initial and terminal freedom, emphasizing that freedom is a virtue to be developed and not simply a status that can be assumed, is preferable to those conceptions of freedom that see it as perfected in the unrestricted maximization of choice. Likewise, the common good should not be reduced to a function of the selfish desires of individuals; it is a good of persons, and must include those goods which are intrinsically social in nature. In opposing the notions of freedom as initial freedom, and thence of the common good as constituted materially and not morally, of social unity as attainable through a joint consent to a philosophical minimum, and of the political order as wholly separated from religious commitment, Maritain therefore appears far removed from many typically liberal political conceptions. Yet, as we saw earlier, he is committed to a form of pluralism. He wants a body politic Christianly inspired, yet one which allows people of diverse understandings of the good to co-operate in the common task. It is this blend of commitment and pluralism that is at once the strength in his criticism of liberalism and the source of potentially serious difficulties.

The issues are focused in the conception, shadowed in *The Rights of Man* and developed in *Man and the State*, of the democratic charter. It is possible, he holds, to obtain public agreement to a charter which would detail personal and social rights of citizens, without obtaining similar agreement regarding the rational justification of those rights. A common creed of this kind, enabling practical co-operation between those of differing theoretical positions, was lacking in nineteenth-century bourgeois liberalism. Because the latter understood democracy as an arena for the clash of ideas, including those prejudicial to the continuance of the democratic arena, it was unable to resist disintegration

[100] *IH* 161 n. 1.

under the force of totalitarian propaganda. Instead, what is needed is a substantial but non-religious civic faith, constituted by the practical rather than the philosophical or dogmatic agreement of citizens. The medieval creed of religion and the modern creed of reason each required the imposition of beliefs which are prejudicial to genuine democracy: common action cannot now be based on agreed religious or philosophical premisses, only on agreed practical conclusions.

In terms of its content, the charter would contain basic items of social and political morality: personal, political, and civil rights; obligations of persons and groups towards the body politic and the State, and vice versa; statements of the ideals of equality, justice, fraternity, freedom, civic self-devotion, and the like; and so on.[101] Certain other conditions are necessary, in addition to jointly accepted practical principles. Maritain adds that citizens must 'similarly revere, perhaps for quite diverse reasons, truth and intelligence, human dignity, brotherly love, and the absolute value of moral good'.[102] And he asserts the right and the duty of education for democracy, since civic peace depends on acceptance of the terms of co-operation framed in the democratic charter. Each religious group must teach the truths of the democratic charter from within its own suppositions, and in order that it does not become reduced to a set of lifeless propositions, those who teach the charter 'must believe in it with their whole hearts, and stake on it their personal convictions, their consciences, and the depths of their moral life'.[103]

There are clear parallels between Maritain's account of the democratic charter and Rawls's account of political liberalism, each citizen or group of citizens justifying in the one case a list of constitutional rights, and in the other certain principles of justice which might include (by plausible extension) the constitutional specification of rights. Maritain's account of the plurality of justifications for the democratic charter, based on the principle that '[a] genuine democracy cannot impose on its citizens or demand from them, as a condition for their belonging to the city, any philosophic or any religious creed',[104] has a clear prima-facie resemblance to Rawls's notion of the overlapping consensus, based

---

[101] See *MS* 112–13 for a fuller (indicative, rather than technical) listing.
[102] *MS* 111.   [103] *MS* 121   [104] *MS* 110.

on the recognition that 'just as on questions of religious and moral doctrine, public agreement on the basic questions of philosophy cannot be obtained without the state's infringement of basic liberties'.[105] There are, however, disparallels. The principal difference may be discerned from the role which Maritain assigns to natural law in relation to the democratic charter. Natural law, of which he gives a broadly Thomist account, albeit with an idiosyncratic understanding of knowledge by connaturality,[106] serves both as the basis for the specification of constitutionally recognized human rights and as the properly Christian justification for those rights. Other creeds will justify those same rights from within their own positions. Rawls, by contrast, proceeds by abstracting from the question of the existence of natural law: the principles of justice are specified by derivation from the very terms on which citizens will co-operate, without any reference to an antecedent moral law, although Christians are welcome to provide a natural law justification for themselves of the ruling principles of justice.[107]

This comparison of the two opens up the intriguing possibility that Maritain's democratic charter supplies the basis for an answer to the kind of criticisms that Grant levelled at Rawls, which we discussed in the previous chapter. It was argued there that Rawls's political conception, because of its circular appeal to the traditions embedded in public culture, rationalizes rather than justifies the liberal democratic values of equality and liberty; and further that

---

[105] Rawls, 'Justice as Fairness', 230.

[106] *MS* 91–2: 'obscure, unsystematic, vital knowledge by connaturality or congeniality, in which the intellect, in order141
to bear judgement, consults and listens to the inner melody that the vibrating strings of abiding tendencies make present in the subject'. On Maritain's theory of natural law, see Paul Ramsey, *Nine Modern Moralists* (Englewood Cliffs, NJ: Prentice-Hall, 1962), 209–32; and also Germain G. Grisez, 'The First Principle of Practical Reason', in Anthony Kenny (ed.), *Aquinas: A Collection of Critical Essays* (London: Macmillan, 1969), 347–8 n. 11.

[107] The contrast between Maritain and Rawls here has some similarities with a contrast drawn by Basil Mitchell between a 'liberal society' and a 'pluralist society'. The former turns on an understanding of liberalism 'which bases itself on a conviction about the nature of man and of his destiny and which insists on the need of the individual for freedom to choose the way he shall live . . . a liberalism which has an explicit metaphysical context' (*Law, Morality and Religion in a Secular Society* (Oxford: Oxford University Press, 1967), 98). The latter idea is not developed very clearly, wobbling between scepticism (which 'denies that there is a truth about life') and an incommensurability thesis (which asserts 'that there is no rational way of achieving agreement' about the ends of life) (see his 'Introduction' to *Law and Justice*, 82/3 (Trinity/Michaelmas, 1984), 86–90).

his political liberalism, by failing to attend to the sociology of a political conception, does not adequately address problems regarding the stability of justice as fairness. By contrast, Maritain is guilty of no such circularity: at least inasmuch as he bases the democratic charter on a metaphysically grounded natural law, he gives as ontologically deep reasons for his conception as it is possible to give. Unlike Rawls, he is willing to base his political theory on an account of what people are, not on a principled avoidance of the question.

Moreover, whatever difficulties the notion may have, Maritain's appeal to natural law has advantages over Rawls's political conception in another area: namely, the role he expects it to play in the background culture. Rawls's absolute separation of political conception and comprehensive doctrines laid him open, I argued, to the possibility of the principles of justice being subverted by the influence of technology on the background culture, and one solution to this which was suggested was some bridging of the divide between public and non-public. Now natural law is one example of a way of addressing precisely this, since it is expected by Maritain to play the role of both public truth and comprehensive doctrine. Furthermore, he also provides a means by which the assertion of natural law can be causally effective within the background culture. In his discussion of the Church, Maritain describes a body which, through its inspirational presence, is a leaven in society, the most important agent in awakening perceptions of natural law. By contrast, Rawls's separation of public and non-public, and his refusal to prescribe for the latter, leaves him with no equivalent, and renders him vulnerable to the difficulties Grant indicated.

The significance of Maritain's doctrine of natural law goes beyond the existence of an institution which seeks to educate people into awareness of it. It also provides for him a support for the hope that people will agree to the public terms of co-operation, a support that is different in kind from that of Rawls. To see this, we need to consider briefly the nature of the ontological grounding of practical agreement for which he argues. The theme is developed at its deepest level in his account of the morality of 'pseudo-atheists' in his article 'The Immanent Dialectic of the First Act of Freedom'.[108] By the 'first act of

---

[108] In *Range of Reason*, 64–85.

freedom' he means the first childhood action performed from the moral motive of pursuing good or avoiding evil rather than from desire of praise, fear of blame, or other heteronomous motives. Logical analysis of such an act shows, first, awareness of the formal distinction between good and evil; second, the existence of a law of human acts; and third, the ordainment in lived act, though not in signified act, towards God as the ultimate good. Thus, in such an act the intellect has an actual but non-conceptual knowledge of God, knowing the Separate Good through a practical and non-speculative direction of the will to its natural end. While grace is necessary for this act to be good, and supernatural faith for it to be salvific, the agent need be conscious of neither of these. Now such an act is not confined to childhood, and is found whenever an adult by means of a decisive act of free will changes the essential direction of his or her moral life.[109] Further, it may be found whatever a person's religious background: indeed, it is found amongst those who are consciously atheists, many of whom have denied the existence of an imaginary entity that is supposedly either immoral or logically impossible, but not the God who is the final object of the reason and terminus of the will. These pseudo-atheists may consciously disagree with Christians about ultimate matters, but they have chosen the moral good, and have therewith an unconscious knowledge of God.

The implications of this for agreement about issues of morality, despite disagreement on speculative matters, are drawn out obliquely in *Man and the State*. Here Maritain asserts that there is 'a sort of unwritten law, at the point of practical convergence of extremely different theoretical ideologies and spiritual traditions'.[110] This is due to a complex 'geology of the conscience' in which common but pre-conscious ethical knowledge is refracted into consciousness through differing rational frameworks,[111] though it is particularly through the Gospel leaven that these apperceptions have been awakened.[112] The undoubted fact of moral disagreement despite the ontological universality of natural law can be ascribed either to different determinations of more basic principles or to the presence of perverted inclinations.[113]

The ontological grounds for agreement regarding practical

---

[109] Ibid. 83.   [110] *MS* 78.   [111] *MS* 80.
[112] *MS* 111.   [113] *MS* 93.

principles are an important feature of the argument for common subscription to the democratic charter. They provide a basis for agreement which runs at a different level from that given by Rawls. Where Rawls provides a number of general (if inadequate) sociological considerations, which appeal to the moral psychology that citizens in a well-ordered society would have or to the educative value of the public acceptance of justice as fairness, Maritain gives a metaphysical theory rooted in an account of natural law.

This certainly avoids the charge of circularity that was levelled against Rawls in the previous chapter, and it gives reasons at a profound level as to why people might be expected to agree to the democratic charter. Nevertheless, it is arguable that Maritain's account is also incomplete, and that, like Rawls, he also needs to address the sociological and educational issues more carefully. After all, it is one thing to provide an ontological rendering of moral psychology which shows why in principle people may tend to assent to the requirements of natural law; it is another to give a psychological-sociological account of the reasons why in practice they often do not assent to them. He refers to the different determinations of more basic principles and the presence of perverted inclinations as explanations for moral disagreement; but there are also reasons why the determinations and distorted inclinations take the form they do, and these are worthy of explanation in their own right. Maritain, one might say, establishes a metaphysics for the relevant social theory, but not the social theory itself.

(c) Dissenters from natural law

Of course, Rawls refused to ground his theory in natural law or anything like it because he wished to avoid basing it on controversial philosophical and moral grounds. And this raises a question for Maritain about the potential intolerance of his position. How can he expect everybody in a modern Western society to agree to the content of a democratic charter based on natural law?

Maritain is aware of some of the difficulties raised by the democratic charter in specifying and adjudicating rights. For example, in his introduction to a UNESCO volume on human rights he alludes to the need for a 'scale of values' to adjudicate clashes between rights, and senses that differences will arise because of the different theoretical justifications of the charter.[114] Elsewhere he comments briefly on how agreement on paper about the list of rights will lead to discord in practice because of the different hierarchies of values related to liberal–individualist, communist, and personalist understandings of the basis of human dignity. But the discussion does not address the problem of the means for resolving these disputes.[115] Nor does he find it unproblematic to say about nations such as France and the United States that 'practically everybody would be ready to endorse all the tenets of such a charter', and indeed in general that 'we have good reason to hope that in all the nations of the world the people—I say the people, whatever the case of their governments may be—would be likely to offer the same endorsement'.[116]

There are hints, however, contained in a discussion of matters of conscience, of the guidance Maritain would offer for legislation concerning those groups or communities who reject natural law morality within a vitally Christian lay state. The general principle is that

the legislation of the Christian society in question could and should never *endorse* or *approve* any way of conduct contrary to Natural Law. But . . . this legislation could and should *permit* or *give allowance to* certain ways of conduct which depart in some measure from Natural Law, if the prohibition by civil law of these ways of conduct were to impair the common good.[117]

The common good, he continues, could be damaged either if communities within the nation whose loyalty to the nation was essential to the common good were constrained from acting on their moral beliefs, even if they deviated from Christian morality, or if many of the citizens were of insufficient moral capacity to follow particular natural law precepts. Such derogations would be allowed not because of some blanket right to pursue the moral career of a group's choosing, but because legal permission for deviant moral codes is a lesser evil for the sake of the common good. Since the purpose of law is to lead to virtue, the adaptations

---

[114] 'Introduction' to UNESCO, *Human Rights*, 15–17.

[115] *MS* 106–7.

[116] *MS* 113. His feelings are no doubt understandable when it is remembered that he was writing at a time when organizations such as the Committee to Frame a World Constitution were being spawned.

[117] *MS* 167–8.

of natural law to the moral traditions of a nation will be as few as possible, and can never be justified because of 'sheer relaxation of morality and decaying mores'.[118]

These derogations could, he suggests, be recognized constitutionally through the granting of charters to those communities or spiritual groups which the legislature in its political judgement recognized.[119] The charters would be adapted as compromises between the public morality and the communal traditions. Therefore, for Catholics the charter would converge towards Church teaching, while in the case of the colonizing of polygamous cultures (to cite Maritain's example) the ill effects of polygamous practices would be limited by the charter and every encouragement given in the direction of natural law requirements.[120] The relation between the individual charters and the overarching democratic charter is not made explicit, though it may be that 'federal' legislation would cover some areas and leave others to the discretion of the communities: thus it is suggested by one commentator that civil legislation would coincide with Church legislation on marriage, education, domestic responsibility for children, the freedom of succession, and so on, but permit divorce or artificial birth control for those religious groups which accepted them.[121]

Natural law must therefore always be the positive pole in the direction of legislation in the lay state of the new Christendom, and there would be degrees of variance from it. In this way, 'the commonwealth would be vitally Christian, and the various non-Christian spiritual groups included in it would enjoy a just liberty'.[122] Maritain appears to envisage as his focal case countries such as France or the United States, in which the dominant moral traditions are rooted in versions of Christianity and are prima facie close to natural law, and in which a few religious minorities would demand separate attention.

There are problems with this. It is intended as a means of avoiding legislation that would be prejudicial to the common good on the grounds of its being unacceptable to particular spiritual

---

[118] *MS* 171.

[119] *FMW* 65–6; *MS* 170.

[120] *FMW* 66 n. 1. For his comments on the approach in relation to the Jews, see his *Anti-Semitism* (London: Geoffrey Bles, 1939), 23–4.

[121] Joseph W. Evans, 'Jacques Maritain and the Problem of Pluralism in Political Life', *Review of Politics*, 22 (1960), 322–3.

[122] *IH* 161.

traditions. Yet it is not at all clear how this is practically sustainable in a plural society in which the interchange of people from different traditions would make the legal problems of enforcing different charters dauntingly complex, not to say morally dubious. To take one example, Paul Ramsey noted the existence in the late 1950s of Protestant clergymen in Spain who could not marry, despite their being allowed to in civil law, because they had been baptized as Roman Catholics.[123] Such an approach via derogations might be possible in the case of, say, native peoples living on geographically separated reserves (though even here significant problems arise). But for the mainstream public of those societies which bear allegiance to the principle of voluntary association and the freedom to change religious affiliation, a different approach to the question of intolerance must be found.

A connected question concerns those countries which are not Christian at all. The issue of whether Maritain's prescriptions apply to wholly non-Christian countries turns on his understanding of the relation of Christianity and natural law. Often, on the one hand, he appears to imply that a natural law commonwealth would *eo facto* be a Christian commonwealth. Thus, for a body politic to be Christianly inspired, it would be sufficient for the people to recognize the value and reasonableness of political conceptions that are in fact Christian, not necessarily to profess Christian faith.[124] And he talks of the democratic charter having arisen through the awakening by the Gospel of the ' "naturally Christian" potentialities of common secular consciousness'.[125] This suggests the characterization of the natural order as unconsciously Christian that was discussed above in relation to the category of 'pseudo-atheists'. On the other hand, it clearly helps if the commonwealth is explicitly Christian: a Christian democracy is a democracy 'fully aware of its own sources'.[126] While 'the political order has its own proper specification', it can and should 'bear in its proper political specification an impregnation of Christianity'.[127] That is, commonwealths are never more truly themselves than when explicitly Christian.

This ambivalence about the relationship of Christianity to natural law raises some issues. If 'Christian' means no more than 'ethical', as some passages suggest, then these problems are not so

[123] Ramsey, *Nine Modern Moralists*, 237.   [124] *MS* 109.
[125] *MS* 113.   [126] *MS* 177.   [127] *IH* 161 n. 1.

great—though it should be said that there are the questions both of how he will describe social orders that see themselves as explicitly Christian and not merely as 'ethical' and, conversely, of whether social orders that are not expressly Christian, but are pursuing the goals of justice and the like, should rightly be understood as (anonymously) Christian. On the other hand, if he is suggesting that the societies which best fulfil their nature are those which are explicitly Christian, he runs a serious danger of legitimating the self-righteousness and hypocrisy that the idea of a Christian society is liable to evoke.

(d) Conclusion: Maritain and the communitarians

We will return to these problems in the final section. By way of summing up the present section, we are now in a position to see how Maritain's political thought addresses the questions about socialization and neutrality that were raised at the beginning of the chapter in connection with the communitarian criticisms of liberalism.

Maritain's Thomism clearly allows him an understanding of agency that is communitarian rather than liberal: instead of a discrete self prior to its ends, metaphysically separable from society and with a given freedom which society functions to protect, Maritain's notion of personality takes it to be fulfilled in, and to that extent constituted by, social communication, its freedom a goal of psychological and moral pilgrimage as well as a metaphysical given.

This understanding of human beings as perfected in society implies the scotching of three characteristically liberal ideas: an instrumentalist conception of the common good, civic unity through shared acceptance of a philosophical minimum, and the laicist state. The rejection of these should not be assumed too quickly to be a move in a communitarian direction, however. Civic friendship, for example, as the basis of civic unity need only mean a willingness to co-operate, without a commitment to shared substantial values. Nevertheless, it is clear that existentially, with a proper Thomist denial of separately subsisting essences, political society will embody shared commitments that will reflect particular determinations of the democratic values of the new Christendom. The same idea is evident when he accepts that the public expression of the civic faith would employ the forms of the

Christian confession most appropriate to the people's particular religious traditions.[128]

Yet Maritain differs from at least the cruder forms of communitarianism through his acceptance of the moral imperative which he derives from the fact of pluralism: against the Romantic conception that anarchy is the only alternative to a substantial and shared conception of the good, he recognizes that in modern societies a form of social peace is enjoyed despite religious and philosophical disagreement.[129] This peace he wishes to be mediated institutionally through the democratic charter. I have suggested some reasons why Maritain thinks that practical agreement might be achievable despite different theoretical premises. But the charter, despite being justifiable to every religious group in terms of its own assumptions, is not straightforwardly neutral: it provides for concessions to the moral creeds of particular groups for the sake of the common good, so long as these are kept in tension with the demands of natural law. Maritain's vitally Christian lay state should be seen not as a neutral state, but as a natural law state with varieties of moral toleration.

4 MARITAIN IN AN AUGUSTINIAN FRAMEWORK

The discussion in the last two sections has left some important questions outstanding. At the end of section 2 I mentioned the problem of how Maritain could assert both that Christendom could be a morally appropriate political order for the Middle Ages and yet that a move towards the new Christendom could be construed as a moral advance. This is a specific instance of the more general issue of whether it is possible to claim both that different political orderings may be genuinely appropriate in different circumstances and yet that some forms of political society are morally preferable to others (or even that one form is supremely preferable, all things considered). And at the end of the previous section I raised some problems with natural law

---

[128] *MS* 172–3.
[129] For communitarianism and political romanticism, see Charles E. Larmore, *Patterns of Moral Complexity* (Cambridge: Cambridge University Press, 1987), 91–131.

charters in ideologically plural societies and with Maritain's account of the relationship of Christianity to natural law.

These problems can be addressed, I shall now argue, by placing Maritain's thought within an Augustinian framework. But to see what this involves, and how an Augustinian political theology might help, we first need an overview of Aquinas's and Augustine's views.

For Aquinas it is natural that humankind is an *animal sociale et politicum*.[130] Society is necessary because of those needs which individuals are unable to satisfy out of their own resources: it provides both 'those things without which life itself would be impossible' and what is necessary 'to achieve a plenitude of life [*ad vitae sufficientiam perfectam*]'.[131] But there could be no social existence unless somebody were set in authority for the sake of the common good:[132] there were inequalities between human beings even in the state of innocence,[133] and it would be wrong if those more knowledgeable and righteous did not exercise their gifts on behalf of the rest.[134] Such natural subjection should, however, be distinguished from slavery, which is a consequence of sin: in the relationship of slavery the master rules for his own benefit, whereas in the political relationship the king rules over a free people for the sake of the common good.[135] The function of the ruler is to secure the virtuous life which is the object of human community.[136] But since it is the final aim of social life to attain the supreme good of the enjoyment of God, and since this cannot be achieved by natural virtue, human government must be subordinate to divine rule.[137] Thus, although kings have the supreme power in temporal affairs, under the law of Christ kings must be subject to priests.[138] From their obligation to assist the virtue of their subjects, rulers must co-operate with the Church by their religious intolerance. Infidels and Jews may not be compelled to profess the faith, because belief is a matter of

---

[130] *De regno*, I. i. 4; in Aquinas, *Selected Political Writings*, ed. A. P. D'Entrèves (Oxford: Blackwell, 1948), 2–83. See Markus, *Saeculum*, 222 n. 3, for the development of Aquinas's terminology for human social nature.

[131] *Commentum in X libros ethicorum ad Nicomachum*, I. i; in *Selected Political Writings*, 188–93.

[132] *ST* I. 96. 4.   [133] *ST* I. 96. 3.

[134] *ST* I. 96. 4. Cf. *Summa contra gentiles*, III. 81; in *Selected Political Writings*, 98–101.

[135] *ST* I. 92. 1 ad 2.   [136] *De regno*, I. xiv. 106; xv. 117–18.

[137] Ibid., I. xiv. 107–8.   [138] Ibid., I. xiv. 108, 111.

the will;[139] their rites, however, are not to be tolerated, unless some benefit can be derived from toleration (the foreshadowing of the true faith in Jewish rituals, for example) or some greater evil averted.[140] Heretics and apostates should be constrained, by force if necessary, to acknowledge their baptismal promises, for their own sake and for the safety of others: their punishment is a just reward for their sin.[141]

Aquinas's political thought represents the working out of an Aristotelian understanding of political authority within a theological context. In its founding of the order of politics on nature, its belief that human government can assist towards virtue, and its acknowledgement that the achievement of that good requires the subordination of political authority to God, Aquinas's understanding of politics echoes wider themes in his theology and metaphysics: notably, the healing and supernatural elevation of nature by grace and the harmonious hierarchy of relations between higher and lower orders of being.

Augustine's different theological cast of thought engenders a different conception of politics, centring principally on the place his historical-eschatological scheme gives to providence. Although he initially toyed with the Neoplatonic notion of political authority as part of a cosmic hierarchy of levels, his developing reflections on history, sin, the Church, and justification issued in a radical reinterpretation of the classical treatment of the political order.[142] Before the Fall, he appears to have believed, there was no political subordination.[143] There is no clear evidence that political authority for Augustine was part of created nature: the principle that rational creatures, made in the image of God, should have dominion only over irrational creatures is naturally taken as excluding political direction (and slavery) from the created order, an inference

[139] *ST* II. ii. 10. 8. Cf. *De regimine Judaeorum*, in *Selected Political Writings*, 84–95, for Aquinas's attitude to the Jews.

[140] *ST* II. ii. 10. 11.

[141] *ST* II. ii. 10. 8, 11. 3.

[142] For Augustine's social thought see esp. Markus, *Saeculum*; see also Herbert A. Deane, *The Political and Social Ideas of St Augustine* (New York: Columbia University Press, 1963); Oliver O'Donovan, 'Augustine's City of God XIX and Western Political Thought', *Dionysius*, 11 (1987), 89–110; and Rowan Williams, 'Politics and the Soul: A Reading of the *City of God*', *Milltown Studies*, 19/20 (1987), 55–72.

[143] See in general Markus, '"De Civitate Dei", XIX. 14–15 and the Origins of Political Authority', in *Saeculum*, 197–210.

strongly supported by his observation that 'the first just men were established as shepherds of flocks, rather than as kings of men'.[144] Unlike the natural authority of parents over children and of husbands over wives, political authority, whose essence is coercion, is a divinely ordained remedy for the Fall. Since it was instituted to restrain sin, it should not be imagined to contribute positively to the final human good: rulers are not divine agents for helping towards salvation, though obedience to them is submission to the hidden will of God. Justice cannot be a defining feature of political society, inasmuch as the failure of earthly commonwealths to be oriented to the true end of human beings means that they will never be able to give human beings their due. Instead, the ends of a particular commonwealth are constituted by a combination of wills (*compositio voluntatum*) of the people agreeing together on the common object of their loves. The *saeculum* represents the temporal life of the two cities in their intertwined, and only eschatologically separated, reality.

R. A. Markus believes that the main lines of Augustine's thought 'point towards a political order to which we may not unreasonably apply the anachronistic epithet "pluralist", in that it is neutral in respect of ultimate beliefs and values'.[145] He further claims that this ' "secularization" of the realm of politics implies a pluralistic, religiously neutral civil community', and that 'Augustinian theology should at least undermine the opposition to an open, pluralist, secular society'.[146] Although he admits that Augustine did countenance and even encourage religious coercion, this bore no structural relation to the general tenor of his political thought; rather, it was part of a pastoral strategy of *disciplina*, aided by his non-libertarian understanding of freedom of choice and (in his earlier thought) by his prophetic interpretation of the Roman Empire.[147] His accept-

---

[144] *De civitate Dei*, XIX. 15; in *The City of God against the Pagans*, trans. G. H. McCracken *et al.* (London: Heinemann, 1957–82), vi. 186–7.

[145] Markus, *Saeculum*, 151.

[146] Ibid. 173.

[147] For coercion as a pastoral strategy, see e.g. *Retractationes*, II. 5. Augustine's attitude to coercion was peculiarly complex; see esp. Markus, *Saeculum*, 133–53, and Peter Brown, 'St Augustine's Attitude to Religious Coercion', *Journal of Roman Studies*, 54 (1964), 107–16 (repr. in *Religion and Society in the Age of Saint Augustine* (London: Faber and Faber, 1972), 260–78); but see also Brown, *Augustine of Hippo: A Biography* (London: Faber and Faber, 1967), 236–40, and W. H. C. Frend, *The Donatist Church: A Movement of Protest in Roman North Africa* (Oxford: Clarendon Press, 1952), 237–43.

ance of religious coercion does not compromise ascribing to Augustine the lineaments of a neutral 'state', so long as the use of that term
is seen as a reasonable extrapolation from the text and is not read
anachronistically into it.[148]

Now much of Maritain's thought, despite his professed
Thomism, bears a greater prima-facie resemblance to Markus's
Augustine than to Aquinas: not only in the connection of politics
with history and the structural place for religious freedom, but also
in respect of the naturalness of equality and the endorsement of
pluralism in civil society. Such a conception, I shall argue through
a closer analysis of Maritain's account of the committed but
pluralist civil society, seriously misprizes Maritain, although this
should not detract from the important differences between him
and Aquinas. Nevertheless, through the process of attending to the
differences between Maritain and Augustine, we turn out to be in a
position to suggest some improvements on Maritain's answer to
our central theological problematic concerning the neutral state
and the debate between communitarians and liberals, and to
address the problems raised by his account.

(a) Maritain and Augustine

There are a number of superficial resemblances between Maritain
and Augustine. For Augustine, the political order is founded
historically through providence; Maritain, as we saw above, also
injects a historical dimension into his political prescriptions.
Augustine finds human beings created equal, allowing natural
subordination only between male and female, parent and child;
Maritain has no place for natural subordination between citizens.
Augustine looks for no more agreement concerning commanding
and obeying than is found in a combination of wills concerning the
things that pertain to mortal life; Maritain unfolds his democratic
charter detailing the practical agreements reached by opposing
theoretical creeds. Indeed, the opinion which Markus accords to
Augustine, that people 'are more easily brought to agree in their
intermediate principles, *vera illa et media axiomata*, as Bacon says,
than in their first principles',[149] could as easily be ascribed to
Maritain. And the general picture presented by Markus of a

---

[148] Markus, *Saeculum*, 72. Markus's account is criticized below.
[149] Ibid. 101.

secular realm, pluralist and non-ultimate, describes Maritain's vitally Christian lay state with some accuracy.

Nevertheless, Maritain is much better understood within the Thomist tradition, despite his many differences from Aquinas. Although, as I argued, he is a historical relativist and a historicist, political order is still part of the natural order. History enters in for him because nature itself is historicized; whereas for Augustine the locus of history in political thought is to be found in the categorization of the realm of politics as a providential dispensation in response to the Fall. For the mature Aquinas the Fall introduced the possibility of coercion into the natural realm of the political, and Maritain no doubt would affirm an analogue of this: but for neither is the Fall intrinsic to the very possibility of political subordination.

Again, for Maritain the political order tends towards virtue, being a divinely appointed agency to assist (albeit indirectly) the journey towards God rather than an instrument for minimizing disorder. Instead of having civil authority serve as a haven against iniquity, so that innocence may be protected in the midst of evil,[150] he finds a positive and creative role in its capacity, by securing the material and moral conditions of the good life of the body politic, to contribute to the welfare of the soul. Further, as in classical and Thomist thought, justice is 'a primary condition for the existence of the body politic':[151] it is not that every kingdom is a gang of criminals unless its ruler is a Christian constantly praying for divine forgiveness, but rather that if a political society is found to be unjust, it is merely a gang of criminals. Government by Christians is not essential to the just society, although Christian leaders would be beneficial because of their awareness of the true sources of democracy and the natural law justification of the democratic charter.

Finally, Maritain's understanding of freedom is more Thomist than Augustinian. If Markus's interpretation of Augustine's account of political freedom is correct,[152] and his concern to secure Augustine for the cause of Berlin's negative liberty gives one reason for suspicion, then his opposition of this to Aquinas's

---

[150] Augustine, *Epistulae*, 153. 6. 16; in *Letters*, iii, trans. Sr. Wilfred Parsons, Fathers of the Church, 20 (Washington: Catholic University of America Press, 1953), 293.

[151] *MS* 10.

[152] Cf. Markus, *Saeculum*, 228–30.

positive conception of liberty makes of Maritain a Thomist. The distinction between the two kinds of liberty in this context might be misleading, inasmuch as both Augustine and Aquinas regard social existence as constitutive of, and not just instrumental to, human fulfilment, and inasmuch as Maritain argues for many rights more regularly associated with negative liberty. None the less, it still makes clear that for Augustine political coercion is a curtailment of liberty, whereas Aquinas thinks that liberty is diminished only if coercion is not for the agent's good. Now, although (as we have seen) Maritain thinks religious coercion wrong in the new Christendom, and although he may well subscribe to the basic principle of the free society that freedom be restricted only when necessary, neither of these implies that he regards legal coercion as such as intrinsically diminishing liberty: if so, his thought would still be compatible with a Thomist view of freedom.

Yet the superficial similarity between Augustine and Maritain prompts the question of what difference adopting a broadly Augustinian political theology would make to Maritain's contribution to the debate between communitarians and liberals, and in particular, whether placing Maritain in an Augustinian framework could address these problems. At this stage we should note that Markus's derivation of an open, religiously neutral society from the *saeculum* as a temporally entwined and only eschatologically separable reality is contentious. Markus grants that the use of the word 'state' is an inference from the text, and would be an anachronism if read into it;[153] but he still maintains that from Augustine's notion of the *saeculum* can be extrapolated the institution of the neutral state. Augustine, he holds, does not have an ideal of the Christian state:[154] he merely wishes to secure a common sense of membership for Christian and unbeliever alike.[155] However, Markus has, by his own admission, difficulties with the emperor's role in coercion: clearly Christian emperors, amongst whose duties are 'to put their power at the service of God's majesty, to extend his worship far and wide',[156] cannot be

---

[153] Ibid. 72.

[154] Against e.g. Michael Wilks, in e.g. 'St. Augustine and the General Will', *Studia Patristica*, 9 (= *Texte und Untersuchungen*, 94) (Berlin: Akademie Verlag, 1966), 487–522.

[155] Markus, *Saeculum*, 102.

[156] *De civitate Dei*, v. 24: 'suam potestatem ad Dei cultum maxime dilatandum maiestati eius famulam faciunt'.

identified *tout court* as the executives of a neutral state. But further, as Oliver O'Donovan well argues,[157] there is no common use of political society towards different ends: only the earthly city has an agreement about the uses of the political order, and it shares a common end in eternal destruction. Markus's stress on membership takes insufficient account of the pilgrim nature of the heavenly city, which merely makes use of the earthly peace during its earthly sojourn. A condition of order is all that is common to the two cities, not a neutral institution.[158]

The *saeculum*, then, does not entail directly the neutral state, but only an earthly peace, of which the heavenly city makes use. All Augustine expects of it is a condition of order, in which people negotiate about such things pertaining to this life as politics can achieve. This disabused understanding of the realm of the political, mindful of its role in restraining disorder rather than its contribution to virtue, provides the background for some answers to the questions we put to Maritain.

It makes clear, first, that a legal and constitutional order does not have to be implicitly or explicitly Christian or to lean towards a Christian understanding of the moral good for it to be a properly political order. Indeed, an Augustinian will be deeply suspicious of the idea of a Christian society (whether it be given communitarian, liberal, or any other complexion) if it refers to anything other than the *civitas caelestis*. An earthly polity can display traces or similitudes of justice, to be sure, but the separation of this from the true source of righteousness means that the only truly virtuous (or, for that matter, truly Christian) thing about it would arise out of its rulers and people humbly kneeling and begging for forgiveness. The opportunity to be tempted by the moral dangers of identifying the best society with a Christian society, while never of course wholly removed, is at least thwarted by the absence of the relevant intellectual category.

Second, by emphasizing the negotiatory aspects of politics, Augustine can address the problems I noted about derogations from a natural-law-based democratic charter. Instead of deviations from the natural law provisions of the charter being viewed as regrettable concessions for the sake of the common good, justice can be done to the complex ideological plurality of society and its

---

[157] O. O'Donovan, 'Augustine's *City of God* XIX'.
[158] Ibid.

inability to be crudely reduced to one overarching tradition with a number of minorities. Legislation, including foundational legislation of this kind, reflects the teeming pressures of the background culture, and not the givens of the moral good: it is formed by negotiation (however stylized, conflictual, class-ridden, etc., the processes of this may be in practice), not by imposition of an ideal.

Of course, it may be that the negotiated outcome of the background culture does indeed seek to reflect Christian moral imperatives in its public doctrine. If so, so much the better for it—at least if those imperatives truly embody justice. Augustine fully grants that, although justice is not properly part of the definition of a commonwealth, 'the better the objects of its united love, the better the people'.[159] While it is not part of the *esse* of the body politic that its law be natural law, none the less, accepting for the purpose of the argument that natural law is a better guide for legislation than other objects of love, such a standard could be taken as part of its *bene esse*. And this would allow us to introduce into this Augustinian framework Maritain's interpretation of natural law as applied to the new Christendom—and so to address the final question put to Maritain. The democratic charter, its status as interpreted in the previous paragraph, could be admitted into an Augustinian political theology as an appropriate political framework for Western-style liberal democracies, without implying either that it is appropriate for all societies past and present or that natural law itself need be historicized. Its provisions would be in line with natural law as much as the people were, and it would provide as much of a public commitment to a natural law framework as the people themselves wished.

(b) Public reasons

I have argued that many of the difficulties raised with regard to Maritain can be resolved by adopting the framework of an Augustinian political theology. Inevitably other issues remain. Probably the most glaring of these was implicit in the discussion two paragraphs above; this concerns his failure to recognize sufficiently the theoretical problems that arise from the differing and probably incommensurable justifications of the democratic charter. How are the conflicts in the adjudication of rights that

---

[159] *De civitate Dei*, XIX. 24.

these will inevitably raise to be resolved without the charter and its interpretation becoming, like politics in Michel Foucault's account, the locus of another 'war pursued by other means',[160] albeit one more precisely circumscribed? Maritain, as we saw above, appealed to natural law both as the basic orientation of the charter and as the grounds for his belief in the possibility of practical agreement. No doubt his confidence with regard to the feasibility of his proposals was aided both by the Christian history of the societies he was principally addressing and by the wide reception granted to the Universal Declaration of Human Rights. Yet the problem in this position is revealed when it attempts to govern an issue such as public policy on abortion. If this is decided on the grounds of an appeal to natural law or to the Christian traditions of the country, a large and influential section of the population will be bitterly aggrieved. Civil war due to competition of interest groups must result from not having public reasons for public decisions: if Maritain is to maintain the ideal of politics as conversation about the good rather than as the balancing of the power of pressure groups,[161] it appears that he must provide a theory of public rationality.

The nature and possibility of such a theory is a topic which lies beyond the scope of the present chapter. Suffice it to say here that the first principle of the possibility of public conversation must be the affirmation of a common world—the existence, that is, of something which that conversation can be about—but also that conversation gives out before truth is recognized by all: political dispositions must be made even when the conditions for public speech and deliberation are less than ideal, and when people remain in disagreement and mutual misunderstanding about what justice requires. This does not imply that the achievement

---

[160] Michel Foucault, *The History of Sexuality: An Introduction*, trans. Robert Hurley (London: Allen Lane, 1979), 93.

[161] Stanley Hauerwas, 'Politics, Vision and the Common Good', in *Vision and Virtue* (Notre Dame, Ind.: University of Notre Dame Press, 1981), 222–40, discusses these alternatives in relation to Niebuhr. David Tracy, 'Religion and Human Rights in the Public Realm', *Daedalus*, 112/4 (Fall 1983), 237–54, curiously thinks that Maritain rejects the ideal of politics as conversation because he holds that parties to the democratic charter are not to ask each other why they subscribe to it. But the charter is to be regarded as an instrument, not for suppressing conversation, but circumscribing its limits: the question addressed here is whether that conversation can be rational or is condemned to being a mask for the underlying play of power.

of such justice as is possible is not a worthy end of action, but only that those who seek it must, with Augustine's judge, pray for ultimate deliverance from the constraints that bind them: 'De necessitatibus meis erue me!'[162]

[162] Augustine, *De civitate Dei*, XIX. 6.

6

The Central Problem of Liberal Constitutional Theory

I INTRODUCTION

The concept of the democratic charter discussed in the previous chapter was elaborated by Maritain in an effort to secure a public definition of the personal and social rights of citizens without resorting to or presuming an agreed justification of those rights: he hoped for a practical moral consensus without philosophical or religious agreement. Natural law was to provide not only the Christian justification for the charter and the specification of the rights listed in it, but also the ontological grounding for the belief that moral agreement was in principle obtainable. In Chapter 5 I argued that Maritain was insufficiently attentive to the problems posed for the democratic charter by its public dependence on conflicting and probably incommensurable rational justifications. These difficulties arose chiefly at two levels: at the level of the theory of rationality, concerning the possibility of adducing public moral reasons as a basis for public action, and at the level of constitutional theory, concerning the potential conflict generated by the commitment of the liberal democratic political order both to individual rights and to majoritarian choice. I noted the former at the end of the last chapter; in this chapter we turn to issues raised by the latter.

Maritain's conception of democracy comprised both a procedural component—namely, the electoral accountability of the government to the people and the use of majoritarian decision procedures at several levels of choice—and a substantive component, which included the rights detailed in the democratic charter. The former was ultimately derived from the right of the people to govern themselves;[1] whereas the latter was based on the demand that the Christian lay polity expound and defend the common

---

[1] *MS* 65; Maritain's defence of the formal component of democracy is discussed in more detail below. That it is termed a 'formal' component does not imply that a commitment to democratic procedures is value-neutral.

tenets which formed the fundamental creed of its social and political life.[2] Yet the relation between the two components, formal and substantial, was never systematically developed: although in one place he asserted that a 'renewed democracy' should be able 'to defend itself against those who would use democratic liberties to destroy freedom and human rights',[3] he gave little guidance concerning either the proper institutional locus for settling conflicts between 'democratic liberties' and 'human rights' or the principles by which such conflicts should be adjudicated. Given the range of his preoccupations in political theory, and his orientation to the concerns of the time, this lacuna was barely reprehensible. But it occurred precisely at the node of a cluster of issues which together form the central problematic of present-day constitutional theory, concerning the nature and propriety of the separation of powers, the value of written and codified fundamental or constitutional law, the justification of judicial review of legislative action, and the alleged conflict between majoritarianism and individual rights.

These are problems which not only confront a full development of Maritain's political theory, but also lie at the core of Western political thought, since they manifest a conflict between its fundamental allegiance to both individual rights (the 'liberal' aspect) and majority rule (the 'democratic' aspect). As a matter of history, it was claimed in Chapter 2, liberals, while supporting equal political rights, have sometimes feared democracy, associating it with popular tyranny and the suppression of the rights of individuals and minorities, and have sought, in line with their habit of stressing the effectiveness of institutions rather than the virtue of citizens, to control majorities through a range of constitutional devices. The most prominent example of this is no doubt the United States Constitution's highly refined scheme of checks and balances, with its co-ordination under the Constitution of functionally separated powers, its system of federal and state governments, and its inclusion of such features as the Presidential veto of Congressional legislation, the bicameral legislature, the senatorial ratification of Presidential appointments, and the judicial review of legislation.

Of these features of the American system, the most discussed in the context of the defence of rights has been the last. Although the

<hr />

[2] *MS* 109.　　[3] *Range of Reason*, 167.

power of the judiciary to declare unconstitutional any law that contravenes the Constitution is not made explicit in the text of the Constitution, none the less, the right of judicial review, and with it the interpretation of the relation between legislature and judiciary as one of potential conflict between majoritarian decision-making and the rights of individuals or minorities has been implicit in American constitutional practice ever since Chief Justice John Marshall's ground-breaking doctrine (formulated in *Marbury* v. *Madison* (1803)) that the American Constitution is fundamentally *law*, and that legal interpretation and adjudication is peculiarly the province of the judiciary.[4]

No such power has been invested in, or seized by, the British judiciary. While a Bill of Rights was passed in 1689, it has been largely repealed, and there exists no written constitution, in the sense of a body of fundamental law codified in a single document, which could be enforced by the courts against Parliament. There have, however, been calls for the incorporation of a new Bill of Rights, perhaps of the European Convention of Human Rights,[5] into British domestic law, for a number of reasons, including the growth of executive power within the British Parliamentary system, the failure of the British governmental machinery to provide prompt (if any) remedies for grievances, and the creeping encroachment on individual and group rights in the name of the 'public interest' or 'national security', particularly in contexts such as Northern Ireland. In the last decade, alleged infringements of rights in connection with trade union membership, press freedom, and governmental secrecy, as well as an increasing concentration of power in the hands of government ministers and senior civil servants, have contributed to making the entrenchment of a written constitution and Bill of Rights into central demands of the largely left-liberal Charter 88 manifesto.[6]

---

[4] 1 Cranch 137 (1803).

[5] The European Convention is already binding on Britain in international law. For the issues concerning its incorporation into British domestic law, see Home Office, *Legislation on Human Rights with Particular Reference to the European Convention: A Discussion Document* (London: HMSO, 1976), 8–19; Joseph Jaconelli, *Enacting a Bill of Rights: The Legal Problems* (Oxford: Clarendon Press, 1980), 246–81.

[6] Text in *New Statesman and Society* (2 Dec. 1988), 10–11. For a full list of reasons for adopting a Bill of Rights and a history of the British debate, see Michael Zander, *A Bill of Rights?*, 3rd edn. (London: Sweet and Maxwell, 1985), 1–42. More recent contributions include Institute for Public Policy Research, *A British Bill of Rights*, Constitution Paper No. 1 (London: Institute for Public Policy Research,

In this chapter I will attempt to develop some theological understanding of the issues of constitutional and political theory connected with the judicial review of legislation, making special reference to the introduction of a Bill of Rights into British domestic law.[7] After giving at an outline of the precise problem and a brief account of some short cuts that do not succeed, I will turn to what is probably the most important general theoretical defence of judicial review, that of Ronald Dworkin. I will then survey some criticisms of Dworkin's position made by John Finnis; I argue that these need supplementing in order to produce a general theological account of the relation of legislature and judiciary. The remainder of the chapter is devoted to developing that account and showing its bearing on the question of adopting a Bill of Rights and judicial review in the United Kingdom.

Before that, however, I should make some remarks on the scope of this chapter. First, although we are principally concerned with the general problem of judicial review in North Atlantic types of democracy, by making special reference to the British system, we can afford to ignore several issues which are irrelevant in that context, and therefore not intrinsic to the general problem, but which are discussed at length in the American literature. Amongst them are federalism cases, in which the Court[8] has to decide issues of 'incorporation' and the relation of state and federal law (although it should be recognized that federalization of the

1990); *idem, The Constitution of the United Kingdom* (London: Institute for Public Policy Research, 1991); Frank Vibert, *Constitutional Reform in the United Kingdom: An Incremental Agenda,* IEA Inquiry Paper No. 18 (London: Institute for Economic Affairs, 1990); National Council for Civil Liberties, *A People's Charter: Liberty's Bill of Rights* (London: National Council for Civil Liberties, 1991); Rodney Brazier, *Constitutional Reform* (Oxford: Clarendon Press, 1991); and Ferdinand Mount, *The British Constitution Now: Recovery or Decline?* (London: Heinemann, 1992). On the state of civil liberties in Britain, see e.g. Geoffrey Robertson, *Freedom, the Individual and the Law,* 6th edn. (Harmondsworth: Penguin, 1989); K. D. Ewing and C. A. Gearty, *Freedom under Thatcher: Civil Liberties in Modern Britain* (Oxford: Clarendon Press, 1990).

[7] There is next to no theological literature on the subject. Reinhold Niebuhr is one interesting exception. He criticizes both Catholic (including explicitly Maritain) and Enlightenment liberal demands for charters of rights, on the grounds that they fail to recognize 'the perennial corruptions of interest and passion which are introduced into any historical definition of even the most ideal and abstract moral principles' (*CLCD* 51–8, at 52), and hence that they neglect the time-boundedness and ideological contamination of such charters.

[8] Throughout this chapter the phrase 'the Court' refers to the US Supreme Court, and 'the court' to the putative UK Court of Human Rights (however titled).

United Kingdom through the transfer of power either to the British regions or to supra-national European institutions would require some governmental body, most likely judicial, to resolve conflicts); separation-of-powers cases, where the judiciary must decide disputes between the legislature and the executive; historical questions concerning whether federal judicial review was constitutionalized by the framers of the US Constitution; and finally, issues of 'substantive due process' taken as issues of the interpretation of the Fifth and Fourteenth Amendments, even though many of the most controversial cases of judicial review (such as *Lochner* v. *New York* (1905)[9] and its successors, and *Roe* v. *Wade* (1973)[10]) have been decided under this rubric.

Second, I will not discuss here questions of the merits of a written constitution in general, but only those questions which pertain to the enactment of fundamental law understood in the sense of a Bill of Rights. Certainly many issues concerning statutory constitutional law overlap with those concerning Bills of Rights (its provisions may not be amended by ordinary legislative process, for example), but they will not receive attention here outside that connection: no doubt the frequent assimilation of fundamental law to constitutional law in American writing is partly due to the US 'Bill of Rights' consisting of the first ten Amendments to the Constitution.

Third, we shall be concerned with judicial review of legislation, not with judicial review of executive action, provision for which is already well established in the United Kingdom; none the less, the discussion is clearly relevant to review of administrative action.

Finally, it should be emphasized that our interest in this context is not with judicial 'innovation' in cases involving either statutory delegation of authority to a court (whether explicit or implicit) or underdetermination of a case by statute law, common law, and judicial precedent, but rather with the judicial declaration of a law's unconstitutionality: not, that is, with the judiciary's role in fulfilling or interpreting the legislature's purpose, but with its capacity for frustrating that purpose.

---

[9] 198 US 45 (1905) (limited hours for workers in bakeries are arbitrary interferences with freedom of contract).

[10] 410 US 113 (1973) (Texas criminal abortion statutes are unconstitutional, etc.).

2 THE PROBLEM OF JUDICIAL REVIEW DEFINED AND SOME UNSUCCESSFUL SHORT CUTS

The teasing, central problem can be formulated more precisely in three ways, which differ according to the principle which is taken as axiomatic. The first, and perhaps the commonest, assumes a procedural understanding of democracy, and makes judicial review the problem: this questions how a system basically committed to electorally accountable decision-making can admit enforceable decisions made by the judiciary, which is composed of people who are appointed rather than democratically elected.[11] The second, impressed perhaps by the US Supreme Court's racial desegregation decision in *Brown* v. *The Board of Education of Topeka* (1954),[12] takes judicial review as fundamental, and with that side-constraint seeks to maximize the power of the legislature.[13] The third takes the principles of both majoritarianism and judicial review to be derived from a common source which should be analysed in order to determine their rank-ordering. One example of such a source might be utility; another might be some understanding of equality; a third might be at the level of rights, with attention paid to both the political rights of equal participation in the political process and the civil (and, perhaps, welfare) rights of citizens.[14]

It is important to remember that there are different formulations of the matter: not all assume, for example, that majoritarianism should be taken as a given and that the undemocratic nature of judicial review is the problem. Which of these three (or others) is adopted will of course depend on the overall political theory from

[11] See John Hart Ely, *Democracy and Distrust: A Theory of Judicial Review* (Cambridge, Mass., and London: Harvard University Press, 1980), 7. Robert A. Dahl thinks the electoral process of 'decisive importance' for democracy (*A Preface to Democratic Theory* (Chicago and London: University of Chicago Press, 1956), 125). Evidently it is also Jon Elster's position (in Jon Elster and Rune Slagstad (eds.), *Constitutionalism and Democracy* (Cambridge: Cambridge University Press, 1988), 1–17) when he enquires why a political assembly should want to bind itself (8–14).

[12] 347 US 483 (segregation of public schools on the basis of race contravenes the equal protection clause of the Fourteenth Amendment).

[13] Not Michael J. Perry's position, but entertained by him (*The Constitution, the Courts, and Human Rights: An Enquiry into the Legitimacy of Constitutional Policy-making by the Judiciary* (New Haven and London: Yale University Press, 1982), 10 n.).

[14] The rights-based approach is adopted by e.g. Rawls, *TJ* 221–34, 350–62.

which the question is approached. But in general terms the underlying issue may be stated as follows: on the assumption (to which we return below) that democratic fairness of procedure and the justice of legislation are both central political goods, how, institutionally, may they both be ensured? Should it be by means of judicial review of legislation? And if so, what should be the constitutional balance of power between legislature and judiciary?

All the accounts just outlined are united in the basic assumption that there is a fundamental tension between legislation by the elected representatives of the people and judicial review of legislation. Some have argued, however, that the tension is merely superficial. For example, it is claimed that in Britain, Parliament can override any judicial opinion not to its liking, and therefore that to the extent that the courts make decisions which are not reversed by statute, they in effect do so as delegates of Parliament. Again, it is urged that because Supreme Court judges in the United States are appointed by the President and ratified by the Senate, and the higher judges in the United Kingdom by the Queen on the advice of the Prime Minister in consultation with the Lord Chancellor, the judges are indirectly elected by the people. Third, at the opposite extreme from the last point, it is suggested that although judges are not popularly appointed, political representatives are themselves rarely responsive to their constituents.

None of these arguments is cogent. The first underestimates the force of practical obstacles, such as the pressures of time on the Parliamentary agenda and the political complications of reversing decisions in emotive moral areas. More important, it neglects the special conditions of entrenchment that would most likely accompany a Bill of Rights, and therefore the particular difficulty Parliament would have in reversing a judicial decision in precisely the most controversial and perhaps evenly balanced cases. The second argument ignores the categorical difference between appointment and election. The former implies the intrinsic inappropriateness of reference to the electorate in a manner which the latter does not: thus the principal reason for appointing, rather than electing, judges has been to avoid accusations of political bias. Certainly the history of appointments of, and decisions by, judges is scarcely a record of detached impartiality,[15] but the solution to

[15] See J. A. G. Griffith, *The Politics of the Judiciary*, 4th edn. (London: Fontana Press, 1991).

this is not (though this would require further argument) popular election of justices. Moreover, at an empirical level, the argument fails to note that on the evidence from the United States, where Supreme Court judges must register their (at least nominal) party allegiances, the degree to which such explicit politicization of appointments affects the Court's judgments is difficult to prove: on the one hand, 'packing' the panel or increasing its number has not always helped, since judges have not always followed the policies which on appointment they might have been expected to pursue;[16] on the other hand, the policies of the Court cannot oppose over the long run the wishes of a stable majority.[17] Either way, there is a sufficiently indirect connection between electorate and the judiciary for the appointment of judges not to be simply equivalent to election by the people. The final argument—that representatives themselves are not very responsive to the electorate—does not do justice, to the extent to which it is true, to the critical importance for democratic government of elections, which are the primary and most effective means of securing such representative responsiveness as is possible.

3 RONALD DWORKIN'S DEFENCE OF JUDICIAL REVIEW

The issue is not resolved, then, by these various arguments that there is no fundamental tension between judicial review and legislation by an elected assembly. A more robust defence is necessary if judicial review and majoritarianism are to be combined in the same constitutional system. The account we will take as a starting-point is that presented by Ronald Dworkin, who is an appropriate choice both because he has treated the underlying theoretical issues with more philosophical awareness and sophistication than any other current defender of judicial review, and because he has integrated his account of the relations of judiciary and legislature into a general anti-positivist jurisprudence and anti-utilitarian liberal political philosophy. In

---

[16] See e.g. Perry, *Constitution*, 126–8.

[17] Dahl provides evidence for the conclusion that 'law-making majorities have generally had their way', though there may have been policy delays of up to 25 years due to Court action ('Decision-Making in a Democracy: The Supreme Court as a National Policy-Maker', *Journal of Public Law*, 6 (1957), 291). Dahl's argument, it should be noted, could be turned either in favour of judicial review (it does not ultimately defeat democracy) or against it (it makes little difference).

addition, his grasp of the deeper issues makes transfer of his arguments to the British constitutional context particularly easy.[18]

Dworkin's theory of judicial review is based on his revisionary understanding of the proper functions of legislators and judges. He agrees with previous legal theorists that courts and legislatures cannot be simply contrasted with each other, the one issuing statutes and the other merely interpreting them, since the law may be vague, may appear to have 'gaps', or may produce conflicting provisions in particular cases. The positivist response to this issue has generally resembled that of Benjamin Cardozo, who argued that where the correct interpretation of the law was unclear, it was the duty of the judge to act as legislator: 'interstitial' adjudication was more akin to creation than to discovery, and the judge 'ought to shape his judgment of the law in obedience to the same aims which would be those of a legislator who was proposing to himself to regulate the question'.[19] Dworkin argues, against this kind of position, albeit in the analytically more refined version developed by H. L. A. Hart, that for two reasons the methods of reasoning employed by judges and by legislators cannot be straightforwardly identified: the first concerns the type of argument which it is appropriate for each to use, the second the nature of adjudication.

The difference between the kinds of argument suitable to each turns on Dworkin's contrast between arguments of policy and arguments of principle. Arguments of policy, he says, 'justify a political decision by showing that the decision advances or protects some collective goal of the community as a whole', while arguments of principle justify a decision by showing that it 'respects or secures some individual or group right'.[20] The distinction between collective good and individual or group rights is the distinction between two types of political aim: within any political theory a political aim is any state of affairs such that 'it counts in favour of any particular decision that the decision is likely to advance, or to protect, that state of affairs, and counts against the decision that it will retard or endanger it'.[21] A 'goal' is a non-individuated political

---

[18] Dworkin's work has been developed largely through scattered essays, the most relevant of which are collected in *TRS* and *MP*. See also his *A Bill of Rights for Britain* (London: Chatto and Windus, 1990).

[19] *The Nature of the Judicial Process* (New Haven: Yale University Press, 1921), 120.   [20] *TRS* 82.   [21] *TRS* 91.

aim, while a right is an individuated political aim which may be pursued even at the expense of goals, should they conflict: rights are 'trumps' over goals. Using this distinction between rights and goals, Dworkin then defines questions of principle as questions about the rights of individuals or groups against each other and the State, and questions of policy as concerned with the overall goal of a society and the appropriate strategy for achieving it.[22] The distinction between arguments of principle and arguments of policy then affords a contrast between the legislature and the courts: while the former should and does use both kinds of argument, the latter should and (Dworkin argues) do only operate with arguments of principle. The fundamental ground for offering this description of the contrast between the two institutions turns on the basic conviction that the demands of justice, of rights and duties, cannot be reduced to what will make the community 'go better' in any utilitarian sense, and that it is the duty of judges to adjudicate in accordance with the rights and duties which they believe people have.[23]

The other strand in Dworkin's insistence that courts are not deputy legislatures is drawn from his theory of adjudication and legal interpretation: even if judges may appeal to principle alone and not to policy in hard cases, they do not simply legislate their own moral principles.[24] The positivist opposition of what is given in law and what is left to the judge's discretion is, he argues, amongst other things both phenomenologically inaccurate, in that judges find that law and precedent are constitutive of, rather than constraints on, their decisions, and morally unjust, in that by implication hard cases are decided by retrospective legislation. Instead, the law must be treated as a seamless web: if a law is insufficiently determinate to decide a case, that is not because it is incomplete and requires to be added to, but because it is too abstract and requires more concrete expression. There is a right answer in hard cases, even if it is disputed and even though there is no rigidly defined procedure for specifying it. For Dworkin this

[22] See 'A Reply by Ronald Dworkin', in Marshall Cohen (ed.), *Ronald Dworkin and Contemporary Jurisprudence* (London: Duckworth, 1984), 263.
[23] Ibid. 266–7; *TRS* 84–8.
[24] See in general 'Hard Cases', *TRS* 81–130. Dworkin has elaborated his position considerably since this paper, but not in ways which affect the present discussion. It should also be noted that a number of interpretive difficulties are elided in this account.

does not imply 'spooky' metaphysical commitments, but only the responsibility of judges to reason in a certain way. The process of legal reasoning is a matter of developing a theory of the law which produces the best 'fit', sufficiently detailed to cover the case at hand, between legal provisions and the history of precedents. Clearly such a process will require judges to use their own judgement: in particular, they may have to elaborate contested concepts by reference to those considerations of political philosophy which they find persuasive. But their convictions will not be *simply* opposed to the community's convictions, since the theory they produce is generated out of their interpretation of the community's convictions as these have been expressed in law and precedent. To the extent, therefore, that it can be said that judges 'innovate', they do so in a manner very different from legislators.

For Dworkin, then, while on the one hand it would be naïve to regard courts and legislatures as utterly distinct in kind, on the other, judges do not *simply* legislate. How then does he move from this account of courts as concerned with principle, and legislatures with policy as well as principle, to a defence of judicial review?

He appeals to the root notion of treating people as equals, the fundamental principle of his political theory. By 'treatment as equals' Dworkin does not mean 'equal treatment'—that is, equal distribution within a society (whether of welfare, material goods, resources, or opportunities)[25]—but a more fundamental conception—namely, 'the right to equal concern and respect in the design and administration of the political institutions that govern them'.[26] Although this right of itself could be satisfied by any of the different kinds of equal distribution, it is not an empty category: amongst the things it guarantees is the claim of all those whose interests will be affected by a decision to be heard in the debate concerning whether the decision will serve the general interest.[27]

More importantly for our purposes, from the right to treatment as equals, Dworkin derives three grounds for the institution of judicial review. First, from this fundamental ideal come the ideas both of democracy and of the rule of law; thus Dworkin treats the central problem concerning majoritarianism and judicial policy-making in the third of the ways outlined earlier, by appealing to a

---

[25] See Dworkin, *Law's Empire* (London: Fontana Press, 1986), 297.
[26] *TRS* 180; cf. 227.   [27] *TRS* 273.

more basic value. But this deeper value implies, Dworkin appears to argue, that 'justice is in the end a matter of individual right, and not independently a matter of the public good',[28] and such a claim for justice can be ensured only by an independent forum of principle. Democracy, when understood as a substantive and not merely as a procedural notion, is enriched rather than impugned by judicial review.

Second, the notion of treatment as equals also explains why certain kinds of justification for legislation are inadequate.[29] Pure utilitarianism or pure majoritarianism, for example, could offer no grounds for opposing the legislature in the case of racially discriminatory legislation which a strong majority of the people want; and so, Dworkin argues, treatment as equals cannot mean merely the numerical equality demanded by these conceptions ('each to count for one', 'one person, one vote'). Rather than the consequences of legislation, it is the types of argument used in defence of proposed legislation which should be scrutinized. Thus, '[r]acially discriminatory legislation is unjust in our own circumstances because no prejudice-free justification is available, or, in any case, because we cannot be satisfied that any political body enacting such legislation is relying on a prejudice-free justification'.[30] And it is for such a scrutinizing role that Dworkin thinks judicial review is justified.

Third, through judicial review, minorities and the poor are treated as equals.[31] Although Dworkin thinks that the power of individual citizens is weakened by instituting judicial review, some citizens are likely to gain more than they lose. In particular, since, on the one hand, the rich have in general more power over the legislature than the poor, and on the other, majoritarianism is by

---

[28] *MP* 32.

[29] *MP* 65–6.

[30] *MP* 66. Ely provides an extended argument in favour of treating legislative or administrative motivation as an appropriate reason for counting something unconstitutional, in cases such as 'suspect classifications' (*Democracy and Distrust*, 135–79). Of course, proof may be mighty difficult; certainly not all offences will be as unsubtle as that of the City of Tuskegee in Alabama, whose boundary lines, having originally been on a square plan, were redrawn so as to form an 'uncouth twenty-eight-sided figure', thereby excluding nearly all the city's black voters (ibid. 139–40).

[31] *MP* 27–8. Dworkin talks here of equality of political power, though he is probably referring to treatment as equals rather than equal treatment; even though his argument at this point appears to be about redistribution (and therefore perhaps concerned with equal treatment), it is better read as an attempt to remedy distortions in the access to power caused by poverty.

definition biased against numerical minorities, judicial review may enhance the power of respectively the poor and (at least) numerical minorities.

All three arguments aim to benefit individuals and minorities, but they are each different kinds of argument. The first turns on the non-reducibility of rights to a function of the collective good, the second on the kind of reasoning for legislation that is impermissible, and the third on the relative distributions of access to political power found in systems with and without judicial review. The third also differs from the other two, at least in respect of the second of its limbs, in the following way: while at a formal level it is a contingent feature of legislatures that the rich have, all else being equal, more power over them than the poor, it is at the same formal level intrinsic to majoritarian decision procedures that minorities will have reduced power. That is, at this formal level only the version of the third argument which refers to the nature of majorities shows an intrinsic problem with majoritarianism; for the other two (and a half) some further argument is necessary to show conclusively that majoritarianism needs supplementing, perhaps by judicial review. Why can the right of moral independence, the ensuring that justice be a matter of individual right, and the rights of the poor not be attended to by a responsible legislature? Why need the judiciary be brought in?

Dworkin answers in the following terms:

Judicial review insures that the most fundamental issues of political morality will finally be set out and debated as issues of principle and not of political power alone, a transformation that cannot succeed, in any case not fully, within the legislature itself . . . It is a pervasive feature, because it forces political debate to include argument over principle, not only when a case comes to the Court but also long before and long after.[32]

The fear which underlies this position appears to be that in legislatures issues are decided by political power; by contrast, judges, who do not have to face re-election, may nurture their thoughts in a somewhat less inhospitable climate. The merits of an issue are for legislators often enough less important than the opinions of (some of) their constituents or their selection committees; they may debate at the level of reasons, but they vote in line with political pressures. The legislature is different from the

---

[32] *MP* 70.

judiciary, not only in its use of arguments of policy, but also in the comparative unresponsiveness of its decisions to the merits of the issues.

This argument of Dworkin's supports judicial review as a necessary addition to a representative assembly in two ways. It suggests, first, the value of reflective debate on political issues, as well as the impetus judicial review gives to public discourse on questions of political and general morality, to a degree which Dworkin thinks will not be supplied merely by Parliamentary debate and its public reporting. Second, and more important, it may provide reasons for believing that the judiciary would generate a superior accuracy of results. Although there is no prima-facie strong reason for thinking the legislature less accurate, the relative independence of the courts from political pressure removes that potential form of distortion: in particular, judges are able to preserve 'speculative consistency' to an extent which legislatures would not ordinarily match.[33]

It might be questioned whether Dworkin's theory is compatible with a commitment to democracy. Amongst canvassed versions of the demand that judicial review be consistent with democracy or else be abandoned, one line of thought allows constitutional adjudication so long as judges 'confine themselves to enforcing norms that are stated or clearly implicit in the written Constitution' (as John Hart Ely defines 'interpretivism')[34]; another version demands that judicial review confine itself to 'process' issues— that is, those issues which concern the effective exercise of democracy—and refrain from matters of substantive morality (Ely's own version of 'non-interpretivism'). Dworkin's account, the argument in either of its forms continues, claims that adjudication of hard cases necessarily brings in the justice's own judgements of value, that this is incompatible with judicial review understood in the terms just given, and therefore that Dworkin's account of interpretation undermines his case for judicial review.

Clearly Dworkin cannot accept that democracy entails a refusal to import any substantive judgements of value into adjudication, since he accepts the former but rejects the latter; the reasons for his

---

[33] Questions of speculative consistency are questions 'that test a theory of rights by imagining circumstances in which that theory would produce unacceptable results' (*MP* 24).

[34] Ely, *Democracy and Distrust*, 1.

rejection of strict constructionism as an approach to legal interpretation were outlined earlier. His answer to this objection must
therefore rest in his argument given above that his conception of
the rule of law, which includes judicial review, enhances rather
than detracts from democracy; for democracy is not understood
merely in a procedural sense, and both democracy and the rule of
law are grounded in the deeper value of treatment as equals which
forms the basis of Dworkin's defence of judicial review.

Dworkin's argument, for a concept of judicial review, then, is
based on his account of the relation between courts and legislatures.
This denies that courts simply legislate in hard cases, both because
of the nature of adjudication and because of the kinds of argument
which it is inappropriate for them to use. Judicial review ensures that
justice is a matter of individual right rather than of an independent
public good, that law is not enacted for certain kinds of reasons, and
that minorities and the poor are treated as equals in their access to
political power. These goods can be secured by judicial review
principally because the courts' freedom from electoral accountability makes them more responsive than representative assemblies to
arguments of principle. This account of judicial review is not
impugned, he claims, by the argument that only strict construc-
tionist accounts of legal interpretation are compatible with democracy; for true democracy, he notes, 'is not just *statistical* democracy,
in which anything a majority or plurality wants is legitimate for that
reason, but *communal* democracy, in which majority decision is
legitimate only if it is a majority within a community of equals'.[35]

4 JOHN FINNIS'S CRITICISMS OF DWORKIN

It will be recalled that Dworkin's defence of his understanding of
the separation of powers turned on a distinction between arguments of principle and arguments of policy, which in turn
depended on a distinction between collective good and individual
right. In his 1985 Maccabean Lecture, John Finnis criticized this
latter distinction on two grounds.[36] The first is familiar and cogent
against many forms of utilitarianism: the idea of a quantifiable
collective good appeals to a notion of an aggregation of different

---

[35] *Bill of Rights for Britain*, 35, emphasis original.
[36] 'A Bill of Rights for Britain? The Moral of Contemporary Jurisprudence',
Proceedings of the British Academy, 72 (1986), 303–31, at 315.

goods which is intrinsically incoherent and fails to recognize the incommensurability of the goods whose commensurability it presumes; there is, in other words, nothing against which individual right can be contrasted.[37] The second is directed against Dworkin's allowance that *in extremis* rights may be overridden by policy. His assertion that 'rights are not absolute and do not hold when the consequences for policy are very serious'[38] does not ultimately take seriously the exclusionary or trumping nature of rights which it has been the centre-piece of his theory to affirm. Instead of rights being defeasible or subject to exceptions under extreme circumstances, they should rather be qualified when they apparently conflict with other rights.[39]

Behind Finnis's criticisms of the notions of the quantifiable collective good and the rebuttable right lies a different conception of the goal of government. Every governmental action aims not at 'collective welfare', which is independent of individual rights, but at the common good, which is itself constituted by individual rights. More precisely, to use the language of Finnis's wider political theory, moral rationality in governmental action implies fulfilment of the basic requirements of practical reasonableness, amongst which is the requirement of 'favouring and fostering the common good of one's communities',[40] but which also includes the attempt to respect every basic good in every act, to admit no arbitrary preferences amongst basic goods, to be efficient within reason, and so on. The common good comprises rights in the sense that lists of rights, exemplified in the various charters and bills of rights, outline the basic features of the common good from

[37] Ibid. 318–21. For the incommensurability of goods, cf. *NLNR* 113–15; Finnis, *Fundamentals of Ethics* (Oxford: Clarendon Press, 1983), 89–90; Joseph Raz, *The Morality of Freedom* (Oxford: Clarendon Press, 1986), 321–66; and Charles Taylor, 'The Diversity of Goods', in *Philosophy and the Human Sciences*, 230–47.

[38] *TRS* 83.

[39] Finnis, 'Bill of Rights for Britain?', 321–2. Cf. *NLNR* 218–21, 223–6; Paul Ramsey, *Deeds and Rules in Christian Ethics*, Scottish Journal of Theology Occasional Papers, 11 (Edinburgh: Oliver and Boyd, 1965). The point is just a logical extension of Dworkin's own distinction between abstract and concrete rights, according to which an abstract right is 'a general political aim the statement of which does not indicate how that general aim is to be weighed or compromised in particular circumstances against other political aims', whereas concrete rights are 'political aims that are more precisely defined so as to express more definitely the weight they have against other political aims on particular occasions' (*TRS* 93).

[40] *NLNR* 125. See *NLNR, passim*, for the basis of Finnis's philosophy of law in his account of practical reasonableness.

the point of view of the bearers of rights.[41] No sense, then, can be given to an opposition between common good and individual right: arguments of policy properly understood just are arguments of principle. The policy–principle distinction cannot ground Dworkin's version of the separation of legislature and judiciary, and the constitutional supremacy of the Supreme Court cannot be derived from the trumping capacity of rights over utility.

Finnis's arguments in this regard are largely persuasive, and I will not pursue them further here. Nevertheless, Dworkin is not committed to utilitarianism as the best general normative approach to political theory, as Finnis recognizes,[42] and this might suggest that Finnis's argument is too narrowly focused. Dworkin treats utilitarianism principally because he thinks that many find it an attractive general theory and that it is at least arguable that 'the best justification of our own legal practice shows utilitarianism as the general background theory supporting most legislation'.[43] He never seriously explores any other background justifications, though he mentions a 'platonic interpretation' which argues that the best conditions for human flourishing are those which will maximize the probability of people living in the manner which is really the most valuable for them,[44] as well as other interpretations

---

[41] *NLNR* 210–18.

[42] Finnis, 'Bill of Rights for Britain?', 317 n. 1. Cf. Dworkin: 'I doubt that in the end any package based on any familiar form of utilitarianism will turn out to be best' (*MP* 370).

[43] Dworkin, in Cohen (ed.), *Ronald Dworkin*, 281. Finnis takes 'neutral utilitarianism' as the working theory, for Dworkin, behind current political practice: this ' "takes as the goal of politics the fulfilment of as many of people's goals for their own lives as possible" . . . and is "neutral toward all people and preferences" . . . so that preferences are to be given full weight even when they "combine to form a contemptible way of life" ' ('Bill of Rights for Britain?', 317; the internal quotations are Dworkin's). He rightly argues that this is 'both flatly unacceptable, and regarded as such in every civilized community' (ibid.), because of the evil preferences it admits into the calculus. But properly it is *restricted* utilitarianism which Dworkin regards as, if not finally the best normative political theory, at least better than unrestricted utilitarianism as a descriptive theory of North Atlantic constitutional states (Cohen (ed.), *Ronald Dworkin*, 281). By restricted utilitarianism he means a version of utilitarianism which admits personal preferences (i.e. preferences about how the agent's life should go) into the calculus, but not external preferences (i.e. preferences about how the lives of others should go). Even so, restricted utilitarianism, whatever its normative merits over against unrestricted utilitarianism, still fails to capture the current political practice of excluding certain *personal* preferences (such as 'a lifetime of immolation in slavery, sexual bondage, or drug-induced fantasy and oblivion' (Finnis, 'Bill of Rights for Britain?', 318)).

[44] *MP* 414.

which take as fundamental political goals the glory of the state, military success, class triumph, or material wealth.[45] Yet the most pertinent interpretation concerns what is surely the most plausible descriptive account of governmental decisions, that which points to the vaguely systematic and only partially theorized congeries of reasons for policies. The question might still be asked whether rights should be accepted as judicially enforceable side-constraints of these laws. The coherence or otherwise of the background justification would here be irrelevant: the judicial enforcement of rights would be sufficiently justified by the fact that, because of actions permitted or required under law, an infringement of rights had in a particular case occurred.

This returns us to the central problematic of the chapter. For the argument as presented in the last paragraph begs the question of whether courts are the uniquely appropriate place for discussing questions of rights, or, more generally, whether they are a suitable forum for enforceable review of legislation. We have seen Dworkin's reasons for thinking so above. But not all have agreed with him: Thomas Jefferson, for example, claimed, by contrast, that Congress was equally competent to judge the constitutionality of laws. On a similar tack, Finnis argues for the supremacy of the legislature from considerations of institutional responsibility and competence.[46] Legislatures, on the one hand, he says, have the responsibility for acting in accordance with the basic requirements of practical reasonableness, for assessing costs and benefits, and for choosing a society's public commitments concerning personal and political morality. Courts, on the other hand, must 'ensure that their decisions are consistent with (i.e. "fit") the derivative, *institutional* rights and principles created by the public commitments already made by the relatively determinate sources which can be the subject of legal *learning*: legislation, custom and judicial precedent'.[47] The construal of open-ended constitutional provisions is not a task for which peculiarly 'lawyerly skills' are suited.

How are we to judge this? Finnis claims that legislatures have the responsibility for making commitments on behalf of a society, and that courts are institutionally better equipped to adjudge the relatively determinate sources of law. However, even if he is

---

[45] *TRS* 365.
[46] Finnis, 'Bill of Rights for Britain?', 328–9.
[47] Ibid. 329, emphasis original.

correct in general terms, without pursuing the question further, we will still need to set his account within a broader theory, since his argument from legislative responsibility and judicial competence suffers from a number of inadequacies.

First, although his account explains why courts on the British model are not best suited to conducting judicial review of legislation or the interpreting a broadly worded fundamental constitutional document, it does not address the possibility of non-judicial review of legislation. That is, the function of review of legislation could be performed by an advisory body which is not part of the judicial system and whose officers are neither elected nor necessarily drawn from the ranks of the judiciary: the Conseil Constitutionnel of the Fifth French Republic is a body of this sort. Here the training of lawyers and the institutional competence of courts would be irrelevant, yet the fundamental question of review by an unelected body of an elected assembly's legislation would still stand.

Second, legislatures are prone to make mistakes. Although on Finnis's account they may be charged with the responsibility for acting in accordance with the criteria of practical reason which he enumerates, they do not always fulfil that responsibility; nor of course do many legislators understand their responsibility in those terms. But even if they did act as Finnis stipulates, they would still occasionally produce legislation which was by independent criteria poor or mistaken, because of the pervasive fact of limited information. That is, on the assumption that there is a right answer to the question of what legislation would meet the criteria of practical reasonableness,[48] legislative procedures are, to borrow Rawls's terms, matters of 'imperfect' rather than 'pure' procedural justice: that is, rather than the procedure defining what will count as just, there are independent criteria of justice, even though no set of institutional legislative procedures can be guaranteed to achieve justice according to those criteria.[49] But if accuracy of results is the primary goal (a premiss we shall discuss below), then institutions of government should be designed so as to maximize sound

---

[48] This assumption will not be defended here, though it would be satisfied by the kind of moral realism assumed throughout this book. Note (i) that this reference to a 'right answer' need not imply that a particular piece of legislation would be *uniquely* correct, and (ii) that the applicability of the concept of imperfect procedural justice merely requires the *belief* that there are independent criteria.

[49] *TJ* 84–6.

outcomes; and if legislative process is a matter of imperfect procedural justice, then it may be that judicial review (or some other institutional arrangement) might serve to improve accuracy.

The third reason is an extension of the second, and echoes some themes mentioned earlier. Legislatures are liable not only to make mistakes, but to do so in a manner intrinsic to majoritarian democracies. Under such systems power may be systematically abused or the rights of some consistently mishandled in a manner peculiar to and inherent in majoritarianism: thus the rights of individuals, of minorities, or of the poor may in different ways fail to be recognized by legislatures because they cannot obtain stable majority approval. A tempting remedy for these problems might be a written Constitution on the US model, which would incorporate both structural provisions (such as the separation of powers) which minimize some distortions of democracy such as self-interested representation or factional tyranny and rights provisions which would insulate certain rights from majoritarian interference.[50] At any rate, it would be inadequate merely to assert the legislature's responsibility, since the possibility of certain kinds of deformation are inbuilt in majority rule.

For these three reasons, then, a full treatment of the issues concerning the incorporation of a Bill of Rights requires not just an account of institutional competence and responsibilities, but also a broader theory of the relation of judiciary and legislature in the context of democratic theory and, more particularly, of the propriety of having unelected bodies pronouncing upon legislation. And since the present investigation is theologically based, we need to see how a theologically grounded account of democracy and political authority bears on the question.

5 DEMOCRATIC PROCEDURES AND JUST OUTCOMES: A THEOLOGICAL PERSPECTIVE

At the beginning of this chapter I said that there was a lacuna in Maritain's thought concerning the relationship between the formal commitment to democratic majoritarian procedures and the substantive commitment to the rights listed in the democratic charter.

---

[50] For the distinction between structural and rights provisions, see Cass R. Sunstein, 'Constitutions and Democracies: An Epilogue', in Elster and Slagstad (eds.), *Constitutionalism*, 327–8.

Maritain did not develop an account either of the institutional locus of adjudication between the two commitments or of the principles which such an institution should follow in adjudicating. There is also a further, deeper tension in Maritain's approach which remains even if one abstracts from the notion of a democratic charter. For if the political authority is ordained to the common good, it would seem to follow that accuracy of the political authority's provisions in respect of the common good is its supreme goal and criterion. Yet the right of people to self-government suggests that (at least for this historical constellation) fairness of procedure through majoritarian democracy is the principal formal criterion of just decision-making. This tension could be resolved either by fencing off some courses of action from the range permissible to representative assemblies or by subordinating in principle the common good to majoritarianism, or conceivably by a mixture of the two. But the first option brings us back to the problem of the locus of adjudication between democratic procedures and codified rights, and also introduces, should judicial review or a similar solution be adopted, the issues of inaccuracy in judicial review; while the second runs severe risks of injustice.[51] Clearly this tension between soundness of result and fairness of procedure, which Maritain never addresses,[52] must be resolved by any theological account of judicial review.[53]

(a) Two models for popular consent

Let us open the political theological considerations by comparing two theological models of popular consent to political authority. Maritain's is a version of the Thomist 'transmission' theory of political authority, found in Cajetan, Bellarmine, and Suarez,

[51] Another resolution of the tension might be through the claim that the formal commitment to electoral democracy and the substantial commitment to the common good refer to different stages in the process of government, the former addressing the question of who will make the decisions, the latter the question of what they will decide. But the same problem arises here: may or may not the government elected do what it wishes, without side-constraints?

[52] 'I am no legislator, nor an inventor of constitutions' (*Scholasticism and Politics*, 115–16).

[53] Note that the common good will of course include fairness of procedure, in terms of (e.g.) treating all with equal concern and respect; formally, there is no tension at the level of the exercise of authority between soundness of outcome and fairness of procedure. Rather, the problem arises at the level of *electoral* participation: here there is a real question, addressed below, concerning whether the common good includes electorally fair—i.e. majoritarian democratic—procedures.

which I propose to call the *conferral* model of consent.[54] According to this, the people 'receive from God the right to self-government and authority to rule themselves in an *inherent* manner'.[55] That is, 'they are possessed of this right and this authority as a "principal agent" (though "secondary" or subordinate with respect to the Primary Cause) which through its own causal power—acting, as everything acts, in the virtue of God's universal activation— invests with authority the one or ones designated'.[56] While God is the ultimate source of political authority, the people are granted the right to be the proximate source of authority. As such, they are entitled to confer authority on the ruler or ruling regime, but they never alienate or transfer their fundamental right to self-government; in this sense, democratic philosophy is the only true political philosophy, though this is compatible with aristocratic and monarchic as well as democratic regimes.[57] The more specific argument for a democratic regime with universal suffrage is never expounded at length, though a passage in the essay 'Democracy and Authority'[58] suggests the line of his thought: universal suffrage, while it is valuable as a weapon against political slavery, is particularly important for its symbolic significance in witnessing to 'the right of human persons to political life, and of the multitude to the constitution of the authoritative organism of the city'.[59] Its symbolic value, he continues, must, however, be given genuine value, through features such as community representation.

By contrast, the *confirmation* model of consent, as I shall term it, does not grant the people the intrinsic right to self-government.[60] On this view, the axiom that all authority is from God is interpreted to mean that God is not only primary cause but also

---

[54] Yves R. Simon, *Philosophy of Democratic Government* (Chicago: University of Chicago Press, 1951), 158–76, claims that these Thomists give a 'unified expression' of the theory (175), and that it is (sketchily) present in Aquinas (158–60).

[55] *MS* 128, emphasis original.   [56] Ibid.   [57] *MS* 129.

[58] In *Scholasticism and Politics*, 89–117.   [59] Ibid. 113.

[60] This model approximates that defended by e.g. Oliver O'Donovan in *The Desire of the Nations* (Cambridge: Cambridge University Press, 1996); I am grateful to him for clarification of a number of issues about it. Clearly it resembles the 'designation' theory, in contrast to the 'transmission' theory, of the traditional discussion (see Simon, *Philosophy of Democratic Government*, 157, 163–4); though the confirmation model makes clear the distinction between the human means of designating those who will exercise authority, which need not be popular, and the necessarily popular (though not necessarily formally instituted) confirmation of that authority.

principal agent in conferring political authority: should a people take part in electing a government, their role in transmitting authority is instrumental rather than (subordinately) self-derived. The fundamental contribution of the people lies in their recognizing (or refusing to recognize) the government's edict, and this recognition is the barest minimum that is necessary for legitimate authority. But of course the divinely ordained good for political authority goes beyond the minimum: it is part of the *bene esse* of political society that the part played by the people lies not just in passive confirmation of authority but in active involvement in lawmaking, perhaps through representative deliberations in Parliament. This role for public consultation and debate concerning the common good is based theologically on the structural analogies between politics and ecclesiology, in this case between the giving of the Spirit at Pentecost and the participation by all in political life. Just as the prophecy of Joel was fulfilled that sons and daughters, menservants and maidservants, would declare the Word of God, so all are freed to speak a word of judgement or encouragement for the sake of the public good. Denial of this right of public speech, which is grounded primarily in the good of the public realm, and not in the right of individuals to say whatever they please, is not strictly tyrannous, inasmuch as legitimate government can proceed without public consultation; but it is autocratic, in that, in making rulings for a society, it refuses that public role for the people.

For the confirmation model, then, the role of the consent of the people lies not in conferring political authority, but in confirming whether it is present; and lack of consent is the sign rather than the substance of a lack of authority. Moreover, it is for the good of the political realm if there is a place for freedom of speech about the common good. But it is worth noting two other differences between the models, in addition to the contrast between the people's intrinsic possession of the right to self-government and their instrumental role in transmitting political authority. First, the conferral model, being based on the people's right to self-government, has the emergent implication of popular participation in political appointment (though further argument would be necessary to reach a specifically majoritarian or representative form of popular participation). Such an implication, though in itself merely conceptual, could with historicist premisses easily lend itself to claims about historical progress towards democracy, of the sort I criticized

Maritain for in the last chapter. The confirmation model, on the other hand, does not of itself lean towards democracy so directly. Second, the two models suggest different answers to the question of whether democratic electoral procedures are intrinsic or incidental to the common good. For the former, democratic fairness of procedure could be conceived to be of intrinsic (even if limited) value, and therefore to be essential for an accurate embodiment of the common good, at least in the historical climate of modern civilization; for the latter, the common good might be achieved without incorporating the right to vote.

How do the two models differ in their approach to the question of judicial review? It turns out that the answer to this depends in part on what formulation of the central problem of judicial review is suggested by each of them. Let us assume first, as we have throughout this discussion so far, that the problem is that decision-making by unelected bodies is incompatible with a commitment to electoral democracy. On this assumption, there is a prima-facie case for thinking that the conferral model's inbuilt leaning towards democracy makes it less open to judicial review and the role of non-elected bodies in government than the confirmation model; the latter, because it does not tend specifically towards popular electoral participation, cannot at this level of generality rule out the role of a non-elected review body.

In fact, on this assumption the conferral model does not rule out the possibility of judicial review, though it is clearer from Yves Simon's work than from Maritain's that there can be limitations on pure democracy within the conferral model. Discussing the party system, Simon accepts that democracy 'may well be saved by a non-democratic principle acting as a check on its enemies',[61] and, concerning the rule of the majority, he allows constitutional restraints on the majority, though he mentions only proportional representation.[62] Yet, if proportional representation is granted as a supposed brake on the majority, there might well be a place for judicial review too, provided that an important constraining principle, derived from the fundamental right of the people to self-government, was accepted: namely, that judicial review be in some sense an expression of, rather than a limitation on, the will of the people. Given this principle, the people themselves would not lose

---

[61] *Philosophy of Democratic Government,* 108.
[62] Ibid. 99–103.

power under a constitution with judicial review—even if their elected representatives would.

This consideration is adduced not in order to show that judicial review is therefore desirable in the British case, but merely that it is at this general level possible within the terms of the conferral model of popular consent, despite that model's predilection for democracy. Neither the conferral model nor the confirmation model finally either excludes or demands judicial review, then, on the assumption that the problem is that of the unelected nature of the court.

(b) A deeper understanding of the difference between the two models

But to put the question in this way is not to draw on the deepest impulses of each theory. In fact, the nature of 'the problem of judicial review' changes in accordance with the theory from within which it is addressed, as will become evident.

(i) The confirmation model   In the case of the confirmation model, we will consider two arguments which purport to rule out judicial review, one which turns on the good of public debate in relation to governmental decision-making, and a second which considers the fundamental legal nature of Bills of Rights.

According to the first argument, judicial review is ultimately problematic on the grounds that it insulates public decision-making from public debate: whereas the well-being of political society depends on the freedom of all to contribute to discussion about the common good, judicial review prevents such contributions. The central problem of judicial review lies not so much in the unelected status of judges, the confirmation theorist would insist, but in its potential for stifling public debate; the reason for defending electoral democracy—namely, its capacity for representing symbolically universal possession of the spirit of prophecy—is precisely the reason for rejecting judicial review. By rendering impermissible the universality of speech in relation to a selected class of public decisions, the role of the judiciary becomes autocratic, compromising the dialectical relation between divinely ordained authority and the popular confirmation of that authority which is given full expression in the right to freedom of speech.

However, this argument does not prove as much as it claims. Certainly it would rule out any form of ultimate judicial supremacy, according to which there was no possibility of redress against a supreme court's rulings. But systems of judicial review do not usually propose this. Even models of direct review, such as that in the United States, allow for legislative response to the Court's rulings, though the entrenchment of the Bill of Rights designedly makes this difficult. Any version of judicial review which made a reality of the dialectical relationship between political authority and the people would fit the confirmation model, at this general level.

The second argument that claims to show that judicial review would be unacceptable within the terms of the confirmation model revolves around the nature of the law contained in Bills of Rights.[63] If it could be shown, the argument goes, that Bills of Rights are not in a significant sense law, it would seem to follow that the court would be acting as a legislature. For in the order of being, laws have to be made before they can be applied, the act of judgment being the twofold process of legislation and adjudication; so, if a Bill of Rights had not been made law (in some significant sense, yet to be determined) by a legislature, the only evident institutional locus for its becoming law would seem to be the judiciary. Such legislative action would seem to subvert the primacy of the legislature, and thus to render judicial review unacceptable.

The case for asserting that Bills of Rights do not contain law might, the argument continues, proceed as follows. A Bill of Rights contains moral teachings about fundamental goods of a society; its provisions are superior to what we might call 'non-fundamental law', not through their capacity for trumping statute laws by being applied directly to particular cases, but in their being embodied in all ordinary legislation. Therefore, when a court applies a provision of a Bill of Rights to a case, it is not merely interpreting a broadly worded or open-ended statute, but is also legislating as well, since no truly legislative act had been performed previously. A Bill of Rights comprises a philosophy of law, and in order to pass into non-fundamental law (so as to be at a level where it can potentially conflict with other non-fundamental law), has to be legislated by the judiciary.

In assessing this argument, how are we to make sense of its distinction between 'law' or 'non-fundamental law' on the one hand and 'philosophy of law' or 'moral teachings' on the other?

[63] This argument is one suggested to me by Oliver O'Donovan; all responsibility for misrepresentation is of course mine.

The distinction no doubt could be seen as drawing inspiration from parallels such as Albrecht Alt's diversion of Israelite law into 'casuistic law' and 'apodeictic law'. According to Alt, the former was adopted from the Canaanites, had its *Sitz im Leben* in everyday jurisdiction, and was concerned only with relations between people, not with Israel's larger destiny. The latter was peculiarly Israelite, was concerned with the unalterable will of God, formed the unconditional guiding principle of the laws, and was associated with the recollection of the ideals of Israelite society at the renewal of the Covenant: the Decalogue is a central example of this latter kind.[64] The two kinds of law are fundamentally different, and the latter (so the argument would go) parallels a Bill of Rights.[65]

In response to this defence of the fundamental difference between two kinds of law, we should note that even in the case of the parallel just cited, the two are of sufficiently similar status for Alt to allow that the two may clash, the apodeictic in such instances invariably taking precedence. And we might note a similar point in the case of a constitution and a law conflicting, by referring to the language of the original *Marbury* v. *Madison* judgment:

So if a law be in opposition to the constitution; if both the law and the constitution apply to a particular case, so that the court must either decide the case conformably to the law, disregarding the constitution; or conformably to the constitution, disregarding the law; the court must determine which of these conflicting rules governs the case.[66]

Both cases suggest that fundamental and non-fundamental law may clash, and therefore that non-fundamental law is law in some relevant sense.

These examples are not enough to settle the issue against the argument just outlined, however. Neither Alt nor Chief Justice Marshall may have had our problem in sight. Nor would it settle the problem to demonstrate that a charter or Bill of Rights was law

---

[64] Albrecht Alt, 'The Origins of Israelite Law' (1934), in *Essays on Old Testament History and Religion*, trans. R. A. Wilson (Oxford: Blackwell, 1966), 70–132. His thesis has been subject to much criticism and amendment since, but this does not affect my use of it.

[65] Indeed, Walter Harrelson (*The Ten Commandments and Human Rights* (Philadelphia: Fortress Press, 1980)), having claimed that the Decalogue is not law in its ordinary sense (12–13), explicitly compares the US Bill of Rights and the Decalogue (191).

[66] 1 Cranch 137 (1803), at 178.

in the appropriate sense because it has been formally incorporated as statute law or has the status of authoritative custom, or whatever.[67] For even if human rights provisions in such a charter were shown to have the appropriate formal status, they might still not be law in the focal sense of the term.

Rather, what matters is surely the degree of specificity a law possesses: the question of whether judges are legislating or adjudicating turns on the quantity of material they have to import. Of course, determining what counts as introduction rather than interpretation, and how much of the former is permissible, are the central questions around which flow the great tides of debate between interpretivists (or originalists) and non-interpretivists (or non-originalists), between judicial activists and believers in judicial restraint. For our present, very limited, purposes we do not have to attempt a resolution of them: all we need to note is that if the difference between the provisions of a formally enacted Bill of Rights and ordinary statute law is principally one of specificity, then the two differ not in kind, but only in degree. That is, there is no basic qualitative difference between 'fundamental' and 'non-fundamental' law with regard to their status as law, and the contrast (to refer back to the original putative distinction) between 'philosophy of law' on the one hand and 'law' on the other is misleading. In both cases judges are attempting to interpret or construe legal provisions, even if the one offers them considerably more scope for using their own judgement than the other. Certainly the greater specificity of non-fundamental law may give grounds for regarding it as a more central or focal example of law, but this is not sufficient to refuse the title of law to more open-textured yet still formally valid examples.[68]

[67] The Universal Declaration of Human Rights and the American Declaration of the Rights and Duties of Man (both 1948) are two international human rights instruments which were not intended to create binding obligations in international law on their signatories: for their juridical status see Paul Sieghart, *The International Law of Human Rights* (Oxford: Clarendon Press, 1983), 53–5.

[68] Where does the difference between Bills of Rights and statute laws lie? Certainly they *seem* very unalike, as an elementary form-critical exercise would demonstrate. But, as argued in the text, that dissimilarity does not derive from the latter being formally law, the former not. Nor is it based on Bills of Rights being statements of moral truths, by supposed contrast with statute laws, as if the latter were devoid of moral content. The difference lies rather in two features: first, statute laws have a greater moral specificity; Bills of Rights being higher up the ladder of abstraction of moral claims; second, they contain particular determinations which are appropriate to particular empirical circumstances, but of themselves of no moral import.

Moreover, in both cases interpretation may require some introduction of material: all courts legislate, to some degree. But from
this it follows that if legislation by the courts is an argument against
judicial review, it would also be in principle an argument against
letting judges construe ordinary statute law. Or, more importantly
for our purposes, it follows that if ordinary adjudication may be
conducted by judges, so in principle may review of legislation. The
second argument against judicial review, in other words, comes to
a similar conclusion to the first. Instead of using the fear of judicial
legislation as an argument against enacting a Bill of Rights, it
would be better to consider the conditions under which such
legislative activities by judges might be compatible with the
supremacy of a democratic assembly.

What might these be? Judges are entitled to construe ordinary
law because of two conditions, which need to be taken into account
when considering possible constitutional arrangements which
would include judicial review of legislation. First, on the confirmation model it is the primary responsibility of a body open to
public debate to introduce content (even if the courts inevitably
will also) and to furnish the judiciary with provisions which are as
specific as is reasonably possible. This constraint may be overriden
for the sake of a Bill of Rights, but not, of course, without cost.[69]

Second, if the constitutional primacy of a democratic assembly
which the confirmation theory demands is to be observed, there
must be some provision for legislative rejoinder to the court's
rulings in review cases. In other words, judicial review can be
justified within the terms of the confirmation theory, but only if
substance can be given to the ultimate constitutional supremacy of
the legislature. How this might be possible we return to below.

(ii) The conferral model   Maritain's theory, by contrast with the
confirmation model, does not have concerns in the same way about
freedom of speech. For since the transmission of authority runs
entirely from the people as principal agent (though as secondary
cause to God as first cause), and since freedom of speech is not
essential to the public confirmation of that authority in the manner
that it is for the confirmation model (although of course it is an
important good), the actions of a judiciary in reviewing human

---

[69] Finnis, 'Bill of Rights for Britain?', 325–31.

rights cases are not intrinsically problematic because insulated from public debate. In the conferral of authority through (say) an act of election, the people can in principle license judicial legislation as much as parliamentary legislation. This is not to argue that on this model the holders of authority are permitted to make any proposals they want: they are still bound by the natural law. Nor is it to say that authority is alienated by the people in a Hobbesian sense: the government holds it *per participationem*, vicariously, while *per essentiam* it still belongs to the people. But it is to suggest that the body politic's natural right to full autonomy cannot exclude judicial review as a manner of exercising that autonomy.

This does not commit the conferral model to judicial review, of course, and we must introduce further considerations if we are to get a grip on the general question of the constitutional superiority of the court or the legislature from the premises of the conferral theorist. To this end we need to look in greater depth at arguments which aim to settle the issue by appealing either to accuracy of results or to fairness of procedure, before turning to a third, more satisfactory, approach.

The first kind of argument, based on an appeal to the principle that, in Rawls's formulation, '[t]he fundamental criterion for judging any procedure is the justice of its likely results',[70] would consider whether an elected assembly or a panel that was not electorally accountable would produce the sounder or more accurate results. In favour of the courts it is often argued, with Dworkin, that the legislature cannot police itself; that the court's independence of electoral accountability implies that there is no reason for it to commit the typical vices of majoritarianism, and at least in that respect would be more accurate (or at any rate no less accurate) than the legislature; that it is a good defence of minorities and individuals, and that the majority would in such instances be acting as judge in its own case; and that it provides a good defence not just of 'participational' values of equal access to the political process and non-discrimination against certain kinds of minority (for which Ely argues), but also of substantive, 'non-participational' moral values.

Yet, for all those who would agree with Henry J. Abraham that no 'sane citizen of the United States would wish to have the

----

[70] *TJ* 230.

ultimate exercise of his or her individual liberties, including the provisions of the Bill of Rights, be at the mercy of partisan political bodies',[71] there are many on the other side who would hold with John Hart Ely that 'Our society did not make the constitutional decision to move to near-universal suffrage only to turn round and have superimposed on popular decisions the values of first-rate lawyers',[72] or with Learned Hand, who did not want 'to be ruled by "a bevy of Platonic Guardians," even if he knew how to choose them, which he did not'.[73] The writers of *The Federalist Papers* were particularly wary of the tyranny of the majority. But the potential threat of the tyranny of the few cannot be neglected either: while the legislature may need guarding, so do the guardians of the legislature.

In general, the argument from accuracy is difficult to assess with any precision. Legislatures indeed have their characteristic distortions; but judges too may have their vices: the fashionable liberal attitudes of the intellectual élite, the dispositional conservatism of stability and conformity. One system has produced *Roe* v. *Wade*; the other the Abortion Act 1967. Undoubtedly any system which gave no role at all to democratic process would be liable to inaccuracy—procedural fairness is an intrinsic part of the common good. But without considerably more evidence (and an account of the values which are to be measured) the criterion of accuracy is not dispositive either way, and certainly not conclusive.

The second kind of consideration would argue for the constitutional supremacy of an elected assembly from the priority of procedural fairness: the question should be settled simply by appeal to the will of the majority expressed through its elected representatives. The problems with this approach were mentioned in our discussion of Dworkin: aside from inherent difficulties in the notion of the will of the majority,[74] there are specific groups liable to be discriminated against under such circumstances—minorities, the poor, the powerless. Whatever vague content 'democracy' may have in public rhetoric, it has more substance than crude major-

---

[71] Henry J. Abraham, *The Judiciary: The Supreme Court in the Governmental Process* (Boston: Allyn and Bacon, [6]1983), 167. Cf. Thomas Nagel, 'The Supreme Court and Political Philosophy', *New York University Law Review*, 56 (1981), 519–24, at 522–3.

[72] Ely, *Democracy and Distrust*, 59.

[73] The quotation is Dworkin's (*MP* 27); the internal quotation is Hand's phrase.

[74] See e.g. Finnis, 'Bill of Rights for Britain?', 306–7.

itarianism. Every democracy needs constitutional brakes of some kind on the majority, though these need not include judicial review. While the criterion of fairness affirms the primacy of the legislature, it cannot rule out a role for those forms of judicial review that are in some sense subordinate to the legislature.

A third approach supports this conclusion. This criterion makes the decisive question that of which institution should be allowed to make the errors, given that both inevitably will. Adopting this approach does not imply a diminished view of the importance of soundness of results. On the contrary, against Hand, if a host of Platonic Guardians perfect in knowledge (like the cherubim) and love (like the seraphim) were to dispense law, it would *in this respect* be proper for them to hold authority. But in the conditions which obtain, where the holders of political authority are distinctly limited in knowledge and benevolence, and where, I have argued, neither systems with judicial review nor systems without it are indisputably more accurate, some other presumption-creating criterion must be sought. The most obvious such criterion appeals to the idea that constitutional supremacy must lie with that body which it is least unacceptable for mistakes to be made by.

To discern which body that would be in a North Atlantic democracy such as Britain, it would be inadequate merely to appeal to the right of tradition. For, first, it is precisely the claim to the right of tradition that is in question: some find that the principle of electoral accountability places final responsibility with Congress or Parliament, others that the country's commitment to the rights of individuals and minorities and to constitutional rule should give ultimate say (short of constitutional amendment) to the judiciary. Second, and more importantly, the right of tradition is merely one consideration, to be balanced by others. The argument cannot proceed simply by accepting inherited beliefs as the only relevant source of judgement, though of course the mere fact of their being inherited and held by the community may have a subordinate place in the argument.

Rather, we must look to the structure of the conferral model for the solution. The relevant feature of the model is the vicarious nature of the authority of those in power. Although, as was argued earlier, the transmission of authority from the people means that the conferral theorist has no worries about judicial review at the deepest level, of the kind that the confirmation theorist finds, this does not imply that the theory generates no presumption about who should be allowed to make mistakes. Indeed, it is here that our initial observation about the conferral theory's inbuilt inclination to democracy takes its place. The body politic's right to full autonomy is expressed, at least in this society, through universal suffrage, and this suggests that, if anybody, it should be the people—through their elected representatives—who should be allowed to make the mistakes about the common good that inevitably will be made. The proper locus of effectual moral and political debate about this society's commitments is the legislature, even if the deliberations of that body may typically be distorted by unbridled passion, self-interest, and the manifold corruptions of a sinful world.

(c) Judicial review in a democratic framework

Both theological models point, therefore, towards a system which gives constitutional primacy to a democratically accountable legislative assembly. Systems which answered to this principle would either contain no judicial review of legislation at all, or would adopt a form of judicial review which allowed some means of popular feedback. This latter approach would not entirely exclude direct judicial review of the US variety, inasmuch as the Court's rulings may always be reversed by constitutional amendment. Yet this system, with no provision for review within the legislative process itself and with constitutional amendment as the only means of overturning the Court's decisions, is relatively clumsy.

There are a variety of other review instruments which give more exact substance to the idea of the legislature's constitutional supremacy. In the case of the US Michael Perry has argued for a functional justification of non-interpretive review in human rights cases.[75] This justification is based on an understanding of America's fundamental commitment as a society to a fallibilist moral evolution, a belief in the existence of a right answer about human rights (and political and personal morality as a whole) without the assumption that the truth has been found. The virtue of judicial review lies in its capacity for dealing with moral and political

---

[75] Perry, *Constitution*, 91–145. A 'functional' justification in this context is one which appeals to the inherent value of judicial review for the Constitution, not to anything in the text of the Constitution or the minds of the original framers.

problems 'non-mechanically'—that is, as a matter of reflection, not of reflex, and by deepening moral understanding through dialogue with Congress. The process of conversation between legislature and judiciary which he envisages is likely to lead to more accurate opinions, he thinks, and therefore to help rather than hinder democracy (understood substantively), because of the self-critical disposition it engenders.

The dialectical nature of the relationship is ensured by the authority of Congress to exert significant political control over the Court. The source of this Perry finds in a rarely used clause of Article III of the Constitution, under which the Court 'shall have appellate jurisdiction, both as to law and fact, with such exceptions, and under such regulations, as the Congress shall make'. Congress may define and thus limit the Court's jurisdiction. Such a power is not one of reversing decisions, which would render the Court a mere delegate of Congress. Nor is it equivalent to constitutional amendment: it is intended to control the value-judgements of justices, not of the original framers. Such a distinction depends on the possibility of distinguishing interpretive from non-interpretive review, which is, of course, controversial.[76] Nevertheless, it is clear that attributing such a power to Congress gives rendering to the principle which I enunciated earlier that judicial review be in some sense an expression of, rather than a limitation on, the will of the people. The Court would not be justified in striking down such jurisdiction-limiting legislation precisely because its own moral legitimacy is tied to its submission to the legislature.

Clearly, similar provisions could be incorporated into any formal recognition of judicial review in the United Kingdom. By that means, respect for the presumption in favour of the legislature as supreme bearer of constitutional authority would be maintained, even if the demands of the common good incited general public recognition of the need for fundamental constitutional change. Moreover, it would make clear that a supreme court's role in such circumstances is properly one of judicial *review*, not of judicial legislation.

---

[76] Ibid. 128–39.

6 CONCLUSION

The problem of the relation between a democratically elected legislature and a rights-protecting judiciary is the institutional reflection of a deep tension within liberal democratic theory. In this chapter I have explored the extent to which theological conceptions of political authority and democracy can be brought to bear on the question. I have argued for a presumption in favour of the constitutional supremacy of the legislature: one model I have discussed bases this on the threat which judicial review poses to the right of public speech; the other urges it on the grounds that, if anybody, elected representatives of the people should be those allowed to make bad decisions on behalf of a society. Such a presumption is defeasible, however, should the exercise of power by the legislature exceed certain limits of tolerability. If judicial review should be implemented, there should be some means of increasing the court's responsiveness to the elected assembly in addition to resorting to the procedures of enhanced majorities or constitutional conventions.[77]

Although the main purpose of this chapter has been to probe some of the theoretical issues underlying judicial review, we cannot conclude without touching on one final question: should a Bill of Rights be introduced into British domestic law? Undoubtedly there are difficulties. Not only are there fears to be addressed: that the explicit politicization of judges would be a source of injustice, that the right of appeal to a supreme court higher than the legislature would spur on an increasingly litigious culture, that the possession of rights would come to be thought inconceivable without the possession of a Bill of Rights, that the perceived significance of legislative enactment would be diminished, and that the legislature would no longer internalize its responsibility to protect rights. Again, if the European Convention of Human Rights were not adopted *en bloc*, there would also be significant problems of incorporation to be overcome: the introduction of a Bill of Rights (let alone an entire constitutional document) would require

[77] In this respect at least, the 'semi-entrenched' model of judicial review proposed by the National Council for Civil Liberties (*A People's Charter*) would be preferable to the model of direct judicial review put forward by the Institute for Public Policy Research (*A British Bill of Rights*). Jaconelli (*Enacting a Bill of Rights*, 23–91) discusses various possible constitutional models.

nationwide all-party support significantly greater than a mere numerical majority; the mass of technical legal and procedural details (including the difficulty of how a sovereign Parliament understood in Dicey's terms can bind itself for the future, and the relation of British constitutional instruments to superior European jurisdictions employing a possibly different enumeration of rights) would have to be negotiated; and, most importantly and controversially, the rights and provisions to be incorporated would have to be specified.

Moreover, there are alternative and intrinsically more democratic improvements compatible with the British system, which would reform Parliament while also strengthening individual and minority rights (I will not comment here on the plausibility of any of them, or of others not listed, or on their compatibility with the arguments presented above): detailed legislation in specific areas (freedom of information, supervision of the security and intelligence services, etc.); a strengthened and reformed House of Lords, allowing special representation of minority and regional interests; greater scope for legislative initiatives by individuals or groups in Parliament other than the government; mechanisms internal to the legislature to counteract discriminatory legislation; formal recognition of constitutional functions for the Leader of the Opposition; a separate Ministry of Justice, thereby ensuring that the Home Office is not responsible for justice and civil rights as well as public order and internal security matters; greater openness of government and access of citizens to executive decision procedures; increased powers for the Ombudsman; and procedures for appointing judges which would ensure a greater chance of political independence.

For all that, a Bill of Rights could turn out to be a force for justice such as could not be achieved by any amount of piecemeal reform. Grievances would be remedied, wrongs righted, and rights vindicated. The excessive power of the executive would probably be restrained. The law would on occasion be expanded to advantage, beyond the point to which Parliament or the executive would be willing to take it. And the moral consciousness of the nation would probably be educated out of its customary torpor on the matter of fundamental liberties. But the dangers of judicial review of legislation must still be taken seriously. Shorn of a corresponding emphasis on the duties of the citizen in addition to those of the State, it might entrench the idea that the fundamental forms of human good can be stated in terms of rights—the abstract, individualist nature of which the British system may anyway rightly have suspected. As importantly, the choice to entrust to the judiciary the power, which they would be unlikely to relinquish, of construing a text whose time-bound nature may in future lend only increasing implausibility to an already precarious understanding of interpretive method, and to diminish the chance of reviewing the decisions thereby made, cannot be undertaken lightly. It is sometimes said that in the United States every political question is ultimately a legal question. What needs to be asked is whether the institution of judicial review ultimately betokens the strengthening of justice or the limiting of the freedom of the Word of God in the public realm.

7

Christianity and Liberal Society

I INTRODUCTION

Dr Josef Goebbels is said to have announced: 'You are at liberty to seek your salvation as you understand it, provided you do nothing to change the social order.' In this statement, which Jacques Ellul describes as 'the great law of the technical society',[1] there can be glimpsed, when set in a different context, both the promise and the danger of the liberal society, both the freedom it offers and the tyranny it portends. A similar tension is expressed in the title of this chapter and the book. By juxtaposing Christianity and liberal society in this way, we both contrast and unite, both criticize and defend. Yet, by suggesting a similarity between liberal and national socialist rhetorics, we also show that this tension between affirmation and denial is not evenly balanced, that no earthly order of politics may be identified with the Kingdom, and therefore that the Church's 'No' to the rulers of this world must be pronounced before its ever qualified and cautious 'Yes'. And further, by intimating through Ellul that liberalism as much as fascism may be imprisoned in an iron cage whose bars are the laws of the technical society, we indicate the partial and limited character of the freedoms which liberalism can offer, and, moreover, suggest an account of the forces which govern and constrict its motions.

In the previous chapters I have attempted to provide a number of cross-sections of liberalism. This has involved looking at various features of liberalism, as they have been expressed by different liberal writers, and examining them from the perspectives of selected Christian thinkers. Whilst each of the studies has been self-standing, there are also some common themes which underlie these, and it is my purpose in this final chapter to draw them together.

This is partly a matter of recalling some of the principal conclusions that have already been reached. Of the four central

[1] Ellul, *Technological Society*, 420.

chapters of the book, those on Niebuhr and Grant were more critical, showing the limits and dangers of liberalism from a theological point of view. Through the discussion of Niebuhr's theology of history, I set out the ground for perhaps the single most important question for a theology of politics: the nature, source, and locus of human salvation. Nineteenth-century liberalism, Niebuhr claimed, saw human fulfilment as the end-point of historical development, as the product of human achievement— doctrines of historical progress and implicit Pelagian theologies walking hand in hand. While some of the detail is disputable, in both his theological method and his understanding of liberalism, Niebuhr's instincts for sniffing out signs of political Messianism were unerring. Indeed, the potential for idolatry is as evident in late twentieth-century dependencies on economic growth and technological progress as in the naïve moral and political progressivism which he fought against.

Some similar concerns underlie Grant's work. Although much of the chapter on Grant involved criticism of one of the most prominent twentieth-century English-speaking theorists of liberalism, the opening discussion of Grant was not intended just to provide a platform for engaging in *Rawlskritik*. Instead, it is that Grant's understanding of the givenness of moral value (rather than its constitution through individual choice) gave him an understanding of the dynamics of technology, which in turn pointed up the potential instability of liberalism and the real possibility of historical decline. One does not have to swallow Grant's technological understanding of modernity neat, or believe in the brute determinism of the future, to be able to recognize the importance of the health of a society's background culture for preserving the goods of liberalism.

The chapters on Maritain and on constitutional theory attempted some aspects of the positive task of laying out a basis for these goods of liberalism. Maritain offered the goal of a new Christendom, criticizing liberalism for its thin conception of human agency, its materialist understanding of the common good, its minimalist account of social unity, and its secularist version of neutrality. He also developed the idea of a democratic charter, a declaration of rights which would act as the point of unity for a society. Some of the underlying theoretical issues raised by this, including the theological bases for democracy, were discussed in the following chapter on Bills of Rights and judicial review.

However, I queried a number of Maritain's themes, suggesting that his thought would be the better for being placed against an Augustinian background. There are real dangers in the idea of a 'Christian society', highlighted in Maritain's failure to give theoretical space to the idea of a non-Christian society and the sense of reluctance which the idea of mere derogations to non-natural-law traditions conveys. An Augustinian political theology, emphasizing the negotiatory nature of politics, can allow that political ordering may take different forms in different societies, and that one polity can be morally preferable to another, yet both be legitimate. In its disabused view of public rationality and its refusal to regard pluralist political forms as regrettable lapses from the norm, Augustinian thought can recognize the dangers of Christianity imposed on a society from above, whilst also allowing that there may be genuine benefits for justice from a Christian political inspiration.

But the task of drawing out the underlying preoccupations of the book is more than one of recapitulation. It is more adequately effected by redrawing the interpretation of liberalism given in Chapter 2 as a result of the criticisms and insights of Niebuhr, Grant, and Maritain, and proceeding from there to a statement of the nature of Christian commitment to a liberal society.

I will start by relating liberalism to the so-called 'turn to the subject' which is often connected with the rise of modernity. Although the pattern of thought that is described covers many of the same features as the interpretation of liberalism in Chapter 2, we are now enabled as a result of the theological analysis of the last few chapters to view it in more sharply defined focus. Through working out a theological response to this, it should begin to emerge how, in relation to liberal political society, a responsible theology will learn to articulate its 'No', and a faithful Church to construct its 'Yes'.

2 THE TURN TO THE SUBJECT

At the centre of liberalism, in common with modernity as a whole, lies the phenomenon often vaguely termed the 'turn to the subject'. In order to explicate what is meant by this, I will group together the set of ideas to which it refers under two headings: (a) the centrality of the will and (b) the loss of transcendence. These, it is hoped, will both illuminate the conceptual background of some of the central features of liberalism, and pave the way for the theological analysis. As will become clear, many of the themes are dependent on the more extended discussions in earlier chapters.

(a) The centrality of the will

In talking of the centrality of the will, I refer primarily and foundationally to the nature of the self and of human agency. As was suggested in the account of George Grant's thought, liberals for the most part have been part of the voluntarist stream of the modern world, identifying the seat of the self in the will or the affections, rather than the reason, and connecting this in part to the freedom of action which it is alleged to make intelligible. From this comes the 'atomism' of individual agents, in which the self is disengaged from anteriorly given ends or obligations, and incorporates contingencies only through choice. Whatever the metaphysical commitments of a particular liberal theory, this self is almost always secured a status which prevents it from being decentred into an indefinite web of relations, however composed. Again, the givenness of the self leads in some liberal writers to a diminishment of the role of training in the virtues and the development of personality, while its detachment from external relations may give rise to neglect of the historicity, particularity, and narrative-formed quality of human lives, and likewise of their fundamental constitution in and by community.[2]

From this is derived the particular emphasis which liberalism places on the justification of political authority to the individuals who have to submit to it. This reflects not just the liberal concern for equality, but also the notion that both the consensual basis of political authority and the range of governmental responsibilities are to be referred to entities more precise than the somewhat vapid 'community'. Again, equality itself, together with the tendencies of liberalism towards universalism and abstraction, can be related to this dissociation of the self from the contingencies of power and status.

---

[2] There are a number of suggestive parallels between this account of the liberal self and Rowan Williams's portrait of Arius's God in *Arius: Heresy, and Tradition* (London: Darton, Longman, and Todd, 1987).

Likewise, the ideas that a liberal society should allow as much liberty to each individual as is compatible with granting such liberty to all equally and that government derives its authority from consent may also be derived from this understanding of the self, as can be seen from its interconnections with the notions of freedom and authority. The detachment of the will from reason and the association of freedom with the former are liable to render freedom a matter of empty choice, directionless, indeterminate, and independent of ends which might make its exercise in one direction rather than another intelligible: in my discussion of Maritain, this was characterized as an emphasis on 'initial' rather than 'terminal' freedom. The corollary of this, widely accepted within the liberal tradition, is that an extension of freedom can be conceived only as an expansion in the number of available options for choice; in social and political terms, this is represented as emphasis on the negative freedom not to be interfered with by others, whether individuals or governments, while the positive freedom of rational self-direction is often understated, and the ultimate fulfilment of freedom in the vision of God and the final redundancy of free choice is rarely stated at all. Correlative to this conception of freedom is the notion that there is no authority external to the will which may command it; the existence of authority easily becomes construed as a constraint on desire, not as an intrinsically intelligible end of action which might give actions their basic rationality. Consequently, all legitimization of political authority is, through the conferral of consent, effectively self-imposed.

Despite the condensation of this account of the centrality of the will, it is apparent how the rationale arises for the various aspects of the claim that social and political arrangements should be justified to everybody who lives under them: the concern for equality, the abstract and universalizing mode of thought, the conception of freedom as the absence of externalized constraint, the denial of authority to that which has not been consented to. Thus, contemporary exponents of liberalism, including Rawls, can be represented as sharing with earlier liberals a background of thought rooted in a single complex of ideas centring on the will.

This does not imply that they all have identical accounts of every item in that complex. For example, Rawls's political liberalism shares in many of the features just described, but is not a consent theory in the sense of requiring the actual or tacit consent of every citizen; it is only to those who share in public reason (appropriately defined) that political liberalism purports to provide justification. Again, the above analysis could be extended to an acceptance of the putative fact–value distinction (an extension made explicitly in the portrait of the structure of liberal beliefs in Chapter 2), since this account of the relation of the will to its ends does not make necessary any grounding of moral obligations in facts about human nature. Yet, while for many liberals this has led to a denial of moral realism, Rawls (to continue with him) has a more complex account; even if he in fact happens to believe that constructivism is correct, he tries to abstract from this question for the sake of obtaining public co-operation.

It would be inappropriate, therefore, to suggest that there are no differences amongst liberals in the nature of their commitment to the various features of this analysis. Nevertheless, even if they disagree amongst themselves, to the extent that they share in the complex of ideas centred on the self as will, and are unaware of the broader implications of those ideas, to that extent they are liable to contribute to the undermining of their own ideals. For—and here I am thinking of Grant—this voluntarism has generated a technological drive to mastery which is working against the liberal values of liberty and equality and, in the name of freedom, contributing towards a real and profound loss. This loss is not just a consequence of the danger to liberty of a civil society which fails to promote publicly the virtue of its citizens, but hopes to ensure justice simply through the excellence of its institutions—a danger which is pertinent to the discussion of judicial review. Nor is it merely that the individualism, universalism, and bent towards abstraction of liberalism may render problematic an understanding of the role of contingency and locality and of membership of non-voluntary and intermediate associations, important though these are for the stable preservation of freedom. Rather, beyond these, it is mediated through all those aspects of the technological society which are chronicled in Grant's writings: the mutation of the natural world into raw material for human creativity, the overcoming of chance and particularity through the imposition of predictability and standardization, the replacement of politics by administration and of justice by convenience. And permeating it all is the religion of progress, the manic reaction to the despair which descends when the burden of meaning is placed on the will.

(b) The loss of transcendence

This last, twofold theme, the immanence of meaning and the drive to progress, leads into the second element in the turn to the subject: namely, the loss of transcendence. Indeed, it shows how the centrality of the will and the loss of transcendence interpenetrate. For, on the one hand, Nietzsche's murder of God, and therewith all forms of transcendental signification, required that the murderers themselves become gods to make themselves worthy of such a deed; and, on the other, the centrality of the will makes problematic its dependence on anything transcending itself. Again, on the one hand, the dynamics of progress conduce to making eschatological fulfilment otiose, while, on the other, the denial of such an eschaton places great demands on earthly politics. It is this last proposition which I will particularly concentrate on under the rubric of the loss of transcendence.

Without an eschatology which transcends and fulfils history, the human aspiration for permanence and stability may translate itself into the project of seeking the Kingdom of God on earth. But such a programme has two kinds of problematic consequences. First, when there is no fulfilment external to this world, the burden of human salvation falls on this-worldly activity and its hectoring necessities. Many of the dangers of this were discussed in the analysis of Niebuhr's critique of liberal progressivism in Chapter 3. The possibility that progress (whether in its nineteenth-century guise of social and political evolution or its contemporary economic and technological guise) might not be assured is repressed from consciousness, and a cultural psychology of denial (whether of human moral limitation or of ecological limits to economic growth) takes its place. Likewise, the morally regulated use of force is liable to become unintelligible: politics comes to be thought of as properly conducted when it takes the form of negotiation which disclaims any reference to power, with the result that the only worthwhile sacrifice becomes 'the sacrificial spirit of statesmen who are resolved to negotiate so that negotiation never fails'.[3] And the coming of the Kingdom of peace on earth leads to the mind-set

---

[3] Paul Ramsey, 'The Uses of Power', in *The Just War: Force and Political Responsibility* (Lanham, Md.: University Press of America, 1968), 17.

of deterrence, the idealist utopianism of a perfect peace guaranteed by the existence of weapons too horrendous to be of any possible political use.[4]

Second, such an immanentization of meaning runs the risk of a potentially tyrannical imperiousness of the political order and the danger of its seeking ultimate value for itself. Without the mediation of transcendence to society, political activity assumes ultimate value, and cannot be seen as the transient and fragmentary thing it is, something properly confined to the discussion of those things that pertain to this life. Rawls, as we have seen, appears to find no problem: in making no stipulation about the content of the different philosophies and religions which might be found in a well-ordered society, he presumably assumes that the practice of piety is irrelevant to the flourishing of his constitutional liberal democracy. But this is short-sighted. Transcendence is unavoidable: either it will be offered through the religion or religions of the society, or it is liable to be established by the demonic absolutization of the liberal state.

3 REASON AND REVELATION IN PUBLIC LIFE

The sum of a theological response to this twofold turn to the subject is of course nothing other than a theological account of liberal political thought: in other words, that which has been the central focus of this book. By dividing the material into the two elements, we are now enabled to respond in two different ways. In relation to the set of phenomena I have described as the centrality of the will, we can outline the content of a theologically informed approach to these issues. In relation to the loss of transcendence, we can discuss the form that the Church's witness in the public realm should take. Of course, as we shall see, content and form are mutually implicating.

(a) The integrated self

I will begin by sketching quickly the outline of a response to the movement of thought centring on the will. At the very end of the chapter on Grant the issue was briefly mentioned of whether an integrated account of reason and will were possible. The potential

[4] See Oliver O'Donovan, *Peace and Certainty: A Theological Essay on Deterrence* (Oxford: Oxford University Press, 1989).

danger of an account of modernity in terms of voluntarism lay in a reaction which denied any role for the will at all, so stressing contemplation that it was liable to make action unintelligible. A more adequate response would identify the 'I' with the composite understanding and willing self, such that the known good would always be pursued, and that alone would be pursued which was known to be good. Instead of divorcing reason from will, leading to a malformed understanding of each and the misprized alternatives of rationalism and voluntarism, a proper moral psychology would make clear the cognitive aspect of agency and the rational appreciation of intelligible ends, while allowing a role for the will (in desiring the end, etc.) in its analysis of action.[5] Theologically, the background for this would be represented through an account of the relationship in Scripture between knowing God and doing his will, between hearing and responding, and between faith and works, and through a doctrine of the Holy Spirit, by whom the renewal of the creation in Christ is mediated to us, restoring our full noetic relationship to reality and giving us moral power through an effectual, desiring love for it.[6]

The notion of agency which is integral to this finds both freedom (as the subjective aspect) and authority (as the objective aspect) coinciding in the one reality. Freedom is not in the first instance the negative freedom of lack of external hindrance, but the positive freedom of the effectual capacity to choose and act in accordance with practical reason. Allied to this, it is not maximized by indefinitely increasing the range of options or refusing them any value other than that imposed by will, but is fulfilled in the rational choice of intelligible goods as an integral feature of genuinely moral agency. Therefore, for the one in whom God is at work, there is the freedom to will and to act according to his good purpose (cf. Phil. 2: 13). But in the fallen state, when the agent's purchase on reality is compromised, freedom becomes the exercise of choice in favour of merely apparent goods, the fantastic nature of which may be disguised from the subject by the very thing which is imagined to be their chief virtue: namely, the derivation of their value from the will. Likewise, authority is not an arbitrary constraint on the naturally expansive human spirit, but that which originates, licenses, and makes possible the rationality of human

[5] See *NLNR* 337–42 for a clear introductory outline of these issues.
[6] *RMO* 109–20.

action. In this sense, basic goods, or intrinsically intelligible ends, may be said to authorize action as at once source and goal within the teleological structure of agency. And for those restored to participation in reality, freedom and authority coincide: the Psalmist runs in the path of the commands of the law, the authoritative expression of created moral reality, for God has set his heart free (Ps. 119: 32); and the writer of the letter of James echoes this sentiment in his talk of 'the perfect law that gives freedom' (Jas. 1: 25).

This conception of authority underlies the composite notion of political authority. Political authority is in part a matter of power: at least one element in genuine authority in the actual conditions that obtain (not if everybody were fully rational, or inhabited a well-ordered society, or whatever) is the sheer capacity to bring effective force so as to secure a semblance of social peace. The brute fact that a political power's say-so receives a response, whether that response is rational or irrational, sincere or for outward show, is one irremovable element in its legitimacy. Nevertheless, political authority is not conferred by power alone; it cannot be reduced to the control of the monopoly of the means of force, nor does the possession of power by the bearers of authority imply that the use of coercion is preferable to non-coercive means of resolving conflicts.

Most importantly, the securing of justice is also an essential element in the composition of political authority; even though it will never be perfected in this world, it remains an intrinsic goal of government. And in general, classical theological accounts further argue for another element, giving in all a threefold analysis of the good of government and the basis of its authority, which comprises *ordo* (the order of power), *iustitia* (the order of justice), and *lex* (the legal order), and articulating the aim of political agency in terms of the highest incidence of the three, such that ideally 'every exercise of power is both legal and just'.[7]

Yet the fallen nature of society, to which the providential imposition of government witnesses, has the consequence that the demands of political authority do not always coincide with the realization of the freedom of political society or of the individuals or communities which compose it. Human freedom,

----

[7] Ramsey, 'Uses of Power', 12.

the subjective reality, does not find its highest fulfilment at the point of intersection with the claims of political authority, the objective reality; true freedom will not be found in obedience to the State (let alone in the identification of the universal State with a particular historical configuration), nor will the perfect correlation of freedom and authority be enjoyed before the eschatological consummation in the heavenly kingdom. This is not only because earthly politics concern things of this life alone, a matter we return to below, but also because, even when going about their proper business, the bearers of political authority are thwarted by ignorance and sin. Beyond their obligation to make specific and authoritative determinations for the sake of the common good, their judgement is subject to arbitrariness simply because of the limitations of their knowledge and love. The rulers who long for deliverance from their necessities finally regret not that their dispositions will not be transparent to all their subjects, but that even if all their subjects were fully rational, their judgements would at times remain opaque.

Nevertheless, in this context is to be placed the role of governmental coercion. This is justified inasmuch as through the sanctions of the law political authority is enabled to direct the actions of its subjects for the sake of the common good; it is not that through some act of consent citizens who suffer punishment should properly recognize in it an actualization of their freedom, as if it were a contract being honoured, albeit to their disadvantage. The notion that a society's arrangements should be justified to its members still has a role, however, even if it does not lie in legitimating distributional (and other) provisions and their corresponding sanctions. Government must be able to show that in reaching judgements it is acting fairly, treating all with equal concern and respect, never ignoring the preferences of citizens even when overriding them, acting for the common good and not for the good of the governors or their favourites alone.

Complementing the role of fairness in governmental action is the role of consent in establishing authority. In the previous chapter I discussed two models of consent: the conferral model, according to which the people have the right under God to confer authority on their rulers, but never alienate their fundamental right to self-government; and the confirmation model, according to which the people confirm the existence of the authority which has been granted to their rulers by God. Here we merely note that, although the conferral model is more usually associated with a liberal conception of government, the confirmation model also connects popular consent and the freedom of the public realm to be addressed by all. The confirmation model, on a plausible interpretation of it, recognizes that the acquiescence of the people under its government is sufficient for legitimate authority; but it also insists that it is for the well-being of political society that this is accompanied by the right of public debate, in which all may contribute to discussion concerning the common good, just as at Pentecost even slaves were given the spirit of prophecy.

This has implications for the notion of public reason. It assumes the possibility of public rationality. Yet, throughout the discussion in this chapter (and earlier), we have noted that the nature of contemporary pluralism make it plausible that there are several rival and incommensurable moralities, which disagree not only about first-order moral issues, but also about what would count as an appropriate way of resolving those disagreements. About the possibilities for public conversation, in view of this, we can say little here, beyond three points. First, the presentation of public reasons will never in this world be free of a component of power; but this does not imply either a reduction of reasons to the interplay of forces or the inappropriateness of such elimination of systematic distortions in rational communication as is possible. Second, the postulation (or acceptance) of the possibility of rationality requires the postulation (or acceptance) of a common world about which discussion is being held, a *focus imaginarius* towards which our truth-claims strive. Third, in extremity and in cases of social breakdown, the conflicts which are normally pursued by the surrogate means of ostensibly rational debate take on a cruder aspect; it is one of the virtues of an Augustinian analysis that it can make sense of the idea that the limiting point of politics lies in war, and can also prescribe moral constraints on the use of power even in times of anarchy.

This completes the barest skeletal framework of a theory of the self, agency, freedom, authority, and political authority, as one possible response to the movement focusing on the centrality of the will in which, I have argued, liberalism has often shared. But we must take one further step. For this movement of thought has had a reciprocal relationship with its social and material circumstances, the thought being worked out in the reality, the reality forming the thought. And this suggests the need not only for practice, but also for a praxis, in order to remove not only ignorance, but also illusion. There is a task, that is, not only of obtaining a better understanding of these issues and then acting on that understanding, but also of acting in order that, out of the changed reality, a better interpretation of the world and of these issues may in turn further inform practice. What would be the nature of such a praxis? Of course, there are all those forms of activity which destabilize the material substructures that give rise to idolatrous reifications. But we should also recall the indispensable element that is echoed by Grant in his references to the rigorous and demanding action of contemplation, remembering, cultivating the practice of attention, seeking out the dissonances in the cultural totality of technology, and searching through its absences for the elusive marks of the presence of the genuinely other, the transcendent.

(b) Revelation in public life

Whether such a project can be carried through without reference to some notion of revelation, whether from this starting-point the transcendent can ever be more than a function of the immanent dialectic of the modern cultural totality, and how revelation can be conceived within this frame of thinking, are questions beyond the scope of the present enquiry. For our purpose it must suffice to accept that through God's self-revelation there has been granted a true knowledge of the world and its Creator which the world has not recognized, and which cannot be had without that revelation. Although the Light gives light to everyone, it is to those who have received him and believed in his name that he gives the right to become children of God.

The second question which therefore arises in relation to a theological critique of liberalism concerns how this revelation can be mediated to society: in other words, what the relationship is between revelation and public life. Before addressing this, two preliminary points must be made. First, theology must finally interpret politics, not vice versa: in the discussion of Niebuhr I hinted at a criticism that in his thought the need of civilization for religion governed the viable options for theology, so that religion was finally in the service of politics. Even if such religion generates a broadly critical or progressivist politics and is not so evidently functional for social stability or conservatism, its identity and authenticity are constantly liable to dilution, if not indeed to betrayal. To avoid this, what is needed is a political analogue of Barth's reversal of nineteenth-century culture-liberalism, an inversion of the question such that, if anything, to put the point crudely, it is the relevance of politics and society to religion which focuses the problematic. In this understanding we begin to see emerging theology's 'No' to liberalism.

Second, this does not imply either treating the State as an arm of the Church in some kind of clerocracy, with its attendant religious intolerance, or an indifference (careless or studied) to the affairs of the earthly city. Some considerations in defence of religious tolerance were gathered together in the chapter on Maritain, and neither they nor the many others will be repeated here.[8] As regards the relation between transcendent truth and public engagement, suffice it to say that if the gospel of Jesus Christ is the gospel of a restored creation, theological reflection on society must extend beyond the elaboration of an ecclesiology; remarks in the spirit of Stanley Hauerwas's comment on the state, 'I do not need a theory of its existence',[9] must be deemed inadequate. If, therefore, there are theological reasons both for religious tolerance and for engagement in and support of the public realm, the Church must discover how its public contribution is to be made within the conditions of some version of pluralism. In this we can see the context of the church's 'Yes' to liberalism.

With these two considerations in mind, we may now ask about the role of revelation in public life. The answer is in two parts, the first concerning the relationship between the claims about political society made in the last section and putative theological justifications for them, the second concerning the nature of the witness of the Church.

(i) The first addresses the theological justification for the procedure adopted in the last section of giving theological support to claims which are in principle public (and remain so, however incommensurable they may happen to be with other claims which

---

[8] See further Robert Song, 'Toleration, Religious', in David Atkinson and David Field (eds.), *New Dictionary of Christian Ethics and Pastoral Theology* (Leicester: Inter-Varsity Press, 1995), 851–2.

[9] In his 'Epilogue: a Pacifist Response to the Bishops', in Ramsey, *Speak Up for Just War or Pacifism*, 175.

are also in principle public). If the truth of these philosophical issues can be settled in principle without reference to revelation, what is the point of the theological supplement? And if the theology has more than a simply decorative role, may it not illicitly be directing conclusions which can supposedly be reached on other grounds? In response to this twofold question, the fundamental principle is that revelation confirms and clarifies natural law. This may be explicated in two propositions.

Without a commitment, on the one hand, to some version of natural law, common to all human beings as fellow members of a created moral order, the morality declared by the Church can have no public value, no claim on those who as yet have not responded to the Gospel. Therefore, when James McClendon, while rejecting natural law, nevertheless asserts that stability, integrity, liberty, and plurality are goods which Christians 'may need to urge upon any social order',[10] we should ask on what grounds he thinks he can help himself to them or give any detailed analysis of their content if they are not to be understood in terms of natural goods of society.

Yet without a belief, on the other hand, in the distinctiveness of the Church's understanding of the natural order, both in its clearer apprehension of the requirements of that order as created but obscured by the Fall and in its unique knowledge of the eschatological transformation of the creation present in Jesus Christ, the proclamation of moral truth by the Church becomes redundant, and with it the understanding of ethics as the form of the Gospel, as itself good news. Thus in John Habgood's assertion that '[i]n terms of the principles by which people should live and societies order themselves, Christians have little to say that could not be said by any reasonable person of good will',[11] and that the Church has no distinctive moral content to offer society, but only a quality of debate, it is possible to find not only complacency about the conflicts and moral tensions between different sections of British society, but also an incipient denial of the Church's calling to preach the restored moral order as part of the good news.

The form of public address by the Church which this account implies must start from a declaration of moral truth, and must not

---

[10] McClendon, *Systematic Theology*, 236.
[11] John Habgood, *Church and Nation in a Secular Age* (London: Darton, Longman, and Todd, 1983), 168.

assume that its imagined public unacceptability (at least over some issues) is a reason for diluting moral norms beforehand. It is only after this initial pronouncement that compromise may be entered upon, if such is necessary to reach public agreement. Indeed, sometimes it is precisely as the Church's statement that such a pronouncement may be of general significance, and precisely as grounded theologically that it may be more than another pressure-group submission. Argument does play a part in public decision-making, and it is the responsibility of the Church to ensure that its own voice is clearly heard in that process.[12]

Concerning the right public positions a society should adopt, there was some discussion in Chapter 5. At the limiting point, the Church would look for enactment of those aspects of its moral teaching which form appropriate material for legislation (not every aspect of the Church's moral teaching falls within the scope of public purview—not every sin should be a crime). Yet, of course, the limiting-point conditions are far from those which obtain in North Atlantic democracies, and compromises are the proper stuff of public negotiation. Sometimes it is argued that highly contro-versial issues, such as the decriminalization of abortion, should be referred to a set of values which are taken to comprise the 'sacred canopy' of a society, the basic agreements which give that society its identity. Now certainly it is proper to appeal to the right of tradition, which in effect this is. But the plethora of interpretations (particularly by Americans) of the true nature of the values of 'our' society make clear the truth—mentioned before—of basic disagree-ment about what that tradition is.[13] Nowhere is this more evident than in the public debate over abortion: save in the unlikely event of a massive migration of opinion, any public resolution of this issue will be unstable, and appeal to the values of a supposed sacred canopy will not prevent this. Such an approach is mis-

[12] See Oliver O'Donovan, *Principles in the Public Realm: The Dilemma of Christian Moral Witness* (Oxford: Clarendon Press, 1984). On other aspects of church pronouncements see especially Paul Ramsey, *Who Speaks for the Church? A Critique of the 1966 Conference on Church and Society* (Edinburgh: Saint Andrew Press, 1969), and *Speak Up for Just War or Pacifism*, 125–47; and Duncan Forrester, *Beliefs, Values and Policies: Conviction Politics in a Secular Age* (Oxford: Clarendon Press, 1989). For some pertinent comments, see David Nicholls, 'Christianity and Politics', in Robert Morgan (ed.), *The Religion of the Incarnation: Anglican Essays in Commem-oration of 'Lux Mundi'* (Bristol: Bristol Classical Press, 1989), 172–88.
[13] In the judicial review context, the variety of opinions about the true values of the USA offered by Perry, Ely, and Dworkin is symptomatic.

prized. Generalizations about 'our being a religious people' (or whatever) should be used not as attempts to forestall the public debate but as substantive contributions to that debate. Tradition, properly understood, is in the first place not an externally imposed side-constraint which regulates legitimate speech, but the continuity over time (and sometimes through rupture) of an argument, part of whose content will indeed be the meaning of that argument's history.

(ii) The second part concerns the nature of the witness of the Church. This again divides into two movements: the one declaring a 'No', the other a 'Yes', to liberal society.

First, the liberal society is not the Kingdom. Only after it has been wholly recognized that liberalism may take on Messianic form, in its philosophy of history and tendency to progressivism, in its susceptibility to technological universalism and utopian pacifism, is it possible to consider the justification of pluralism or the institutions of a liberal society. Indeed, as I argued earlier in this chapter, liberalism's claims to objectivity and fairness are liable to blind it to its own special kind of tyranny and absolutism. Liberal society as much as any other social order may be sacralized, and stands in as great a need of challenging and, if necessary at times, changing.

The institutional form of this standing refusal is the Church. The tendency of Niebuhr's approach to place theology in the service of politics is entirely of a piece with his failure to develop any significant ecclesiology. If he had developed an understanding of the Church as the unique eschatological sign of the coming Kingdom, as that which, by its existence, defines the world as world, and by its life, shows to the world its worldly nature, he might have been able to appeal to it as a living demonstration of the relativity and transient nature of politics, and to do so with an effectiveness which the jeremiads of a single prophetic figure could never hope to achieve alone. Likewise, this notion of the Church as the sign of the Kingdom indicates my agreement with Hauerwas against Paul Ramsey that 'the church's social task is first of all its willingness to be a community formed by a language the world does not share'.[14] When it conceives its primary task as that of forming an ethos or a culture, or creating the virtues by which a

---

[14] Hauerwas, *Against the Nations*, 11.

liberal democratic (or any other) society will be sustained, it has betrayed its first vocation.

Yet, second, the Church is not to be simply a refusing Church. Despite the violence and impermanence of political society, political authority is to be affirmed as the divine disposition for violent and unruly creatures. While such affirmation can never preclude the option of selective conscientious objection, when, for example, a society undertakes to preserve itself at the expense of the intentional killing of innocents, whether actual (in the case of prenatal abortion) or conditional (in the case of the nuclear deterrent), the 'No' to liberal society must be followed by a careful and tentative 'Yes'.

Thus my initial agreement with Hauerwas should be followed by disagreement: while he rightly argues that Richard John Neuhaus's definition of democracy as limited government removes the possibility of any empirical tests to show when it becomes unlimited, his pacifism leads him to identify one of the marks of the beast-state with its right to command its citizens' consciences to take up arms in its defence, a right reserved by democratic as much as totalitarian states.[15] Democracies do properly have the right to call on their citizens to bear arms; the denial that war can or should be an instrument of politics places inordinate demands on politics, particularly when the loss of transcendence has given ultimate significance to historical ends. While the Church cannot accept the function of defending liberal democratic (or any other) society as the sole or primary rationale of its being, it is legitimate for it to elaborate principles of justice in declaring and fighting wars, in order that it may live 'a quiet and peaceable life in all godliness and dignity' (1 Tim. 2: 2). And it is also proper for it to distinguish between democracy and tyranny; in criticizing the fragile liberalism of the Weimar Republic, and thereby easing the way for the coming of the Third Reich, the German Christian theologians ended up serving neither Church nor nation faithfully.

Of course, the demands of the State in relation to war may become demonic: when, for example, the defence of a nation is imagined to require participation in the social act of the conditional intention indiscriminately to kill enemy non-combatants. And there are many other respects in which liberal society may overstep its

---

[15] Ibid. 126–30.

limitations: when it fancies that progress to a historical perfection is possible, when it represses from its consciousness its inevitable dependence on the possession of power, when it becomes enslaved by its passions in obeisance to the dynamics of technology. Yet precisely when we use the language of principalities and powers in the context of such overreaching, we indicate that, just as they are fallen angels, so here the struggle is against perversions of divinely ordained goods. Thus the limited justice secured by political authority is a good, albeit partial and fragmented, and the task of authentic prophetic witness lies both in denunciation, in preaching that the kingdom of this world is not the kingdom of God, and in annunciation, in declaring that those in authority have been appointed by God, and that for conscience's sake (though only as far as conscience judges) they are to be obeyed.

The Church has the task of mediating transcendence to society, then, both by its declarations of moral truth in the public realm and by being 'formed by a language which the world does not share', with the courage to stand firm against demonic usurpation and the love to seek workable likenesses of justice. The Church is needed by liberal society precisely because of its orientation to eternity, and fails both itself and the people amongst whom it sojourns if it secularizes itself or becomes so busied with the historical that it becomes mindless of the eternal. However, the Church is to be subservient not to the demands of society, but only to its call to signify the eschatological Kingdom. With regard to the question of a State-established Church, for example, the primary question is not whether the Church endangers liberal pluralism, but whether establishment compromises the Church's purity and faithfulness to its first calling. Therefore we can agree with George Lindbeck that '[r]eligious communities are likely to be practically relevant in the long run to the degree that they do not first ask what is either practical or relevant, but instead concentrate on their own intratextual outlooks and forms of life',[16] when we affirm that 'practicality' or 'relevance' are never the first words to which the Church listens. Yet the integrity of the Church can never, ultimately, be contrasted with its historical effectiveness, since history is under the governance of a providence which vindicates and brings to eschatological fulfilment the order of creation to which

---

[16] George A. Lindbeck, *The Nature of Doctrine: Religion and Theology in a Postliberal Age* (London: SPCK, 1984), 130.

the Church witnesses. In being faithful, we trust, we can finally never be less than supremely relevant; for the greater our faithfulness, the greater our likeness to the one through whom the creation came to be and in whom all things in heaven and earth will be brought together.

4 THE ETERNAL CITY

Dorothee Soelle writes: ' "The real exile of Israel in Egypt was that they had learned to endure it." The real exile of Christians in the First World is that we have learned to endure it.'[17] In attempting a critical theological analysis of liberalism, we have encountered the dominant political ideology of the modern Western world, and tried to identify some of the kinds of unfreedom to which we have become inured and from which we need liberation. Soelle describes our cultural captivity in terms of 'consumerism' and 'hedonistic fascism'.[18] While it is difficult not to be sympathetic to these descriptions of First World societies, or to recognize the kind of loss of humanity which they portray, I have pursued an analysis which incorporates them in a broader historical and intellectual framework, and to some extent relocates the problems. This analysis relates consumerism to the emancipation of the passions, and thence to the growth of technology and the triumph of the will. But it also shows that liberation from our modern forms of bondage may require a remembrance of the eternal and a sense of the transcendent: at the centre of modernity, and tightly entangled with the centrality of the will, is oblivion of anything that is not temporal. Yet, I have argued, liberalism, as one aspect of modernity, cannot finally sustain itself without such a transcendent reference. The question is where that presence of the eternal is to be found, united with the historical in order that historical action may be intelligible, but without being confused with it.

In so far as liberalism is subservient to technology and oriented to historical utopianism, it must be repudiated. In so far as it offers

[17] Dorothee Soelle, ' "Thou Shalt Have No Other Jeans Before Me" (Levi's Advertisement, Early Seventies): The Need for Liberation in a Consumerist Society', in Brian Mahan and L. Dale Richesin (eds.), *The Challenge of Liberation Theology: A First World Response* (Maryknoll, NY: Orbis Books, 1984), 5. The internal quotation is from Martin Buber, *Tales of the Hassidim* (New York: Schocken, 1947), ii. 315.
[18] Ibid. 7.

opportunities for contributing to a social order less unjust than the alternatives, it must be affirmed. Some time in the future there may be in the ascendant a constellation of human sins other than the one we live under now: we do not need to learn to endure subjection to the principalities whose sign is technology. But the fact of continuing sin cannot yet be escaped, even though we are promised that the night is far gone: the present world order must be endured for a little while longer. The need for such endurance does not imply the reification of any particular set of sinful structures or practices. (Augustine was not Constantinian in any sense that includes absolutizing the State: indeed, by denaturalizing it, he profoundly subverted its deepest pretensions.) But it does indicate that we must be grateful for, and ready to assist towards, such precarious justice as this world affords. (The *City of God* was partly written to ease fears that Christians could not recognize the claims of social order at all.) It also means that we should be gravely sceptical about any final dissolution of the differences between the two cities before the dawning of the eternal day.

We have limited imaginations and do not fondly entertain the thought that the Church survived the end of one civilization and may yet find itself witnessing the demise of another. It is not a habit of those amongst whom the Church sojourns to ponder the fact that the Eternal City was sacked by the barbarians. Yet, although the nature of such a loss may be less graphically impressed on us than it was on the inhabitants of an earlier Western empire, we at least have the benefit of the meditations of one who was there. In finding the *saeculum* to be the temporary intermingling of the two eschatological cities in an earthly peace, Augustine made clear the limits of political possibility; and in doing so, he showed how the heavenly city is to relate this fragile earthly peace to the lasting heavenly peace, that final peace 'which is so truly peaceful that it should be regarded as the only peace deserving the name . . . a perfectly ordered and completely harmonious fellowship in the enjoyment of God and of one another in God'.[19]

---

[19] *De civitate Dei*, XIX. 17; in *City of God*, vi. 198–9.

SELECT BIBLIOGRAPHY

ALLARD, J.-L.; BLANCHET, C.; COTTIER, G.; and MAYEUR, J.-M., *L'Humanisme intégral de Jacques Maritain* (Paris: Éditions Saint-Paul, 1988).

AQUINAS, *Selected Political Writings*, ed. A. P. D'Entrèves (Oxford: Blackwell, 1948).

ARBLASTER, ANTHONY, *The Rise and Decline of Western Liberalism* (Oxford: Blackwell, 1984).

ASHCRAFT, RICHARD, *Revolutionary Politics and Locke's* Two Treatises of Government (Princeton: Princeton University Press, 1986).

AUGUSTINE, *The City of God against the Pagans*, trans. G. H. McCracken *et al.*, Loeb Classical Library (7 vols., London: Heinemann, and Cambridge, Mass.: Harvard University Press, 1957–72).

BARRY, BRIAN, *The Liberal Theory of Justice: A Critical Examination of the Principal Doctrines in 'A Theory of Justice' by John Rawls* (Oxford: Clarendon Press, 1973).

BARS, HENRY, *La Politique selon Jacques Maritain* (Paris: Les Éditions Ouvrières, 1961).

BARTH, KARL, *The Christian Life*, trans. Geoffrey W. Bromiley (Grand Rapids, Mich.: Eerdmans, 1981).

BELLAH, ROBERT; MADSEN, RICHARD; SULLIVAN, WILLIAM M.; SWIDLER, ANN; and TIPTON, STEVEN M., *Habits of the Heart: Individualism and Commitment in American Life* (Berkeley: University of California Press, 1985).

BERKHOF, HENDRIK, *Christ and the Powers*, trans. John H. Yoder (Scottdale, Pa.: Mennonite Publishing House, 1962).

BERLIN, ISAIAH, *Four Essays on Liberty* (Oxford: Oxford University Press, 1969).

BRAMSTED, E. K., and MELHUISH, K. J., *Western Liberalism: A History in Documents from Locke to Croce* (London: Longman, 1978).

BRAZIER, RODNEY, *Constitutional Reform* (Oxford: Clarendon Press, 1991).

BROWN, PETER, 'St. Augustine's Attitude to Religious Coercion', *Journal of Roman Studies*, 54 (1964), 107–16; repr. in *Religion and Society in the Age of Augustine* (London: Faber and Faber, 1972), 260–78.

——*Augustine of Hippo: A Biography* (London: Faber and Faber, 1967).

BROWN, ROBERT MCAFEE, *The Essential Reinhold Niebuhr: Selected Essays and Addresses* (New Haven and London: Yale University Press, 1986).

BULLOCK, ALAN, and SHOCK, MAURICE, *The Liberal Tradition: From Fox to Keynes* (London: Adam and Charles Black, 1956).

CAIRD, G. B., *Principalities and Powers: A Study in Pauline Theology* (Oxford: Clarendon Press, 1956).

Charter 88 Manifesto, *New Statesman and Society* (2 Dec. 1988), 10–11.

CLARKE, PETER, *Liberals and Social Democrats* (Cambridge: Cambridge University Press, 1978).

COHEN, MARSHALL (ed.), *Ronald Dworkin and Contemporary Jurisprudence* (London: Duckworth, 1984).

COLLINI, STEFAN, *Liberalism and Sociology: L. T. Hobhouse and Political Argument in England, 1880–1914* (Cambridge: Cambridge University Press, 1979).

COLLINS, IRENE, *Liberalism in Nineteenth-Century Europe* (London: The Historical Association, 1957).

CONDORCET, ANTOINE NICOLAS DE, *Sketch for a Historical Picture of the Progress of the Human Mind* (1795), trans. J. Barraclough (London: Weidenfeld and Nicolson, 1955).

COOPER, JOHN W., *The Philosophy of Freedom: The Legacy of Jacques Maritain and Reinhold Niebuhr* (Macon, Ga.: Mercer University Press, 1985).

CRANSTON, MAURICE, *Freedom: A New Analysis* (London: Longmans, Green & Co., 1953).

——'Liberalism', in Paul Edwards (ed.), *The Encyclopaedia of Philosophy* (8 vols., New York: Macmillan and Free Press, 1967), iv. 458–61.

DAHL, ROBERT, *A Preface to Democratic Theory* (Chicago and London: University of Chicago Press, 1956).

DANIELS, NORMAN (ed.), *Reading Rawls: Critical Studies on Rawls' 'A Theory of Justice'* (Oxford: Blackwell, 1975).

DAVIS, HARRY R., and GOOD, ROBERT C. (eds.), *Reinhold Niebuhr on Politics* (New York: Scribner's, 1960).

DEANE, HERBERT A., *The Political and Social Ideas of St Augustine* (New York: Columbia University Press, 1963).

DOERING, BERNARD E., *Jacques Maritain and the French Catholic Intellectuals* (Notre Dame, Ind.: University of Notre Dame Press, 1983).

DOUGLASS, R. BRUCE, and HOLLENBACH, DAVID (eds.), *Catholicism and Liberalism: Contributions to American Public Philosophy* (Cambridge: Cambridge University Press, 1994).

DUNN, JOHN, 'Justice and the Interpretation of Locke's Political Theory', *Political Studies*, 16 (1968), 68–87.

——*The Political Thought of John Locke: An Historical Account of the Argument of the 'Two Treatises of Government'* (Cambridge: Cambridge University Press, 1969).

——'The Politics of Locke in England and America in the Eighteenth

Century', in J. W. Yolton (ed.), *John Locke: Problems and Perspectives* (Cambridge: Cambridge University Press, 1969), 45–80.

DUNN, JOHN, *Western Political Theory in the Face of the Future* (Cambridge: Cambridge University Press, 1979).

——*Rethinking Modern Political Theory: Essays 1979–83* (Cambridge: Cambridge University Press, 1985).

DURKIN, KENNETH, *Reinhold Niebuhr* (London: Geoffrey Chapman, 1989).

DWORKIN, RONALD, *Law's Empire* (London: Fontana Press, 1986).

——*A Bill of Rights for Britain* (London: Chatto and Windus, 1990).

ELLUL, JACQUES, *The Technological Society* (New York: Vintage Books, 1964).

ELSTER, JON, and SLAGSTAD, RUNE (eds.), *Constitutionalism and Democracy* (Cambridge: Cambridge University Press, 1988).

ELY, JOHN HART, *Democracy and Distrust: A Theory of Judicial Review* (Cambridge, Mass., and London: Harvard University Press, 1980).

EVANS, JOSEPH W., 'Jacques Maritain's Personalism', *Review of Politics*, 14 (1952), 166–77.

——'A Word on Maritain', *Review of Politics*, 19 (1957), 131–4.

——'Jacques Maritain and the Problem of Pluralism in Political Life', *Review of Politics*, 22 (1960), 307–23.

——(ed.), *Jacques Maritain: The Man and His Achievement* (New York: Sheed and Ward, 1963).

EWING, K. D., and GEARTY, C. A., *Freedom under Thatcher: Civil Liberties in Modern Britain* (Oxford: Clarendon Press, 1990).

FINANCE, JOSEPH DE, 'La Philosophie de la liberté chez Maritain', *Recherches et Débats* (Centre Catholique des Intellectuels Français), 19 (July 1957), 95–116.

FINNIS, JOHN, *Fundamentals of Ethics* (Oxford: Clarendon Press, 1983).

——'A Bill of Rights for Britain? The Moral of Contemporary Jurisprudence', *Proceedings of the British Academy*, 72 (1986), 303–31.

FORRESTER, DUNCAN, *Beliefs, Values and Policies: Conviction Politics in a Secular Age* (Oxford: Clarendon Press, 1989).

FOX, RICHARD WIGHTMAN, 'Reinhold Niebuhr and the Emergence of the Liberal Realist Faith, 1939–45', *Review of Politics*, 38 (1976), 244–65.

——*Reinhold Niebuhr: A Biography* (New York: Pantheon, 1985).

FRANKEL, CHARLES, *The Case for Modern Man* (London: Macmillan, 1957).

——'Progress, The Idea of', in Paul Edwards (ed.), *The Encyclopaedia of Philosophy* (8 vols., New York: Macmillan and Free Press, 1967), vi. 483–7.

FREEDEN, MICHAEL, *The New Liberalism: An Ideology of Social Reform* (Oxford: Clarendon Press, 1978).

FUKUYAMA, FRANCIS, *The End of History and the Last Man* (London: Hamish Hamilton, 1992).

GARDET, LOUIS, 'La Culture chrétienne et le dialogue des cultures', *Recherches et Débats* (Centre Catholique des Intellectuels Français), 19 (July 1957), 148–65.

GILKEY, LANGDON, 'Reinhold Niebuhr's Theology of History', *Journal of Religion*, 54 (1974), 360–86.

GINSBERG, MORRIS, 'Progress in the Modern Era', in P. P. Wiener (ed.), *Dictionary of the History of Ideas* (5 vols., New York: Scribner's, 1973), iii. 633–50.

GODWIN, WILLIAM, *Enquiry Concerning Political Justice* (1793), abridged and ed. K. Codell Carter (Oxford: Clarendon Press, 1971).

GOUGH, J. W., *The Social Contract: A Critical Study of its Development*, 2nd edn. (Oxford: Clarendon Press, 1957).

GRANT, GEORGE, *The Empire: Yes or No?* (Toronto: Ryerson Press, 1945).

—— 'Have We a Canadian Nation?', *Public Affairs* (Institute of Public Affairs, Dalhousie University), 8 (1945), 161–6.

—— 'Philosophy', in *Royal Commission Studies* (Ottawa: King's Printer, 1951), 119–33.

—— 'Plato and Popper', *Canadian Journal of Economics and Political Science*, 20 (1954), 185–94.

—— 'The Uses of Freedom—A Word and our World', *Queen's Quarterly*, 62 (1956), 515–27.

—— *Philosophy in the Mass Age* (Toronto: Copp Clark, ²1966).

—— 'An Ethic of Community', in Michael Oliver (ed.), *Social Purpose for Canada* (Toronto: University of Toronto Press, 1961), 3–26.

—— 'Conceptions of Health', in Helmut Schoek and James W. Wiggins (eds.), *Psychiatry and Responsibility* (Princeton: Van Nostrand, 1962), 117–34.

—— 'How Deception Lurks in The Secular City' (review of Harvey Cox, *The Secular City*), *United Church Observer* (1 July 1966), 16–17, 27.

—— Review of Ellul, *The Technological Society*, *Canadian Dimension*, 3/3–4 (1966), 59–60.

—— 'A Conversation on Technology' (with Gad Horowitz), *Journal of Canadian Studies*, 4/3 (1969), 3–6.

—— 'Nationalism and Rationality', *Canadian Forum*, 50 (1971), 336–7.

—— 'Ideology in Modern Empires', in J. E. Flint and G. Williams (eds.), *Perspectives of Empire* (London: Longmans Group, 1973), 189–97.

—— ' "The Computer does not Impose on us the Way it should be Used" ', in Abraham Rotstein (ed.), *Beyond Industrial Growth* (Toronto: University of Toronto Press, 1976), 117–31.

—— 'Faith and the Multiversity', *Compass*, 4 (1978), 3–14.

GRANT, GEORGE, Conversations, in Schmidt (ed.), *George Grant in Process*, 13–21, 61–7, 101–9, 141–7.

—— 'Nietzsche and the Ancients: Philosophy and Scholarship', *Dionysius*, 3 (1979), 5–16.

—— 'The Case against Abortion', *Today Magazine* (3 Oct. 1981), 12–13.

—— 'The Triumph of the Will', in Denyse O'Leary (ed.), *The Issue is Life: A Christian Response to Abortion in Canada* (Burlington, Ont.: Welch Publications, 1988), pp. 156–66.

—— Tapes 1, 2 & 3, 'Ideas' (Canadian Broadcasting Association, n.d.).

GRAY, JOHN, *Mill on Liberty: A Defence* (London: Routledge and Kegan Paul, 1983).

—— *Hayek on Liberty* (Oxford: Blackwell, 1984).

—— *Liberalism* (Milton Keynes: Open University Press, 1986).

—— and SMITH, G. W. (eds.), *John Stuart Mill's* On Liberty *in Focus* (London and New York: Routledge, 1991).

GREEN, T. H., 'Lecture on "Liberal Legislation and Freedom of Contract"' (1881), in R. L. Nettleship (ed.), *Works* (3 vols., London: Longmans, Green & Co., 1885–8), iii. 365–86.

GRIFFITH, J. A. G., *The Politics of the Judiciary*, 4th edn. (London: Fontana Press, 1991).

GUTMANN, AMY, 'Communitarian Critics of Liberalism', *Philosophy and Public Affairs*, 14 (1985), 308–22.

HABGOOD, JOHN, *Church and Nation in a Secular Age* (London: Darton, Longman, and Todd, 1983).

HARLAND, GORDON, *The Thought of Reinhold Niebuhr* (New York: Oxford University Press, 1960).

HARPHAM, EDWARD J. (ed.), *John Locke's* Two Treatises of Government: *New Interpretations* (Lawrence, Kan.: University Press of Kansas, 1992).

HARRIES, RICHARD (ed.), *Reinhold Niebuhr and the Issues of Our Time* (London and Oxford: Mowbrays, 1986).

HARTZ, LOUIS, *The Liberal Tradition in America* (New York: Harcourt, Brace and World, 1955).

HAUERWAS, STANLEY, 'Politics, Vision, and the Common Good', in *Vision and Virtue* (Notre Dame, Ind.: University of Notre Dame Press, 1981), 222–40.

—— *Against the Nations: War and Survival in a Liberal Society* (Minneapolis: Winston Press, 1985).

HAYEK, F. A., *Individualism and Economic Order* (London: Routledge and Kegan Paul, 1949).

—— *The Constitution of Liberty* (London: Routledge and Kegan Paul, 1960).

HEIDEGGER, MARTIN, *The Question Concerning Technology and Other Essays* (1952–62), trans. William Lovitt (New York: Harper and Row, 1977).

HOBHOUSE, LEONARD T., *Liberalism* (1911) (repr. New York: Oxford University Press, 1964).

——*The Metaphysical Theory of the State* (London: George Allen and Unwin, 1918).

——*Social Evolution and Political Theory* (New York: Columbia University Press, 1911).

Home Office, *Legislation on Human Rights with Particular Reference to the European Convention: A Discussion Document* (London: HMSO, 1976).

HUDSON, DEAL W., and MANCINI, MATTHEW J. (eds.), *Understanding Maritain: Philosopher and Friend* (Macon, Ga.: Mercer University Press, 1987).

Institute for Public Policy Research, *A British Bill of Rights*, Constitution Paper No. 1 (London: Institute for Public Policy Research, 1991).

——*The Constitution of the United Kingdom* (London: Institute for Public Policy Research, 1991).

JACONELLI, JOSEPH, *Enacting a Bill of Rights: The Legal Problems* (Oxford: Clarendon Press, 1980).

JUNG, HWA YOL, *The Foundations of Jacques Maritain's Political Philosophy* (Gainsville, Fla: University of Florida Press, 1960).

KANT, IMMANUEL, 'On the Common Saying: "This May be True in Theory, but it Does not Apply in Practice"' (1793), in Reiss (ed.), *Kant's Political Writings*, 61–92.

——'Perpetual Peace: A Philosophical Sketch' (1795), in Reiss (ed.), *Kant's Political Writings*, 93–130.

——'The Metaphysic of Morals' (1797), in Reiss (ed.), *Kant's Political Writings*, 131–75.

KEGLEY, CHARLES W., and BRETALL, ROBERT W. (eds.), *Reinhold Niebuhr: His Religious, Social and Political Thought* (New York: Macmillan, 1956).

KROKER, ARTHUR, *Technology and the Canadian Mind: Innis/McLuhan/Grant* (Montreal: New World Perspectives, 1984).

LARMORE, CHARLES E., *Patterns of Moral Complexity* (Cambridge: Cambridge University Press, 1987).

LASKI, HAROLD J., *The Rise of European Liberalism* (London: George Allen and Unwin, 1936).

LINDBECK, GEORGE A., *The Nature of Doctrine: Religion and Theology in a Postliberal Age* (London: SPCK, 1984).

LOCKE, JOHN, *Two Treatises of Government* (1689), ed. Peter Laslett (Cambridge: Cambridge University Press, 1960).

——*Epistola de Tolerantia* (1689), ed. Raymond Klibansky, trans. J. W. Gough (Oxford: Clarendon Press, 1968).

LUKES, STEVEN, *Individualism* (Oxford: Blackwell, 1973).

McCANN, DENNIS P., *Christian Realism and Liberation Theology: Practical Theologies in Creative Conflict* (Maryknoll, NY: Orbis Books, 1981).

McDonagh, Enda, *The Declaration of Religious Freedom of Vatican Council II* (London: Darton, Longman, and Todd, 1967).

MacIntyre, Alasdair, *After Virtue: A Study in Moral Theory* (London: Duckworth, 1981).

——'The Idea of an Educated Public', in Graham Haydon (ed.), *Education and Values* (London: Institute of Education, University of London, 1987), 15–36.

Macpherson, C. B., *The Political Theory of Possessive Individualism: Hobbes to Locke* (Oxford: Oxford University Press, 1962).

——'Democratic Theory: Ontology and Technology', in *Democratic Theory: Essays in Retrieval* (Oxford: Clarendon Press, 1973), 24–38.

Mann, Golo, 'Reinhold Niebuhr und die Kritik der Liberalismus', *Merkur*, 12 (1958), 131–44.

Maritain, Jacques, *The Things That Are Not Caesar's* (1927), trans. J. F. Scanlan (London: Sheed and Ward, 1930).

——*Religion and Culture* (1930), trans. J. F. Scanlan (London: Sheed and Ward, 1931).

——*Anti-Semitism* (London: Geoffrey Bles, 1939).

——*Scholasticism and Politics* (1940), trans. Mortimer J. Adler (London: Geoffrey Bles, 1940).

——'The Conquest of Freedom', in Ruth Nanda Anshen (ed.), *Freedom: Its Meaning* (1940); repr. in Joseph W. Evans and Leo R. Ward (eds.), *The Social and Political Philosophy of Jacques Maritain: Selected Readings* (London: Geoffrey Bles, 1956), 28–46.

——*Redeeming the Time* (1941), trans. Harry Lorin Binsse (London: Geoffrey Bles, 1943).

——*Christianity and Democracy* (1943), trans. Doris C. Anson (London: Geoffrey Bles, 1945).

——*The Range of Reason* (London: Geoffrey Bles, 1953).

——'Introduction' to UNESCO, *Human Rights: Comments and Interpretations* (London and New York: Allen Wingate, 1948), 9–17.

——'On the Philosophy of Human Rights', in UNESCO, *Human Rights: Comments and Interpretations* (London and New York: Allen Wingate, 1948), 72–7.

——*Reflections on America* (New York: Scribner's, 1958).

——*The Peasant of the Garonne: An Old Layman Questions Himself about the Present Time* (1966), trans. Michael Cuddihy and Elizabeth Hughes (London: Geoffrey Chapman, 1968).

Markus, R. A., *Saeculum: History and Society in the Theology of St Augustine*, rev. edn. (Cambridge: Cambridge University Press, 1988).

Meyer, Donald B., *The Protestant Search for Political Realism, 1919–41* (Berkeley and Los Angeles: University of California Press, 1960).

MILL, JOHN STUART, *On Liberty* (1859), in Mary Warnock (ed.), *Utilitarianism* (London: Collins, 1962), 126–250.

—— *Utilitarianism* (1861), in Mary Warnock (ed.), *Utilitarianism* (London: Collins, 1962), 251–321.

MITCHAM, CARL, and GROTE, JIM, *Theology and Technology: Essays in Christian Analysis and Exegesis* (Lanham, Md.: University Press of America, 1984).

MITCHELL, BASIL, *Law, Morality and Religion in a Secular Society* (Oxford: Oxford University Press, 1967).

MONSMA, STEPHEN V. (ed.), *Responsible Technology* (Grand Rapids, Mich.: Eerdmans, 1986).

MOTT, STEPHEN CHARLES, *A Christian Perspective on Political Thought* (New York: Oxford University Press, 1993).

MOUNT, FERDINAND, *The British Constitution Now: Recovery or Decline?* (London: Heinemann, 1992).

MULHALL, STEPHEN, and SWIFT, ADAM, *Liberals and Communitarians* (Oxford: Blackwell, 1992).

MURDOCH, IRIS, 'Against Dryness: A Polemical Sketch', *Encounter*, 16/1 (Jan. 1961), 16–20; repr. in Stanley Hauerwas and Alasdair MacIntyre (eds.), *Revisions: Changing Perspectives in Moral Philosophy* (Notre Dame, Ind.: University of Notre Dame Press, 1983), 43–50.

MURRAY, JOHN COURTNEY, SJ, *We Hold These Truths: Catholic Reflections on the American Proposition* (London: Sheed and Ward, 1960).

—— *The Problem of Religious Freedom* (London: Geoffrey Chapman, 1965).

NAGEL, THOMAS, 'Moral Conflict and Political Legitimacy', *Philosophy and Public Affairs*, 16 (1987), 215–40.

National Council for Civil Liberties, *A People's Charter: Liberty's Bill of Rights* (London: National Council for Civil Liberties, 1991).

NEUHAUS, RICHARD JOHN, *The Naked Public Square: Religion and Democracy in America* (Grand Rapids, Mich.: Eerdmans, 1984).

NIEBUHR, H. RICHARD, *Christ and Culture* (New York: Harper and Row, 1951).

NIEBUHR, Reinhold, Review of Maritain, *Freedom in the Modern World*, *Saturday Review* (8 Aug. 1936); repr. in Cooper, *The Philosophy of Freedom*, 172.

—— 'Ten Years That Shook My World', *Christian Century*, 56/17 (26 Apr. 1939), 542–6.

—— 'A Faith for History's Greatest Crisis', *Fortune*, 26/1 (July 1942), 99–100, 122–31.

—— 'The Sickness of American Culture', *Nation*, 166 (6 Mar. 1948), 267–70.

—— 'Intellectual Autobiography', in Kegley and Bretall (eds.), *Reinhold Niebuhr*, 3–23.

NIEBUHR, REINHOLD, 'Reply to Interpretation and Criticism', in Kegley and Bretall (eds.), *Reinhold Niebuhr*, 431-51.

—— *The Godly and the Ungodly: Essays on the Religious and Secular Dimensions of Modern Life* (London: Faber and Faber, 1959; originally published as *Pious and Secular America* (1958)).

—— *Nations and Empires: Recurring Patterns in the Political Order* (1959; repr. London: Faber, 1960).

—— 'The Truth in Myths', in Ronald H. Stone (ed.), *Faith and Politics* (New York: George Braziller, 1968), 15–31.

NOZICK, ROBERT, *Anarchy, State, and Utopia* (Oxford: Blackwell, 1974).

O'DONOVAN, JOAN E., *George Grant and the Twilight of Justice* (Toronto: University of Toronto Press, 1984).

—— 'The Battleground of Liberalism: Politics of Eternity and Politics of Time', *Chesterton Review*, 11 (1985), 131–54.

O'DONOVAN, OLIVER, *Principles in the Public Realm: The Dilemma of Christian Moral Witness* (Oxford: Clarendon Press, 1984).

—— 'Augustine's City of God XIX and Western Political Thought', *Dionysius*, 11 (1987), 89–110.

—— *The Desire of the Nations* (Cambridge: Cambridge University Press, 1996).

PASSMORE, JOHN, *The Perfectibility of Man* (London: Duckworth, 1970).

PAVAN, PIETRO, 'Declaration on Religious Freedom', in Herbert Vorgimler (ed.), *Commentary on the Documents of Vatican II* (5 vols., London: Burns and Oates; New York: Herder and Herder, 1967–9), iv. 49–86.

PERRY, MICHAEL J., *The Constitution, the Courts, and Human Rights: An Enquiry into Constitutional Policymaking by the Judiciary* (New Haven and London: Yale University Press, 1982).

PLAMENATZ, JOHN, 'Liberalism', in P. P. Wiener (ed.), *Dictionary of the History of Ideas* (5 vols., New York: Scribners, 1973), iii. 36–61.

PLASKOW, JUDITH, *Sex, Sin and Grace: Women's Experience and the Theologies of Reinhold Niebuhr and Paul Tillich* (Lanham, Md.: University Press of America, 1980).

POPPER, KARL, *The Open Society and its Enemies*, 6th edn. (2 vols., London: Routledge, 1966).

RAMSEY, PAUL, *Nine Modern Moralists* (Englewood Cliffs, NJ: Prentice-Hall, 1962).

—— 'The Uses of Power', in *The Just War: Force and Political Responsibility* (Lanham, Md.: University Press of America, 1968), 3–18.

—— *Who Speaks for the Church? A Critique of the 1966 Conference on Church and Society* (Edinburgh: Saint Andrew Press, 1969).

—— *Speak Up for Just War or Pacifism: A Critique of the United Methodist Bishops' Pastoral Letter 'In Defense of Creation'* (University Park, Pa.: Pennsylvania State University Press, 1988).

RAUSCHENBUSCH, WALTER, *Christianity and the Social Crisis*; excerpts in Benson Y. Landis (ed.), *A Rauschenbusch Reader: The Kingdom of God and the Social Gospel* (New York: Harper, 1957).

——*A Theology for the Social Gospel* (1917) (Nashville: Abingdon Press, 1945).

RAWLS, JOHN, 'Fairness to Goodness', *Philosophical Review*, 84 (1975), 536–54.

——'The Basic Structure as Subject', *American Philosophical Quarterly*, 14 (1977), 159–65.

——'Kantian Constructivism in Moral Theory', *Journal of Philosophy*, 77 (1980), 515–72.

——'Justice as Fairness: Political not Metaphysical', *Philosophy and Public Affairs*, 14 (1985), 223–51.

——'The Idea of an Overlapping Consensus', *Oxford Journal of Legal Studies*, 7 (1987), 1–25.

——'The Priority of Right and Ideas of the Good', *Philosophy and Public Affairs*, 17 (1988), 251–74.

RAZ, JOSEPH, *The Morality of Freedom* (Oxford: Clarendon Press, 1986).

Recherches et Débats (Centre Catholique des Intellectuels Français), 19 (July 1957).

REES, JOHN C., 'A Re-reading of Mill on Liberty', *Political Studies*, 8 (1960), 113–29.

REISS, HANS (ed.), *Kant's Political Writings* (Cambridge: Cambridge University Press, ²1991).

RICHTER, MELVIN, *The Politics of Conscience: T. H. Green and his Age* (London: Weidenfeld and Nicolson, 1964).

ROBERTSON, GEOFFREY, *Freedom, the Individual and the Law*, 6th edn. (Harmondsworth: Penguin, 1989).

RUGGIERO, GUIDO DE, *The History of European Liberalism* (Oxford: Oxford University Press, 1927).

RYAN, ALAN, *The Philosophy of John Stuart Mill* (London: Macmillan, ²1987).

——*J. S. Mill* (London: Routledge and Kegan Paul, 1974).

SANDEL, MICHAEL J., *Liberalism and the Limits of Justice* (Cambridge: Cambridge University Press, 1982).

SAUVIGNY, G. DE BERTIER, DE, 'Liberalism, Nationalism and Socialism: The Birth of Three Words', *Review of Politics*, 32 (1970), 147–66.

SCHMIDT, LARRY (ed.), *George Grant in Process: Essays and Conversations* (Toronto: House of Anansi Press, 1978).

SCHUURMAN, EGBERT, *Technology and the Future: A Philosophical Challenge*, trans. Herbert Donald Morton (Toronto: Wedge Publishing Foundation, 1981).

Second Vatican Council, *Dignitatis Humanae Personae* (Declaration on

Religious Freedom), in Walter M. Abbott, SJ (ed.), *The Documents of Vatican II* (London: Geoffrey Chapman, 1965), 675–96.

SHELL, SUSAN MELD, *The Rights of Reason: A Study of Kant's Philosophy and Politics* (Toronto: University of Toronto Press, 1980).

SIEDENTOP, LARRY, 'Two Liberal Traditions', in Alan Ryan (ed.), *The Idea of Freedom* (Oxford: Oxford University Press, 1979), 153–74.

SIMON, YVES R., *Philosophy of Democratic Government* (Chicago: University of Chicago Press, 1951).

SOELLE, DOROTHEE, '"Thou Shalt Have No Other Jeans Before Me" (Levi's Advertisement, early 1970s): The Need for Liberation in a Consumerist Society', in Brian Mahan and L. Dale Richesin (eds.), *The Challenge of Liberation Theology: A First World Response* (Maryknoll, NY: Orbis Books, 1984), 4–16.

SONG, ROBERT, 'Toleration, Religious', in David Atkinson and David Field (eds.), *New Dictionary of Christian Ethics and Pastoral Theology* (Leicester: Inter-Varsity Press, 1995), 851–2.

STONE, RONALD H., *Reinhold Niebuhr: Prophet to Politicians* (Nashville: Abingdon Press, 1972).

STRAUSS, LEO, *Natural Right and History* (Chicago: University of Chicago Press, 1953).

TAYLOR, CHARLES, *Philosophy and the Human Sciences: Philosophical Papers 2* (Cambridge: Cambridge University Press, 1985).

TRACY, DAVID, 'Religion and Human Rights in the Public Realm', *Daedalus*, 112/4 (Fall 1983), 237–54.

TURGOT, A. R. J., 'A Philosophical Review of the Successive Advances of the Human Mind' (1750), in *Turgot on Progress, Sociology and Economics*, trans. and ed. Ronald L. Meek (Cambridge: Cambridge University Press, 1973), 41–59.

VIBERT, FRANK, *Constitutional Reform in the United Kingdom: An Incremental Agenda*, IEA Inquiry Paper No. 18 (London: Institute for Economic Affairs, 1990).

VOEGELIN, ERIC, 'Liberalism and its History', *Review of Politics*, 36 (1974), 504–20.

WALDRON, JEREMY, 'Theoretical Foundations of Liberalism', *Philosophical Quarterly*, 37 (1987), 127–50.

WILLIAMS, HOWARD, *Kant's Political Philosophy* (Oxford: Blackwell, 1983).

——(ed.), *Essays on Kant's Political Philosophy* (Cardiff: University of Wales Press, 1992).

WILLIAMS, RAYMOND, 'Liberal', in *Keywords: A Vocabulary of Culture and Society* (Glasgow: Fontana, 1976), 148–50.

WILLIAMS, ROWAN, 'Politics and the Soul: A Reading of the *City of God*', *Milltown Studies* 19/20 (1987), 55–72.

WINK, WALTER, *Naming the Powers: The Language of Power in the New Testament* (Philadelphia: Fortress Press, 1984).

——*Unmasking the Powers: The Invisible Forces that Determine Human Existence* (Philadelphia: Fortress Press, 1986).

——*Engaging the Powers: Discernment and Resistance in a World of Domination* (Minneapolis: Fortress Press, 1992).

WOLFF, ROBERT PAUL, *Understanding Rawls: A Reconstruction and Critique of* A Theory of Justice (Princeton: Princeton University Press, 1977).

WOLIN, SHELDON, *Politics and Vision: Continuity and Innovation in Western Political Thought* (Boston: Little, Brown and Co., 1960).

ZANDER, MICHAEL, *A Bill of Rights?*, 3rd edn. (London: Sweet and Maxwell, 1985).

INDEX

Abraham, Henry J. 205
agency, human 40, 100, 129–30, 151–2,
    158–9, 216, 221
    see also self; voluntarism; will
Albert the Great 143–4
Alt, Albrecht 202
Aquinas, Thomas 4, 131–2, 143–4,
    166–7, 169–70, 197 n. 54
Aristotle 31, 88 n. 8, 89, 91, 121, 128, 129
Arius, Arianism 15, 216 n. 2
atomism 129–30, 216
    see also individualism
Atonement 55, 79
Augustine 70, 77, 121, 122, 143, 167–
    73, 175, 215, 233
authority 34, 150, 217, 221–2
    political 17–18, 43, 44, 166–7, 197–8,
    216, 222–3
autonomy 10, 21, 26–7, 31, 41, 47, 85,
    154
    freedom of autonomy (Maritain)
        150–1; *see also* freedom, terminal
    see also freedom; Kant, Immanuel

Bacon, Francis 169
Barth, Karl 1, 51 n. 7, 66, 226
Bellarmine, Robert 196
Bentham, Jeremy 24
Berlin, Isaiah 21, 46, 75 n. 112, 170
Beveridge, William 38
Bill of Rights 7, 179, 180, 200, 202–4,
    210–11
    England (1689) 178
    US 180, 201, 206
    see also judicial review; rights
Boethius 150
Brown v. *The Board of Education of
    Topeka* (US Supreme Court) 181
Bultmann, Rudolf 53

Cajetan, Thomas de Vio, Cardinal 196
capitalism 17, 38, 42, 87, 95, 98, 112,
    124, 132, 134
    see also liberalism, economic
Cardozo, Benjamin 184
Charles II, King of England 17

Charter 88, 178
Christendom 135, 141, 148, 165
    see also new Christendom
Christian Democracy 4, 137, 163
Christology 55 n. 21, 68, 78, 82, 122,
    138–9
Church, the 17, 91 n. 23, 158, 213, 227–
    8, 229–32, 233
    see also Church and State; ecclesio-
    logy
Church and State 134–7, 142, 166, 226,
    231
    see also Church; liberalism; state
Clark, J. C. D. 9
coercion 18, 22, 29–30, 31, 35, 39, 41,
    138, 144, 168, 170, 171, 223
common good 30, 134, 143, 152–5,
    161–2, 191–2, 196, 198, 199, 223
communitarianism 7, 106–7, 128–30,
    164–5, 171, 216
Comte, Auguste 153
Condorcet, Marquis de 43, 71
conferral model, *see* consent
confirmation model, *see* consent
Conseil Constitutionnel (Fifth French
    Republic) 194
consent 18, 29, 37, 40, 217–18, 223
    conferral model of 197, 198–200,
    204–8, 223–4
    confirmation model of 197–9, 200–4,
    223–4
Constant, Benjamin 39 n. 94, 102
consumerism 18, 49, 98, 107, 232
contract 29, 96, 223
    see also social contract
creation 16, 55 n. 21, 62, 120–1, 123,
    167, 226, 227
    see also natural law

Dahl, Robert 183 n. 17
Darwin, Charles 89
Declaration on Religious Freedom
    (Vatican II) 144–5
democracy 27, 46, 155–6, 176, 186–7,
    189–90, 195, 196, 198–200, 206–7,
    230